African Footballers in Europe

African Footballers in Europe traces the social and economic evolution of African football and examines the strategies and resources that players mobilise in their migrations, with a particular focus on 'Give Back Behaviours' (how players contribute to their countries or communities of origin). It shines new light on contemporary migrations, labour markets in sport, and processes of development in Africa.

Using a multidisciplinary approach and Weberian methodology to analyse players' 'Give Back' behaviour, the book highlights the complex rationale behind this behaviour, based on a combination of social, cultural, and economic elements. It features interviews with former and current African professional players, providing a vivid picture of the role of communities in players' migration projects, the allure of the European football market, and investment initiatives that can contribute to local and regional development.

This is a vital read for academics, researchers, and students of sport sciences, sociology of sport, sport management, sociology, geography, political sciences, management, sociology of Africa, migration studies, sociology of the labour market, and economic sociology. It is also an important resource for professional organisations, NGOs, football agents, football administrators, federations, confederations, and governments.

Ernest Yeboah Acheampong (PhD) is Lecturer in the Department of Health, Physical Education, Recreation and Sports at the University of Education, Winneba, Ghana, and Associate Researcher in the Laboratory of Sport and Social Environment at Université Grenoble Alpes, France. His research interests are in African football, footballers' migration and mobility, football coaching, youth football and education, sport for development, and the giving back phenomenon.

Malek Bouhaouala is Associate Professor in the Socioeconomics of Sport at Université Grenoble Alpes, France. He coordinates a research programme on ecosystem innovation in the mountain sports industry and is President of the think tank University and Enterprise Alliance of Grenoble (AUEG). His research interests are sport and tourism, leisure and society, mountain sports, entrepreneurs, sport consumers, and the giving back phenomenon.

Michel Raspaud is Professor of Sport Sociology at Université Grenoble Alpes, France. His research focuses mainly on sociology and history of mountaineering, high altitude adventure tourism, and international football (Africa, Brazil, Romania).

:al Research in Football

Editors:

Critical Research in Football book series was launched in 2017 to showcase the and multi-disciplinary breadth of debate relating to 'football'. The series de- 'football' as broader than association football, with research on rugby, Gaelic gridiron codes also featured. Including monographs, edited collections, short ks and textbooks, books in the series are written and/or edited by leading ex- s in the field whilst consciously also affording space to emerging voices in the , and are designed to appeal to students, postgraduate students and scholars are interested in the range of disciplines in which critical research in football nects. The series is published in association with the *Football Collective*, www. tballcollective.org.uk.

ilable in this series:

otball Fandom, Protest and Democracy
porter Activism in Turkey
han Irak

ican Footballers in Europe
ation, Community, and Give Back Behaviours
st Yeboah Acheampong, Malek Bouhaouala, and Michel Raspaud

ball in Fiction
tory
cGowan

all as Medicine
ibing Football for Global Health Promotion
by Peter Krustrup and Daniel Parnell

//www.routledge.com/sport/series/CFSFC

Critical Research in Football

AFRICAN FOOTBALLERS IN EUROPE

MIGRATION, COMMUNITY, AND GIVE BACK BEHAVIOURS

Ernest Yeboah Acheampong, Malek Bouhaouala, and Michel Raspaud

ROUTLEDGE

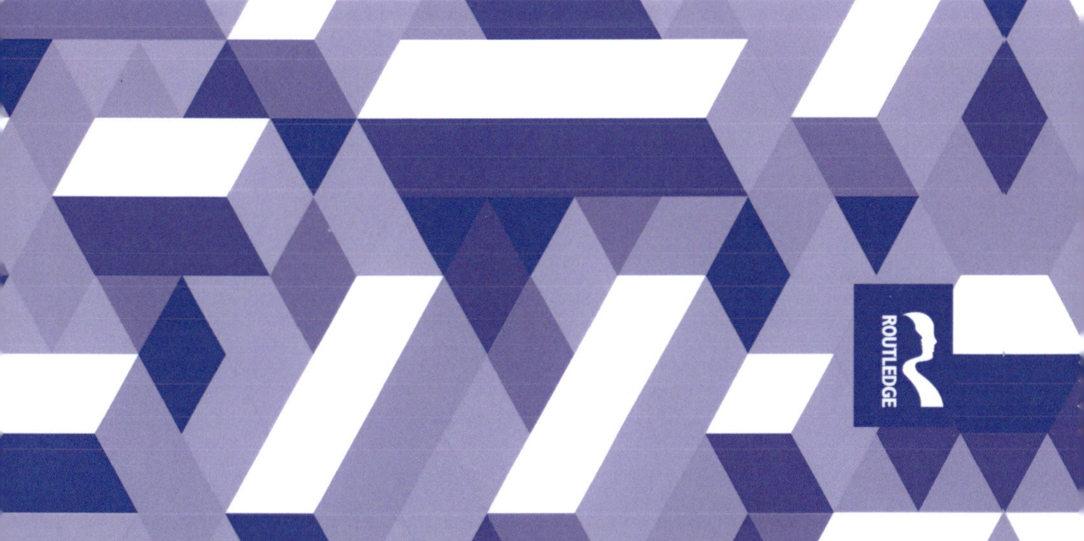

African Footballers in Europe

Migration, Community, and Give Back Behaviours

Ernest Yeboah Acheampong,
Malek Bouhaouala, and
Michel Raspaud

LONDON AND NEW YORK

First published 2020 by Routledge

2 Park Square, Milton Park, Abingdon, Oxon OX14 4RN
605 Third Avenue, New York, NY 10017

Routledge is an imprint of the Taylor & Francis Group, an informa business

First issued in paperback 2021

Publisher's Note

The publisher has gone to great lengths to ensure the quality of this reprint but points out that some imperfections in the original copies may be apparent.

British Library Cataloguing-in-Publication Data
A catalogue record for this book is available from the British Library

Library of Congress Cataloging-in-Publication Data
A catalog record has been requested for this book

ISBN: 978-0-367-26297-6 (hbk)
ISBN: 978-1-03-217711-3 (pbk)
DOI: 10.4324/9780429292422

Typeset in Goudy
by codeMantra

Contents

Preface

As a former semi-professional player from the developing world, I set out to become an example for the youth who are so obsessed with football that some abandoned school to focus only on the game. Some of the words the community use to describe early football enthusiasts in Africa are lazy, blunt-headed, visionless, nothing to do, incapable, low-minded, etc. I wanted to refute this erroneous impression by proving that football players have the capabilities to become academics and contribute to the scientific knowledge bank. After two decades, the same players have become social icons, achieved high social status and above all, provided some socioeconomic opportunities for society via their investment initiatives among others. I started to develop my human capital in the area of sport because of my passion for football. I nursed an ambition to become a medical doctor but there was a sudden twist towards sports. My new ambition deepened to the point of becoming a professional footballer abroad, but this could not materialise.

After attaining my second master's degree in Sports Management from the FIFA Master, one of the leading sports management programmes in Europe, I was inspired as the first Ghanaian to be one of this great alumni. I decided to serve as a conduit to transmit the knowledge and experience acquired to young ones playing actively in the domestic leagues in Ghana. Through my international network, an alumnus from the FIFA Master connected me to Anthony Baffoe, who coincidentally was looking for someone with my pedigree to steer the affairs of the budding union from its observer status to membership status. Based on the extensive briefing of his concept, I opted to support as a volunteer and got appointed as the General Administrator/ Coordinator of the Professional Footballers Association of Ghana (PFAG) as a former semi-professional. We were inaugurated in December 2009 and started working seriously towards achieving the set target member status of FIFPro. My reasons for supporting the union were:

(a) to contribute towards achieving the member status of FIFpro as a former player and
(b) to have answers to my implicit curiosity regarding how some professional players manage their football resources in their communities.

During my two years' stay at the PFAG, I met a lot of African professional footballers both retired and active through the various meetings and events of the union and established contacts with many. Through my interaction with them, I conceived the idea of putting together some documents based on their experiences and sporting knowledge which could provide an effective tool for young boys and girls in Africa desperate for a professional career abroad. Beyond that, it was helping me find answers to my mind-bothering questions. Similarly, these professional experiences can prepare the youth sufficiently for a better future transition after a professional football career abroad. Many of the professional footballers I spoke with mentioned the word 'giving back to society' in their own small ways to support the cause of their communities (with players' remittance). Since I wanted to know more about their usage of football resources and sporting capital, I decided to investigate further, and that served as an inspiration for my PhD thesis research. Here, another FIFA MASTER Alumnus connected me to his former thesis director, Michel Raspaud (Professor in Sociology of Sport) in the Laboratory of Sport and Social Environment (SENS) at the Université Grenoble Alpes, who coincidentally had worked on football in Africa aside from his interest in the sport. Professor Michel Raspaud also discussed scrutinising my research proposal on African professional footballers with his colleague in the same department, now an Associate Professor, Malek Bouhaouala, with a background in economic sociology. I was ecstatic about their positive response because they found my research proposal innovative and interesting. This journey of satisfying my curiosity exceeded my expectations when I finally defended my PhD thesis on 2 June 2017, in the department of Sport and Social Environment (SENS) at the Université Grenoble Alpes, France. The results of this innovative and interesting PhD research inspired the authors (Ernest, Malek and Michel) to share the fascinating conclusions of the thesis with a wider audience in order to appreciate some unique aspects of African culture through the Give Back Phenomenon (GBP). According to the recommendations of the external assessors, the new topic was intriguing and has prospects for development in society. This has contributed to producing new knowledge of African footballers' migration to the European leagues, by highlighting the link between the evolution of African football, footballers' migration strategies and the Give Back Phenomenon

In this book, we explain how African players used ingenious approaches to become footballers via street football activities which is a common characteristic among social groups in the communities. For instance, through their social groups, young boys could walk long distances to go and play football with other boys from different towns or villages as a way of expressing themselves and to have fun with what they have passion for. An explanation is provided of how players could graduate from the streets to find themselves in the big stadiums in Europe. This also enlarges our understanding of the shift in perspective of African football, its societies and the evolution of the European football market, which created inspiration for the best talents to move to their leagues. Indeed, some of the processes players went through to become professional players abroad are intrepid, adventurous and risky, which is rarely acknowledged. The book provides an understanding and enlightenment of African footballers' Give Back Behaviours (GBB) that supported examining key hypotheses including the past and current studies on migrants' relations with their communities of origin, particularly with reference to the context of professional football.

Regarding the specificities of footballers' process of migration, social status, and level of incomes, their GBB may be specific and also tied to differentiation. Based on the above observations, further consideration is given to the different socioeconomic causes that tend to affect their GBB. This GBB is a complex issue in African societies regarding their culture and family settings that may limit the economic rationality of the individual actors. Through this book, we share with our audience how the GBB is consubstantial to player migration projects, migration strategies, and itineraries to Europe, which are based on their aspirations and ambitions, due to the limited opportunities they have back home. We again discuss both players' experiences and lessons in dealing with parents, family, relatives, extended family, friends, coaches and the communities in relation to the GBB. These are cleverly supported with glowing interviews of former and current professional players narrating their football career paths, difficulties, memorable moments and achievements from the communities of origin to the Global North.

In this book, we contribute to new knowledge and provide vivid information in clarifying this issue through the analysis of cultural, social, and economic factors underpinning the GBB of African footballers in Europe. The book illustrates the evolution of African football and identifies the strategies and resources football players mobilised in facilitating their migratory process and professional itineraries. When migrants and professional footballers have achieved a high social and economic status, how do they manage this 'Give Back' Phenomenon in relation to their communities of origin? Should we consider the GBB as resulting from African footballers' economic rational choice or from a complex socioeconomic phenomenon which may be based on the interaction of economic and non-economic factors or individual and/or collective logics? To achieve this, we provide a multidisciplinary analysis based on a socioeconomic model which opens new perspectives on research concerning professional football and local interpretation of socioeconomic development in African countries.

The subject of the Give Back Phenomenon and behaviour of African professional footballers is new but highly connected to classical subjects such as athletes' migration, African football evolution, sport and local development, etc. This book will enrich the current curricula or inspire some universities in creating new courses or curricula out of it. The book is suitable to serve a diverse audience of academics, researchers, students in Faculties of Sports Sciences, sociology, geography, political sciences, management, etc. as well as professional organisations like NGOs, football agents, FIFPro, UNFD, players' unions, football administrators, federations, confederations, Governments, FIFA, UEFA, etc. These audiences are critical because they are concerned about the migration process, migration itineraries, professionalisation strategies, the evolution of African football, footballers' incomes, footballers' socioeconomic behaviours, and the mobility of African players in the European leagues.

Before writing this book, we had published three peer-reviewed papers: 'African footballers' life cycles according to the analysis of transfer value along their career path', 'African Footballers' Migration to Europe: Shifting Perspectives and Practice' and 'Socioeconomic analysis of African footballers' migration to Europe: Elements for decision making in the game's development.' Each of the publications focuses on African football migrations, the evolution of African football and socioeconomic contributions of players to society. All these together provide the reader with a series of diverse statements that surround the GBB of players which inspired this work.

African Footballers in Europe: Migration, Community, and Give Back Behaviours charts a new course in understanding how their football resources and sporting capital via their socioeconomic investment initiatives can impact on society. As is the case for this book, it develops new prospects in the area of how African players can invest in appropriate socioeconomic ventures that can support the good cause of society rather than indiscriminately giving out money to promote their fame.

We would like to give special thanks to Professor Claude Sobry (Université Lille 2, France) and Professor Lanfranchi Pierre (De Montfort University, Leicester, United Kingdom and CIES/FIFA Scientific committee member), who served as external assessors for their insightful and useful suggestions, and Ellis Kofi Akwaa-Sekyi (PhD) for his time and efforts spent severally reading on various draft chapters and offering valuable comments. We are also particularly, thankful to the reviewers for their constructive comments that have improved the book's content, and to those friends of ours, we salute you for your support and contributions. Finally, we would like to express our appreciation to the Series Editor and Rebecca Connor for their cooperation and support.

Introduction

Background and rationale

The migration of sport athletes continues to feature in the sport industry and academic circles. Some scholars have attributed the continuous migration to the evolution of the European football labour market and its EU policies on sport. This has contributed to increasing the movement of footballers from developing countries to the European leagues as observed during the 1990s (Acheampong and Bouhaouala 2019; Darby 2014; Poli 2010, 2015). Around the same period, the migration process of African footballers was reformed through the ingenious approach of becoming professional footballers in leagues abroad. The new development significantly increased African footballers' level of incomes and improved their social status and social recognition in their countries of origin while engendering their visibility internationally.

Indeed, the structure and professionalism of the UEFA leagues have enhanced greatly their socioeconomic importance and made them become the face of African football and social cohesion in their communities and beyond. Concurrently, these professional players maintain strong contact with their local communities, families, relatives, and friends due to social norms and cultural values or economic interests or personal goals. This sociocultural responsibility and the values they share with their communities reflect an important role that leads to the expectation of high socioeconomic demands from them. For instance, classical migrants from Africa who moved abroad had the expectation of high economic earnings to enable them to assist and support their families, relatives, and some community members. This raises the question of the nature of African footballers' relationships with the communities of origin in terms of 'Give Back Behaviours'(GBB). The reasons why they support their communities and how they justify these behaviours are captured in this book.

Essentially, classical migrants from Africa to Europe are basically attracted for economic reasons and with the purpose of supporting their families, parents, and communities, which are influenced by their social norms, the commitment towards their families and the social status they want to achieve. Some feel obliged to give back having enjoyed different kinds of support and financial contributions invested in their migration project. These various supports indirectly make family members and the community expect a return on investment (ROI) because they played a decisive role in their migration process.

In this book, we provide insight and explain how African footballers' Give Back Behaviours inspired us to examine the key hypotheses including the past and current studies on migrants' relations with their communities of origin in the context of professional football. Considering the specificities of footballers' process of migration, social status and level of incomes, their GBB may be explicit and varied depending on the level of leagues in Europe. Based on the above observations, we explore further to understand the different socioeconomic causes that tend to affect their GBB.

This book brings new knowledge and information to clarify this issue through the analysis of cultural, social, and economic factors underpinning the GBB of African footballers in Europe. Beyond that, it draws on the evolution of African football, the identification of strategies and resources that football players mobilised to facilitate their migration process and professional itineraries. When players achieve a reputation as a professional footballer abroad, which promotes their social and economic status in society, how do they manage the Give Back Behaviours in relation to their communities of origin? Should we consider the GBB as resulting from African footballers' economic rational choice or as a consequence of complex socioeconomic phenomena which may be based on the interaction of economic and non-economic factors or individual and/or collective logics?

In this book, we defend the concept that GBB is consubstantial to Africa and Europe migration and migrants' communities. In line with this, we highlight the role of economic and non-economic factors (social and cultural) that can orient African footballers' Give Back Behaviours towards their families, relatives, and communities. African players' GBB may be determined considering the return on investments (Becker 1993) or values and norms (Weber 1978 [1922]) or the embeddedness in social relations (Granovetter 1985, 2017) or the institutionalised networks (North 1990; Volery 2007) related to footballers' migration. In sum, a thorough analysis of players' GBB may be based on the combination of social, cultural, and economic factors in their socioeconomic approaches (Swedberg 2003).

Also, we carefully considered distinctive approaches that can help to explain their GBB including players' contributions to human capital development (Becker 1993), through the ROI, which cannot be the only explanation for footballers to give back but also includes non-economic causes. Giving back can be a condition to maintain the giver's social status and relationship with their communities of origin. Similarly, the GBB may be considered as a social and economic contribution confirming their success as a migrant in respond to their communities' expectations. To understand the dynamics, we employed socioeconomic approaches based on the contribution of Weberian methodology (Bouhaouala 1999, 2007) that provided a meso-analysis combining individualist and holist causes in the determination of African footballers' GBB, This shows the extent to which the interests and values of utilitarian rationality and socio-cultural determinism intermingle in the decisions and choices of the actors.

Max Weber defended this approach with the consideration that the individual is neither totally independent of society nor totally subservient to it. The Weberian ideal types of behaviours illustrate how economic and non-economic causes may influence human actions. In that sense, we avoided giving prevalence to the under-socialised or over-socialised (Granovetter 2017) approach in our analysis of the GBB. This research relied on a qualitative survey together with an extensive database developed to include biographies and autobiographies of African players. The qualitative survey approach was based on scores of interviews conducted with high-profile professional players from Africa. The interview questions were based on literature-based indicators, which are at odds with Weberian socioeconomic approach. These were organised and developed using the analysis grid regarding the survey themes (see Table 4.3). The book outcomes show that African footballers' behaviours in terms of their giving back depend largely on complex socioeconomic logics of action determined by their economic interest, social norms, and cultural beliefs. The findings highlight three main categories;

(1) The social and economic evolution of African football. This explains how communities and families' perception of football, specifically as a professional career, has evolved positively. Establishment of football structures and sporting facilities, juvenile leagues and football academies in developing countries. The emergence of some of these football amenities allowed us to identify one evolution with three distinct periods from the 1980s to the 2000s showing the evolution of social perception, football structures, and migration strategies:

 (a) controversial vision: football vs. school (the 1980s).
 (b) shared vision: football's gradual shift from social to professional activity (the 1990s).
 (c) professional football as an opportunity (the 2000s).

(2) Typology of players' migration itineraries: These are linked to the evolution of African football and the growth of the European football labour market. It contributed to identifying the interconnection between players' strategies, football structures, network profiles and other resources available to them. The three different itineraries observed were:

 (a) collective resource-based
 (b) formal networks resource-based
 (c) individual resource-based.

(3) Four types of Give Back Behaviours: These were identified based on certain factors that structure the GBB typology:

 (a) involvement of social structures (family, community, etc.) and football institutions (academy, clubs, etc.);
 (b) social norms and values and cultural beliefs;
 (c) economic interests and ROI;

(d) nature of resources mobilised; and
(e) targets of the give back phenomenon.

Identifying good reasons (Boudon 1995) regarding the 'give back' approach permitted us to describe and explain the complex phenomenon, supporting the development of a typology of the Give Back Behaviours targeting four types of groups with specific actions:

(a) hybrid family
(b) cross-closed family
(c) shared family
(d) shadow family

Finally, the book has various chapters describing in detail to our readers African professional players' GBB considering the evolution of African football in the context of the European football labour market, the role of communities and how players manipulated the system, mobilised resources from parents, families, friends and the communities to facilitate their migration project. This helps us to understand how the various contributions from the latter could impact the players' GBB to society through robust analysis and discussion, which the origin of the text.

Bibliography

Acheampong, E. Y. and Bouhaouala, M. 2019. 'African footballers' life cycles according to the analysis of transfer value along their career path: a case study of Ghanaian players', *Sport in Society–Cultures, Commerce, Media Politics*, doi: 10.1080/17430437.2018.1551366.

Becker, G. 1993. *Human Capital: A Theoretical and Empirical Analysis with Special Reference to Education*. 3rd edition. Chicago: University of Chicago Press.

Boudon, R. 1995. *Le juste et le vrai: études sur l'objectivité des valeurs et de la connaissance*. Paris: Fayard. [Trans. *The Origin of Values*. 2001. New Brunswick/London: Transaction.]

Bouhaouala, M. 1999. 'Micro-mentalités et logiques d'actions des dirigeants des petites entreprises dutourisme sportif: contribution à une sociologie économique du sport.' Thèse de Doctorat de l'Université Joseph Fourier Grenoble 1.

Bouhaouala, M. 2007. 'Micro-mentalités et logiques d'action des entrepreneurs dirigeants de petites entreprises', *Revue Internationale PME*, 20: 2.

Darby, P. 2014. 'International football migration and Africa: Feet drain or feet exchange', *More than a Game, Sports, Society and Politics: Panorama Insights into Asian and European Affairs*, January 2014.

Granovetter, M. 1985. 'Economic action and social structure: The problem of Embeddedness', *American Journal of Sociology* 91 (3): 481–510.

Granovetter, M. 2017. *Society and Economy, Framework and Principals*. Harvard: The Belknap Press of Harvard University Press.

North, C. Douglass. 1990. *Institutions, Institutional Change and Economic Performance*. Cambridge: Cambridge University Press.

Poli, R. 2010. 'African migrants in Asian and European football: Hopes and realities', *Sport in Society: Cultures, Commerce, Media, Politics* 13 (6): 1001–1011. doi:10.1080/ 17430437.2010.491269.

Poli, R., Ravenel, L. and R. Besson, R. 2015. 'Exporting countries in world football', *CIES Football Observatory Monthly Report*, 1–10.

Swedberg R. 2003. *Principles of Economic Sociology*. Princeton and Cambridge: Princeton University Press.

Volery, T. 2007. 'Ethnic entrepreneurship: A theoretical framework.' In *Handbook of Research on Ethnic Minority Entrepreneurship: A Co-Evolutionary View on Resource Management*. Cheltenham: Edward Elgar, pp. 30–31.

Weber, M. 1978 [1922]. *Economic and Society: An Outline of Interpretive Sociology*, translated by Ephraim Fischoff *et al.*, 2 vols. Berkeley: University of California Press.

1

African football, migration, Give Back Behaviour, and economic rationality

Introduction

This chapter discusses a brief history of African football and its transformation from 1957 and how it has impacted its footballers' migration to leagues abroad. The Confederation of African Football (CAF) manages and organises football and other football-related activities on the Continent. Since its inception, CAF competitions have evolved from four countries' participation to 24 as of 2019. Despite this achievement, some studies have outlined various issues that hinder the progress of African football though the people have passion and pride for football. These include barriers such as underdevelopment and lack of professionalism of the sport on the African continent which continue to fuel players' movement abroad (Acheampong 2018a; Darby 2002, 2007a, 2007b, 2014; Lanfranchi and Taylor 2001; Poli 2006a, 2006b, 2010). Some of these challenges in African football development have lured its best players to the European football market. As at the 2014/2015 season, as many as 1,084 players from 44 different African countries were playing and/or played in the 30 professional leagues from the 13 UEFA countries.

To move abroad, a player may depend largely on resources from families, relatives, and the communities in support of their migration project. Thus, they perceive moving abroad as the only option to become professional footballers (Darby 2010), while acknowledging the efforts of parents, family members, extended family and the community that contribute in different ways from finances, social relations, and networks, to facilitate their migration to leagues abroad (Acheampong 2018b; Büdel 2013; Darby 2014; Poli 2010; van der Meij and Darby 2014). This shows how the latter provide valuable resources in different forms, all to get their young boys, siblings and friends with football talent to have a professional career abroad. This is because achieving a professional footballer status abroad can provide them with substantial incomes some of which are remitted to support activities of families, relatives, and society in their countries of origin. In some cases, the financial rewards from their football profession are seen as long-term provisions for family members, extended family, and friends' sustenance (de Vasconcellos Ribeiro and Dimeo 2009). This support in various forms according to the players' rationality may demonstrate their appreciation by giving something back to families, relatives and communities in return for their different contributions.

The chapter analyses the migration process of African players to Europe and examines how their professional achievement impacts their decision making in relation to society. This helps to gain insight and explain what actually influences players to give something back after becoming successful professionally abroad. To our readers, this chapter begins by exploring African football and its footballers' dynamics in understanding some issues facilitating their migration to leagues abroad. In the next section, we describe how players migrate in the context of professional football and the kind of support they receive from their families, relatives and communities to facilitate their migration project, because African football seemed not to have provided them with better opportunities back home (Acheampong 2018b). Such information is important as it provides a platform to understand the way players appreciate families, relatives, and communities' contributions via their Give Back Behaviour. Lastly, we discuss whether players' Give Back Behaviour is based on economic rationality or determined by values to satisfy society.

African football and footballers in perspective

Modern African football became autonomous during the post-colonial period to affirm the birth of the young nations' identities. Football, like all types of sports, was one of the central elements that played a role in the international positioning during the Cold War. African football has evolved from the four pioneering and independent countries of Egypt, Sudan, Ethiopia, and South Africa. These countries later founded and organised the Confederation of African Football (CAF) which was established in 1957. Even though South Africa could not compete in its maiden event held in Sudan because of multiracial issues, Egypt became the African football leader and the eventual winner. After the colonial era, a few African independent countries started to participate in the tournament. Here there was no qualifying series before a country could make it to the final tournament. This was before 1962 when there was limited number of participating countries for AFCON tournaments. Until the shift in African football, the number of participating countries rose from 12 in 1992 through a direct elimination approach. Participating countries increased from 16 in 1996 until 2019 when the number rose to 24. The Africa Cup of Nations (AFCON) competition is now held biennially in odd years as the biggest event in the continent. The declared overall winner of AFCON represents the continent at the FIFA Confederation Cup. CAF has 55 full members zoned into six geopolitical regions; North zone, West zones A and B, Central zone, Central-East zone and Southern zone (CAF website 2019).[1]

In Africa, football has become an integral part of many countries after its introduction in colonial times (Alegi 2010). Football has supported the integration of many communities in the new African nations by improving their feeling of belongingness. It has also provided socioeconomic opportunities for individuals, groups, institutions, and the community. CAF's new introduction of the Championship of African Nations (CHAN) to create opportunities for domestic leagues' talents is a novelty that offers socioeconomic benefits for participants through international exposure (Acheampong 2017).

The various CAF competitions have improved the standard of play, display of individual qualities and potentials that attract foreign media attention, scouts, football agents, and foreign clubs at their events. National teams with a high ratio of foreign-based players improve the level of play for those African countries (Darby 2014, 78) in domestic and international competitions. The trend has continued since the beginning of the twenty-first century with more participation of foreign-based players than the home-based players (Acheampong, Bouhaouala, and Raspaud 2013). This has positively impacted the team performance of some African nations especially Cameroun, Senegal, and Ghana at the FIFA World Cup competitions. Today, African football, with the South American countries, is the world's biggest provider of professional players to the larger European football market (Acheampong and Bouhaouala 2019).

Indeed, African football is not without challenges. The evolution of European football continues to attract international footballers including those talents from Africa to their leagues (Lanfranchi and Taylor 2001). Also, FIFA's financial and technical support to member associations in Africa has not been enough to accelerate football development on the African continent. The weakness of African states in providing positive perspectives to young people and the CAF's lackadaisical attitude lead to its footballers moving abroad for greener pastures. As contended by Acheampong (2018a), football talents are not only seeking professional opportunities outside African borders but also migrate in order to overcome the limited opportunities back home.

The fact is that African players are scattered around leagues abroad; 1,084 of them were found in 30 professional leagues from the 13 UEFA countries. The majority, representing over 51.56 per cent, are in the top five European leagues (see Table 2.1). In leagues abroad, African player wages/salaries increase considerably compared to other sectors in their countries. On average, some African players in the elite leagues can earn between €15,000 and €100,000 or more as wages/salaries. Those in leagues one, two and three, respectively, can also earn around €10,000–50,000, €5000–20,000 and €2000–10,000[2] (see Acheampong 2018b). Some few high-profile players earn more than €150,000 as wages per month in prestigious European clubs.

These socioeconomic and professional opportunities have contributed strongly to increase the migration of young players far from their communities and countries. This gives them the possibility of achieving new professional status and gaining prestigious social status abroad as well as in their own countries, which empowers them economically and increases their visibility. At the same time, the status of successful migrants increases their families' and communities' expectations in terms of remittances and economic assistance. In the professional football context these are the parameters of a framework for understanding how socioeconomic factors can influence players' economic behaviour regarding their economic investments and societal initiatives in their communities of origin. This is detailed in the subsequent sections on players' GBB to society.

African professional footballers in the context of migration

The migration of football players to elegant leagues and clubs is a continuation of a trend that began in the 1870s when English clubs employed the talented Scottish footballers (Goldblatt 2006, 47). This made migration become dynamic in the context of globalisation. This is catching up with feminisation of migration (female footballers: see Agergaard and Tiesler 2014; Booth and Liston 2014; Williams, 2014). It also encompasses the distinct migration destinations and the transformation of labour flows into the international transfer market of football. Some scholars (Darby 2000, 2002, 2007a, 2010, 2014; Lanfranchi and Taylor 2001; Poli 2006a, 2006b, 2010) have outlined the various concepts of migration but in this book, the focus is on the migration of African players as part of broader international migration of footballers in the transfer market.

Migration emanated from historical perspectives and has since played a crucial role which cannot be disregarded in terms of drawing on football migrations (Taylor 2007) in the sense that migration has created a means for football talents to cross borders, nations and continents to fulfil their dream projects. In Africa, more football talents are eager to migrate abroad than ever before in modern history because of major global changes, the growth of the international football markets, and the weakness of local socioeconomics situations, etc. The African continent persists in being characterised by poverty, high unemployment rates, presence of repressive governments, collapse of educational systems, agricultural reforms with disastrous consequences for countries. Weak political management and poor African football markets continue to intensify the migration of its talents to leagues in Europe (De Haas 2008). Despite some of these challenges, the benefits for migrants' households, community and families can be enormous when they are professionally successful abroad. This is one reason why families, relatives, friends, and the community find it necessary to always support their siblings moving abroad (Acheampong 2018b).

Playing in leagues abroad comes with its own opportunities and difficulties but African football migrants may feel relieved as they have access to many things that can improve their socioeconomic lives back home. This tends to fuel the migration of the best football talents from Africa to European leagues, which is nothing new (Darby 2014; Lanfranchi and Taylor 2001). The best players from Africa are desperate to move abroad in exchange for their talent and potentials in the pursuit of career ambitions as a professional footballer. These players not only seek professional football opportunities outside African borders but also move in order to overcome the limited opportunities back home which rarely empower them, rather influencing their migration abroad (Acheampong 2018b).

Alongside the push and pull factors affecting the migration of footballers, the main motive for international footballers to go to leagues and clubs abroad is based on economic rewards and prospects in anticipation for their services (Lanfranchi and Taylor 2001). Due to the limited opportunities at home for some African players, migration abroad provides an avenue for them to achieve social upward mobility which is prestigious in the local communities. For the players to accomplish this, families, relatives, the community, organise human, material, and social resources to support their migration project abroad because European football tends to dominate the sport worldwide. Such support from the family, relatives, friends, and the community may have some influence on players' economic behaviour when they decide to do investments in the localities. In that case, the players become socially indebted to them (Acheampong 2018b) and this can be observed through their giving back behaviour.

Give Back Behaviour is consubstantial to African migration

As African young people, footballers have identified limited opportunities at home as a barrier to their personal, social and professional projects for which only migrating abroad can provide an alternative. Moving abroad to play professional football can provide them with substantial economic incomes, some of which can be allocated to support activities of the families, community, and society at large in their countries of origin. Darby (2014) argues that optimists view the migration of African footballers to elite leagues abroad as an opportunity to provide them with the sort of exposure and earnings that not only contribute to the development of football but also allow the individuals to escape poverty and act transnationally in ways that potentially facilitate 'development' at home. Some contributions of players can be observed from the various social and economic investments which they offer to society (Acheampong 2018b). Players' behaviour in social terms reflects the rationality behind their investments support in the communities. This determines how players' rationale can be inspired by their objectives, values, conceptions and interests so that they may give important meaning to their economic behaviour (Bouhaouala 1999, 2008).

Others may disagree with how the optimists view the migration of African footballers abroad, but this book goes further to identify African players' economic behaviour in supporting their families, friends, and households with their football earnings and sporting capital in the communities. Giving something back to families, households, friends, and the community may represent their social contributions towards their professional career abroad. An example of this giving back model is seen from the perspective of a football academy in Africa, 'Right To Dream Academy' registered as an NGO in Ghana.

In Right to Dream (RTD) Academy, there is a form of giving back scheme based on 'credit' accumulation. Here, recruit trainees are introduced to a credits system that should be earned through personal achievements in education and football, and for their involvement in community projects, foundations, and entrepreneurial activities in African contexts (Darby 2013,50). Trainees are only asked to sign a declaration of 'give back' to support their communities. This impersonal contract does not fit with their culture, objectives, conceptions, or interests. According to Bouhaouala (1999, 2007), individuals' values, objectives, conceptions, and interests should influence their economic behaviour in relation to whatever rational initiatives and formal structures they want to support local development with. Apparently, the RTD model hardly permits trainees to be part of the decision-making process regarding their giving back model as embedded in their education and socio-cultural context. This model, which is adapted to the rationalist Western culture based on a collective and impersonal system of solidarity, does not fit with the African's socio-cultural rules and norms managing the social relationships in terms of giving back. This makes the scheme unclear regarding what best informs the decisions of trainees to accept and contribute to the credits system of the academy.

Indeed, many trainees are from low-income communities who recognise their recruitment as an opportunity and rarely interrogate it. Similarly, parents, families, relatives, and the community have failed to ask relevant questions about the principle of their 'giving back scheme' in the academy. RTD's approach is a formal rational strategy that presents giving back as an impersonal and formal model. This book advances the argument on their giving back scheme in relation to other professional players from Africa. These are our observations from their concept — (i) does their scheme fit into the social norms and cultural values of many African communities? (ii) what is the underlying rationale behind the RTD concept? and (iii) are trainees being coerced to give something back (which may contradict their personal values or objectives or interests or conceptions) and or otherwise? Though the RTD model purports to target low-income communities and the vulnerable in the society, there is a need to figure out what best explains individuals' contributions concept in a broader context.

A female footballer[3] from West Africa rejected a monetary reward after playing for her country in an international competition. She recognised her participation as a social contribution to her country because they provided her exposure and visibility that led to her migration abroad. The player's decision was not based on achieving a specific economic aim like profits or gains but for the respected values associated with the wearing of national team colours like honour, social recognition, and patriotism (Acheampong 2017).

Some footballers[4] have investments in social projects out of sports and with sports to support their communities (Mensah 2010).[5] They established public libraries, community centres and hospitals, promoted educational initiatives, were ambassadors of UNDP and UNICEF to promote humanitarian projects. Others just give back to their families, relatives or friends, etc. without any national or international framework of visibility. The general backgrounds of these players' socioeconomic logics and cultural obligation explain the rationality behind their behaviour which may affect their community embeddedness and personal interests. Because those former players' social contributions were based either on their values, conceptions, objectives, or on interests that reflected in their various social projects, they invested their resources to the benefit of families, community, or society.

In short, the players' investment projects in different forms can reflect their economic rationality, which demonstrates the significant meaning they give to their actions (either value-oriented or cultural, affection/emotional or rational strategy) and may drive a good cause in society. The players' Give Back Behaviour is linked to their professional status achieved after migrating abroad in pursuit of their career ambitions in football.

Give Back Behaviour, is it economic or value-oriented?

The migration projects of African players are facilitated by either families or friends or relatives or the community or networks or agents as they pursue their professional football aspirations abroad. Support enjoyed from families, relatives, friends, football agents or sport agency and the community may have some influence on their rationality concerning their economic and non-economic initiatives. This may reflect how they behave and how they interpret the support they get from others and how they might want to give back when successful professionally. George Ekeh, a former Nigerian international, recalled the support he had from his family when he finally decided to play football after his secondary education.

> People who had completed university, have no jobs and some graduates were loitering in the streets without jobs and that the future just looks bleak. The next tendency for me was to invest in something that I could see a better future from and that was football.[6]

His decision was rational, but he did not consider the high risk of being unsuccessful, though he qualified for university education. He appreciated the immense contributions of family members as they provided him with training kits and material resources that supported his football career path to leagues abroad. Apart from him investing in his personal businesses, he supported his immediate family with regular remittances to improve their livelihood. His logic depicts formal rationality through the financial support of his family for them to sustain their welfare. African players interviewed disclosed that they have received various forms of support from the society and this often tends to influence their rationality when it comes to sending remittances back home. These supports are to empower some members of the community making them become financially independent through the provision of job opportunities so that it can improve the social welfare of siblings, families, and others in society.

Sometimes, players' economic behaviour to the community members may reflect their state of mind linked to cultural and emotional or affective perspectives. This could be likened to their value orientation as well. For instance, when he was asked how important the African community was to his football career, Victor Wanyama[7] recalled: 'You need to remember where you came from and as much as you can to help them especially the kids who are in need so, is a great initiative.' As a graduate of street football, his social connections with the social groups supported his integration and informal training in the community. This made him identify some of the challenges young boys must handle at that level when searching for a professional opportunity, such as getting football kits and equipment. Encouragement and advice on football career are barely provided for young boys in their social group. Thus, providing them with resources like funds, sports kits and others will go a long way to improve on their talent. Wanyama acted from an emotional or affective stimulus (Weber 1978) emerging from his childhood association with the street football activities and finds it important to contribute meaningfully to societal causes. Thus, he expects not to receive anything in return but to impact young boys' talent which reflects his value-orientation towards improving life skills of people in the community.

Others show their appreciation to the society by establishing charity foundations to educate, develop and protect the young boys in the communities. A former Cameroonian international footballer, Mbvoumin has set up a charity foundation across Africa with a branch in Europe; he explained how it is helping to control and protect young players' migration, as his contribution to society. He invests his sporting capital and experiences, efforts and resources to protect the young ones from exploitation. He said:

> I think my life (goal) was not to win awards with what am doing because I'm a former African player, I faced some problems, I met a lot of African young players even younger than me facing very difficult issues than me. And I said, what is my responsibility or what can I do as a former player for my community and country. This is, why I decided to create Foot Solidaire (Association Culture Foot Solidaire -CFS).[8]

The social initiative to support young players back home and abroad has earned him international awards like Trafficking in Persons (TIP) Award (2008) and the Jackie Robinson Humanitarian Award (2015), all received in the USA, in recognition of the positive effects his CFS foundation has had on humanity in the fight against child trafficking. The rationality behind his non-economic behaviour (humanitarian model) is related to his value-orientation and affection for society, belief in the value being seen in his deliberate actions. In addition, African players exhibited either social or economic behaviour or both directed towards improving social welfare and their future livelihood after an active football career. In sum, African players' Give Back Behaviour through their economic action tends to focus mainly on their socioeconomic rational decision and value-orientation approach.

Conclusion

The limited opportunities at home for young players' development from the communities have strongly supported the best talents to search for a reputation as a professional footballer in Europe. African players used their internal resources (talents, savings, etc.) and other resources to achieve their professional dreams abroad, since becoming a professional footballer comes with its economic prospects, social status and national recognition. African players' ability to manage some of these achievements in relation to their Give Back Behaviour mirrors the significant meaning they assigned to their contributions and support in various ways to the good cause of families, relatives, friends, and the communities. We revealed how some players invested their efforts, knowledge transfer and sporting capital via social and economic activities to support the social welfare of families, relatives, and the communities. Others made socioeconomic rational choices as well as value-oriented decisions as their valuable contributions to the society that had supported them to get this far in their professional careers.

Notes

1. Geopolitical zoning of CAF member associations. http://www.cafonline.com/en-us/caf/cafzones.aspx.
2. Players' earnings were calculated on a monthly basis without bonuses and other incentives.
3. Courtney Dike rejected $7000 paid to her by the Nigerian Football Federation for participating in 2014, U-20 Women's World Cup.
4. Joseph Yobo, John Paintsil, Mohamed Aboutrika, Aaron Mokoena, and John Utaka.
5. Ten African Footballers with a Social Conscience (the writer explained some African players who are into social projects in their communities and beyond).
6. Interview with George Ekeh, on 20 April 2016.
7. Interview with Victor Wanyama was recorded on Kwesé TV Sports, on 23 August 2017.
8. Interview with Jean-Claude Mbvoumin, on 7 October 2015.

Bibliography

Acheampong, E. Y. 2017. 'Socioeconomic analysis of the Give Back phenomenon: Professional footballers in Europe and their assistance to the communities of origin in Africa.' PhD diss., Université Grenoble Alpes, France.

Acheampong, E.Y. 2018a. 'How does professional football status challenge African players' behaviour?', *Soccer & Society*, doi:10.1080/14660970.2018.1541797.

Acheampong, E.Y. 2018b. 'Giving back to society: evidence from African sports migrants', *Sport in Society*, doi:10.1080/17430437.2018.1551367.

Acheampong, E. Y. and Bouhaouala, M. 2019. 'African footballers' life cycles according to the analysis of transfer value along their career path: a case study of Ghanaian players', *Sport in Society*, doi:10.1080/17430437.2018.1551366.

Acheampong, E. Y., Bouhaouala, M. and Raspaud, M. 2013. 'Influence of African professional players on AFCON tournaments.' Presented at the 15th ACAPS congress in Grenoble, France.

Agergaard, S. and Tiesler, N. Clara. 2014. *Women, Soccer and Transnational Migration*. Routledge.

Alegi, P. 2010. *African Soccerscapes: How a Continent Changed the World's Game*. Athens, OH: Ohio University Press.

Booth, S. and Liston, K. 2014. 'The continental drift to a zone of prestige: women's soccer migration to the US NCAA Division 1 20002010.' In S. Agergaard and N. C. Tisler (eds), *Women, Soccer and Transnational Migration* (53–72). London and New York: Routledge.

Bouhaouala, M. 1999. 'Micro-mentalités et logiques d'actions des dirigeants des petites entreprises du tourisme sportif: contribution à une sociologie économique du sport.' Thèse de Doctorat de l'Université Joseph Fourier Grenoble 1.

Bouhaouala, M. 2007. 'Micro-mentalités et logiques d'action des entrepreneurs dirigeants de petites entreprises', *Revue Internationale PME*, 20: 2.

Bouhaouala, M. 2008. *Management de la petite entreprise des loisirs sportifs, une approche socio-économique*. Bruxelles: De Boeck Université, Collection New Management.

Büdel, M. 2013. 'An ethnographic view on African football migrants in İstanbul', *Cilt* (Ankara Üniversitesi) 68 (1): 1–20.

Darby, P. 2000. 'The new scramble for Africa: African football labour migration to Europe', *The European Sports History Review* 3: 217–244.

Darby, P. 2002. *Africa, Football and FIFA: Politics, Colonialism and Resistance*. London: Frank Cass.

Darby, P. 2007a. 'Out of Africa: The exodus of African football talent to Europe', *Working USA: the Journal of Labour and Society* 10 (4): 443–456. doi:10.1111/j.1743-4580.2007.00175. x.

Darby, P. 2007b. 'African football labour migration to Portugal: colonial and neocolonial resource', *Soccer and Society* 8 (4): 495–509.

Darby, P. 2010. '"Go outside": The history, economics and geography of Ghanaian football labour migration', *African Historical Review* 42 (1): 19–41. doi:10.1080/17532523.2010.483793.

Darby, P. 2013. 'Moving players, traversing perspectives; Global value chains, production networks and Ghanaian football labour migration', *Geoforum* 50: 43–53. http: //dx.doi.org/10.1016 /j. geoforum.2013.06.009.

Darby, P. 2014. 'International football migration and Africa: Feet drain or feet exchange', *More than a Game, Sports, Society and Politics: Panorama Insights into Asian and European Affairs*, January 2014.

De Haas, H. 2008. 'The myth of invasion: The inconvenient realities of African migration to Europe', *Third World Quarterly* 29 (7): 1305–1322. doi:10.1080/0143659 080 2386435.

De Vasconcellos Ribeiro, C. H. and Dimeo, P. 2009. 'The experience of migration for Brazilian football players', *Sport in Society* 12 (6): 725–736.

Goldblatt, D. 2006. *The Ball is Round, A Global History of Soccer*. Riverhead Books, ISBN 978-1-59448-296-0.

Lanfranchi, P. and Taylor, M. 2001. *Moving with the Ball: The Migration of Professional Footballers*. Oxford: Berg.

Mensah, K. N. S. 2010. 'African football icons that never lost touch with home plight.' http://www.goal.com/en/news/1717/editorial/2010/07/21/2035384/. Accessed 19 May 2015.

Poli, R. 2006a. 'Africans' status in the European football players' labour market', *Soccer and Society* 7 (2–3): 278–2291. doi:10.1080/14660970600615369.

Poli, R. 2006b. 'Migrations and trade of African football players: Historic, geographical and cultural aspects', *Afrika-Spectrum* 41 (3): 393–414.

Poli, R. 2010. 'African migrants in Asian and European football: Hopes and realities', *Sport in Society: Cultures, Commerce, Media, Politics* 13 (6): 1001–1011. doi:10.1080/17430437. 2010.491269.

Taylor, M. 2007. *The Association Game: A History of British Football*. Harlow, UK: Pearson Longman.

Van der Meij, N. and Darby, P. 2014. 'No one will burden the sea and then never get any benefit: Family involvement in players' migration to football academies in Ghana.' In J. Harris and R. Elliot (eds), *Football and Migration* (159–179). Abingdon: Routledge.

Weber, M. 1978 [1922]. *Economy and Society*. 2 Volumes. Eds. G. Roth and C. Wittich, Berkeley: University of California Press.

Williams, J. 2014. *Women, Soccer and Transnational Migration*. London: Routledge.

2

Give Back Behaviour spectacle, football labour markets, sports migration, and connection with communities

Introduction

This chapter sheds light on what other studies have reported on the Give Back Behaviour (GBB), which is complex in nature. The GBB may represent the act of supporting others with an interest in improving their social welfare in the communities. It can be difficult to understand what actually influences people to give something back to society. As such, we explore the various theories and models to help explain this GBB occurrence focusing on the specific case of football migrants from Africa. In doing so, we employ Weberian methodology and economic sociology approaches to integrate both the individual and societal explanations. Our rationale here is to provide a general context describing how the literature assists in briefly analysing the GBB concept, the evolution of a European football context and labour market, evolution of African football, relationship between African and European football, migration from Africa to Europe, typologies of football migrants in the context of globalisation and African football migrants in Europe. Further discussion on the above improves our understanding of all the processes of migration in the context of globalisation and diverse strategies espoused to achieve players' professional ambition and aspiration in the European leagues. This can go a long way to influence African players' GBB to society. The way the players sustain this relationship after situational changes with the communities of origin is appropriately highlighted. Tables, figures, and a map are used to illustrate the migration of players from Africa to Europe. The chapter ends with a summary of how this process can have effects on decision making in terms of players' GBB.

General context

Understanding the rationale behind players giving something back to their communities is not as simple as it may appear. Various literature was reviewed to assist, develop, and design a framework to explain the rationality behind professional players' decision making regarding 'Give Back Behaviour' (GBB) to their communities of origin. The GBB may represent the act of supporting others with an interest in improving the welfare of society. GBB can also demonstrate an appreciation in return for the individual or group contributions to one's progress in life. The literature provides insight into different theories and models that contributed to explaining why professional players accept the idea of supporting society via their socioeconomic initiatives to improve their social welfare. The action of African players to support others may depend on their subjectivity, social and economic reasons, and on the behaviour of significant others, which can influence their courses of decision making (Weber 1978 [1922]).

Here, the analysis of social and economic interactions underlying players' specific economic behaviour is given preference. This charts a new course on the application of socioeconomic analysis of sport migrants in terms of giving something back to the community and social groups of origin. It does so by also assessing the rationale behind professional footballers' choices to support society, engaging with the use of Weberian methodology and economic sociology approaches to integrate both the individual and societal explanations. The literature gathered also serves as a heuristic tool to analyse and explain how African football evolved, African football development, and other factors that facilitate the migration process and itinerary of African players to the European leagues. African footballers' destination of play is not only the conclusion of their migration project but also a strategy to better their social lives including their families, parents, relatives, and the community.

The theories and models identified, coupled with thorough examinations of other relevant documents, contributed to developing an extensive database on African professional players abroad. The review of literature produced some vital indicators, which aided the design and construction of an analysis grid with specific characteristics tracing the career trajectories of African players and how they sustain relationships with their families, relatives, friends, and the communities of origin and diasporas. Essentially, the extensive review undertaken, examining the itineraries of African players from their local communities to moving abroad, helped in understanding its effects on their GBB to society. The literature further contributes to explaining the importance African players attach to their economic behaviour in term of their socioeconomic investment initiatives in the local communities.

The literature supports the discussions and interpretations of how economic and sociological theories and models identified can contribute to illustrating the rationale behind the players' GBB to their countries of origin. Detailed explanations from the theories and models helped to firm up the theoretical framework connected directly to the GBB of African players.

Evolution of European football context and labour market

Football (soccer) in Europe tends to dominate worldwide. This is due to the convergence of many structural factors (economic, sociological, and 'footballistical').

Indeed, the European context is very attractive in terms of economic level, quality of life, and political stability. In this favourable context the attractiveness of European football as well as the game's performance and marketability all increased. In comparison with African football, there is a big gap in socioeconomic context, the game's level, the quality of competitions, and attractiveness of leagues. Then, the footballers' economic value on the African continent, level of play, mediatisation and commercialisation aspects remain weak. According to some scholars these factors may facilitate the movement of other international talents to their leagues, which may provide a one-directional perspective on athletics mobility (Agergaard and Tiesler 2014). Others defined them as the push or pull factors that support the mobility of football players to Europe (Lanfranchi and Taylor 2001). The evolution of European football has really positioned itself ahead of many places and competitions because of the leagues' ability to absorb nationals from other continents. At the same time, it shows the uniqueness of the European football market in the sport industry. Elsewhere, football as a professional sport provides means to understand the behaviour of the labour market in Europe. Sloane's (1971) study distinguished the model of European sport from the North American model and challenged that the league rather than individual clubs is the relevant 'firm' (decision-making unit). In Britain, the management of the English Premiership has structured and positioned their league in a manner that has attracted foreign investors to become owners and/or shareholders of some prestigious clubs. This demonstrates the huge capital investments in the league, making it appealing to global viewership and recognised as one of the best in the world.

European leagues and competitions serve as a marketing strategy for clubs and federations to attract foreign supporters and sponsors globally. Here, some clubs have started to undertake pre-season tours of other countries as a way of promoting their leagues in those territories. This provides a two-way benefit for the donor and host countries when their migrated talents become successful in the leagues. Conversely, it can have negative effects on both donor and host countries as well (Maguire, Jarvie, Mansfield, and Bradley 2002, 37). From the mid-1990s the major five European championships (English, Spanish, German, Italian, and French) have dominated as the host to many international players across the continents (Poli, Ravenel and Besson 2016). This is nothing new as their leagues are professionalised, structured, competitive and above all, provide socioeconomic potentials. That tends to increase the percentage of migrant footballers in clubs each year (Poli *et al.* 2016), to the extent that some clubs within the distance of 100 km along borders or regions recruit talented minors to recoup returns on investment (ROI) after the resale of their playing rights in future transfers. This aspect of the book tries to understand the European football labour market and how it has benefited individual African footballers and clubs in their transactions within the international transfer market (Acheampong and Bouhaouala 2019).

The evolution of football dated far back into the 1950s with the debates on the subject. Contemporary football is the leading global sport in terms of its audiences and commercialisation across all the continents. This has made European football gain popularity together with its associated economic earnings and quality of international players in the leagues. In brief, football has metamorphosed to a level all of its own. The early 1990s saw the total improvement in the game when FIFA together with its confederations strategised to establish a strong relationship with the media industry as partners. Sugden and Tomlinson (1998) argue that the prominent role of FIFA and UEFA in the marketing of the sport with their tournaments such as the FIFA World Cup and the UEFA Champions League, attract global viewership not only because of its quality but also the blend of international players.

These international players migrate to Europe but are more attracted to the top five leagues of Spain, England, Germany, Italy, and France. These leagues provide the players with considerable earnings and at the same time promote their socioeconomic status and the chance for development. Again, these leagues also have the highest economic level due to the broadcasting rights and sponsorships, which increase in value upon subsequent renewals (Sugden and Tomlinson 1998), which has led to making them more attractive to international players because of their professionalism, enticing other corporate and multinational sponsors. Football undoubtedly is the most popular sport in the world, and it has the highest value of all sports, as revealed in the Deloitte (2008) report as big business (Giulianotti 2005; Kunene 2006). The same Deloitte report outlined the Football Money League, with the top 20 richest clubs in Europe, whose revenue increased by 11 per cent to €3.8 billion during the 2006/2007 playing season. This shows the 'big five' European leagues of Germany, England, France, Spain, and Italy, hosting the most popular football leagues of the world, and accounting for the highest amount of revenue (€8.4 billion and wage costs of €5.5 billion)[1]-(see Poli, Rossi, and Besson 2012).

The same European leagues, according to the report of UEFA in 2011, had the most revenues and the highest player transfer turnover in the football labour market. The huge media coverage, increasing sponsorship and viewership worldwide of the European football have contributed to the game's growth. The game's popularity, broadcasting rights, and the sponsors have also facilitated the transformation of European football, as professional players, particularly the stars, continue to bask in a pool of wealth. An article published on 29 October 2015 by Matt Hamilton reported on the 200 Best Paid People in Football Today.[2] 'In Football/The Business of Sport' showed the weekly earnings or wages of players and their respective clubs. Table 2.1 shows the first 20 footballers on the list out of the 200-survey conducted.

This explains how clubs' budgets can increase regarding the income of players and it is important for them to expand their business models if they want to survive looking at the huge wage demands of best professional players in the marketplace. This development puts much stress on clubs to find extra finances to maintain them and sign on the best talents to help guarantee staying in the football business. Among the top 20 international players with high wages are two African professional players with the majority of the rest coming from the

Table 2.1 Displays of first 20 richest international footballers' wages for 2015 in perspective

	Name	*Weekly Wages (£)*	*Club*	*Country*	*Continent*
1	Lionel Messi	313,461	Barcelona	Argentina	Latin America
2	Cristiano Ronaldo	288,000	Real Madrid	Portugal	Europe
3	Wayne Rooney	285,000	Manchester United	England	Europe
4	Zlatan Ibrahimovic	275,000	PSG	Sweden	Europe
5	Gareth Bale	256,000	Real Madrid	Wales	Europe
6	Asamoah Gyan	226,923	Shanghai SIPG	Ghana	Africa
7	Yaya Toure	220,000	Manchester City	Cote D'Ivoire	Africa
8	Sergio Agüero	220,000	Manchester City	Argentina	Latin America
9	David de Gea	200,000	Manchester Utd	Spain	Europe
10	Bastian Schweinsteiger	200,000	Manchester Utd	Germany	Europe
11	Eden Hazard	200,000	Chelsea FC	Belgium	Europe
12	Luis Suàrez	200,000	Barcelona	Uruguay	Latin America
13	Diego Costa	185,000	Chelsea FC	Spain	Europe
14	Thiago Silva	185,000	PSG	Brazil	South America
15	Rahim Sterling	180,000	Manchester City	England	Europe
16	Fernando Torres	180,000	Atletico Madrid	Spain	Europe
17	Blaise Matuidi	166,154	PSG	France	Europe
18	David Silva	160,000	Manchester City	Spain	Europe
19	Cesc Fàbregas	156,000	Chelsea FC	Spain	Europe
20	Toni Kroos	156,000	Real Madrid	Germany	Europe

European territories. The European players get more benefits than those foreign players regarding the highest wages, which confirms the general migration framework. The huge budgets show how the European football market attracts the best international players globally to their clubs and leagues. On the part of African professional players, the wages are very high compared with what they were earning back in Africa clubs and leagues before moving abroad.

Due to the game's development, its economic potentials and stakeholders' contributions have significantly transformed the sport in relation to its global penetration. This demonstrates how the game has evolved to bring in more finance and its associated benefits for players and leagues in Europe, thanks to the role of the new market of football that continues to provide clubs with the opportunity to meet their expenditures and improving their revenue streams. This is making clubs business-oriented, with players having authority to manage and control their contractual rights and movement in the leagues. The European laws and rules of the EU commission and their application in the football market persistently play a significant role in the movement of international players across borders, nations, and continents to their leagues.

The sport market has not only evolved in the industry but also other sporting disciplines as well, improving their commercialisation perspectives. The European laws and rules of the EU Commission and their application in the football market persistently play a significant role to facilitate the movement of its Member States' citizens. Alongside this, some new legal decisions made after the Bosman ruling open wide the possibilities for non-EU players to play within EU clubs as non-foreigners: Bosman 1995, Malaja 2002, Koplak 2003, Simutenkov 2005, Kahveci 2008, Bernard 2010; and the Cotonou Agreement with 78 countries of the African, Caribbean, and Pacific Group (except Cuba) (see Piraudeau 2017, 22–25). With football, players have their commercial roles which are being used by companies, organisations, and other institutions to market their products. For instance, Pelé from Brazil shared his experience thus: 'Companies have wanted to associate themselves with me since I was a teenager. The first time I was approached to give my name to a product was when I had just started at Santos' (Pelé, born in 1940).[3]

The above statement explains how the game of football appeals to many companies in order to promote and market their products. The extent of using players for a commercial purpose signifies the growth of the football industry that can inspire other talents to strive and achieve such a goal. The economy of football has been the driving force behind changes in the international football labour market and continues to intensify the mobility of players worldwide. Apart from this, football has become truly globalised to support the mobility of international players. This contributes to the understanding of specific behaviours in the football market that may influence players' choice to join leagues in Europe. The economy of football creates a strategy for international players to have options making career decisions in the pursuit of their football profession.

The European football labour market helps to explain the evolution of professional players' wages and clubs' revenue streams. Transformation in the economy of football has brought benefits to the stakeholders, particularly players who have become more mobile in the international transfer market or the labour market of football than before. The promotion of the European leagues has become visible in almost every corner on the Africa continent, enticing young African talents eager to move to those leagues as they see a better future there than wallowing in unstructured leagues across some African countries.

The best African talents able to join those prestigious leagues and clubs in Europe have their earnings increased which can support their families or households back home (Darby 2014). This presents an opportunity for talents from Africa to explore ways and means of moving to leagues abroad. Thus, to achieve a reputation as a professional footballer, they see migrating to Europe as the *only means* to realise that dream (Lanfranchi and Taylor 2001). This is because European football is important economically as well as sociologically, while African football is struggling to maintain professionalism status due to asymmetric development of the game on the continent. Football development and economic conditions in Africa rarely empower talents and potentials to become professional footballers. Dynamism in the European football market provides a vital platform to assess how African football has evolved, leading to the uncontrollable exodus of its best talents abroad.

Evolution of African football context

African countries seem to have achieved some equality on the football pitch despite their overall struggles in national and international football development (Eugene Augustus 2011). Countries from CAF have chalked up more success in the FIFA U-17 World Cup tournaments since its inception in 1985 to the present than five other confederations,[4] thus winning 8 trophies out of the 18 competitions held so far. Other achievements include winning gold and bronze medals at the International Olympic Games.[5] African football has seen a little progress in its organisation of AFCON competitions as a big event on the continent. For example, the AFCON 2012 competition was beamed to a wider global audience thereby attracting viewership of over 3 billion as a historic event for CAF as reported by the CAF media secretary in the same year.

CAF's CHAN competition is a novelty on the part of the organisers. Competitions of CAF may have contributed a little to the level of football in Africa, yet much more needs to be done on its football development. Various CAF competitions have improved the standard of play and players' quality, attracting a high number of foreign-based players to its AFCON tournament. AFCON tournaments have attracted foreign media attention, scouts, football agents, and foreign clubs to the biggest football event in Africa. More participation of foreign-based players in AFCON has continued since the 2000 compared with the home-based players.[6] Despite European clubs benefiting directly from the best pool of exported African talents, it has gone a long way to improve their level of skills, quality of play and mental attitude which are brought to bear on AFCON competitions. AFCON and other international competitions continue to provide opportunities for both foreign-based and home-based players getting offers abroad and to other leagues in Africa (Acheampong 2017). This supports the statement from a CAF technical study committee member that

> revolution in the level of play, technical development, top foreign coaches to observe the game, with a lot of reforms in the coaching aspects and preparations by national teams has contributed to the beauty of AFCON competitions presently. Foreign-based players have made the AFCON tournaments gain more recognition as it attracts a lot of foreign scouts and viewership globally. It has played a role in the continuous player migration with financial benefits, yet players should not forget to give some back to their countries in return.[7]

This demonstrates how the AFCON tournaments have contributed and facilitated players' mobility to leagues abroad in relation to socioeconomic benefits for players.

At the senior World Cup competition, an African country is yet to reach the semi-final stage, with the farthest a country has advanced being the quarter-final stage, credit to Cameroon (1990), Senegal (2002), and Ghana (2010). This achievement is not encouraging for a continent with abundant raw talents and can explain some challenges facing its football development. The sluggish approach of African football growth is a setback in the present day, intensifying its talents' mobility to other continents. Several scholars have engaged in discussions on African football talents migrations. For instance, Bale (2004) discussed the patterns, problems, and post-coloniality of African footballer migrations; Poli (2010a, 2010b) explained the presence of African footballers in Europe and Asia; Büdel (2013) advocated moving beyond the categorisations of African migrations; and Darby (2014) highlighted an extension of European clubs' recruitment of highly skilled talents from Africa and Latin American to obtain value for money.

Contextually, we cannot ignore the attractiveness and exodus of African players based on the economy of the European football market. That includes the effect of the decision of the Bosman ruling (1995) and bilateral trade agreements between EU and non-EU countries,[8] which also support the process of international players' migration to leagues abroad. Indeed, the persistent hardship of the economic conditions in Africa hardly creates the needed opportunities and empowerment for young people to have a better future. As such, the best African players desirous to pursue a career in professional football abroad have no patience to compromise with unstructured leagues and the neglect of their welfare. Some of these situations may inform the decision of individuals to find options that can help them to achieve their professional football dream.

AFCON tournaments have seen some changes, particularly with many professional players' participation[9] but these have been insufficient to convince the world of its football growth due to the frequent migration of its best talents and potentials abroad. The regular participation of more foreign-based players in AFCON competitions tends to enhance the quality and standard of the continent's game. Also, FIFA's continuous scanty support in terms of finances and technical aspects to member associations in Africa has done little to accelerate football development on the continent. All these supports from FIFA rarely reflect significantly on football development in Africa, making the future unclear for its talents who are forced to redirect their energies to leagues abroad.

National football associations and local clubs are sometimes soaked in social canker, mostly similar to those found in the African governments such as corrupt leaders, insufficient training facilities, lack of funding, disputes between ethnic football clubs, and biased refereeing (Eugene Augustus 2011) that invariably retard the progress of the game and its economy drive. Despite these challenges, Africa was able to host successfully the FIFA World Cup 2010 in South Africa for the first time in its history where FIFA made economic gains from the competition.

Yet not much has been done to improve on the continent's football from its struggling to meet the modern trend of football management. This means CAF has more years ahead of its football development if they really want to catch up with the standard achieved by UEFA.

Indeed, CAF's ability to minimise the exodus of African talents to leagues overseas and prevent exploitation by those unscrupulous agents (Darby 2007) can protect its best talents from falling prey to such situations. Thorough analysis from the way African football is organised, managed, and promoted provides the integral actors (players) with little hope and limited opportunities at home to develop, let alone becoming true professionals. Thus, the *only way* for the players to 'make it' is to embrace the migration opportunity towards the new market of football in Europe. This new market offers them alternatives to their mobility project as they pursue a career in football abroad.

The few signs of progress made in African football from the organisational level to international competitions do not reflect on its professional status in a broader context of its structural football development. Some of these structural issues are an incentive for African players to seek options outside these situations. Careful analysis of the issues elaborated here plays a role in facilitating players' strong desires towards migration opportunities abroad. Hence, over-reliance on migration which can only support their football career aspirations and ambitions abroad.

Relationship between African and European football

The new market of football (European football market) has been a stimulus for the mobility of international players towards their career abroad. Similarly, Lanfranchi and Taylor (2001, 2015) demonstrated how this migration has existed from the 1930s, as footballers from Africa moved to Europe. Most of the players came from Angola and Mozambique who were recruited by Benfica, Sporting and Porto clubs during the colonial period (see De Melo 2011; Cleveland 2013). At the same time, players from Black Africa and North African colonies were drafted by Metropolitan French clubs from the 1st and 2nd divisions. In the vein, there existed a North African Championship between clubs of Algeria, Morocco, and Tunisia from 1921 to 1956, and a North African Cup from 1931 to 1956 (Auvray 1995). All these facilitated the detection and recruitment of footballers from the French North African colonies, as well as the Arab natives of the 'Pieds-Noirs'. For example, during the French Championship in 1963–4 for the 1st and 2nd professional divisions, 65 players of the 706 listed[10] were born in Africa (9.2 per cent), 46 from North Africa and 21 from Black Africa, and 27 of the totals (41.5 per cent) were French 'Pieds-Noirs' or of Spanish origin (Elliott and Harris 2015).

The presence of some African players from the 1930s in Portuguese and French leagues continues to create opportunities in the new market of football and that tends to influence their mobility decisions to leagues abroad. Based on this, literature and knowledge on mobility tend to structure the movement of different sets of social objects (Elliot and Urry 2010; Urry 2007). From those mobility experiences, players from Africa manoeuvre through the system by relying on certain factors in the new football market to facilitate their mobility project abroad.

Mobility is a life, where possible, one is only alive if one can be mobile, make the social life of people free from human incidents and cultural constraints that can impede one's progress (Urry 2010). In line with Urry's mobility concept, the mobility of African players abroad should look beyond colonial and neocolonial ties (Darby 2007) because they have their independence to make choices for themselves. This makes the agency of African players pivotal in their mobility choices to pursue a career in football abroad.

The concept of mobility has been theorised in a different context to the mobilities model alluded to in scholarships of sports labour migration. But we consider the mobility of African players towards the European football market. Urry's (2010) mobility notion provides an understanding of the agency of players' mobility in relation to their destinations of play abroad whether they are pushed to choose from the opportunities that abound in the new football market or otherwise. To settle on mobility opportunity, players must consider *where to move, how to move, how to get there and why that choice* so that it reduces their uncertainty as well as making the wrong decisions.

The European football market shapes and reshapes the destination of play for international footballers' relocation activities in their spin patterns (Rial 2008; Roderick 2012) and lived experiences (Agergaard and Tiesler 2014). Footballers' mobility can be either upward or downward depending on their situations (Roderick 2012). Upward mobility permits players to migrate in a relatively trouble-free manner as 'just happening' considering their skills, quality and performance. De-selection and downward mobility are not so easily explained by players, as it captures various things that players hardly can control, such as relationship with the manager, teammates, and decisions of club officials to hire or fire managers (Roderick 2012).

Roderick (2012) argues that most mobility events in footballers' careers are downward and driven by de-selection from their team rather than upward mobility and the free choices of players. In Africa, the limited opportunities at home for players continue to drive them to the European football market. Aside from African players' desire to play in Europe, their development abroad through specialised training programmes improves their quality and potentials that offer them value increase (Acheampong and Bouhaouala 2019), presenting them with upward mobility in leagues. In leagues abroad, some African players may experience downward mobility along their career paths. This usually occurs when African players have limited playing time, changes in club coaches or managers, errors committed in a match and mere dislike by club handlers or coaches. According to Carter's (2014, 167) mobility concept, it should provide footballers with the free will and power to make their own choices. But in the international football labour market, a player's quality and performance determine their mobility choices. This again supports players' upward mobility as per their club choices. In the case of African female players, some clubs rely greatly on agents and intermediaries in producing transnational mobility abroad (Agergaard and Ryba 2014). This situation may prevail in the mobility of African male players, but it is not a common feature because they have control in managing their movement abroad which is dependent on their quality and performance. African players experience upward mobility when moving to the top five European leagues, which tends to be commensurate with their value increases as well (Acheampong and Bouhaouala 2019). In this area, the mobility of players draws on conditions that enable movement of choice and that is relevant for their progress in the industry. African players' mobility may depend on the opportunity to be mobile in the European football market space.

The European football market offers players certain conditions that can push them to achieve their professional ambitions and aspirations. At the same time, it provide players with the opportunity to become self-sufficient as well as boosting their social upward mobility in their communities (Esson 2013) when they are successful. What happens when they are not successful? Some consequences for the unsuccessful ones can be found in the studies of Büdel (2013), where some ambitious African migrant players became unemployed in Turkey.

The new market of football may have its own challenges, yet FIFA continues to reinforce regulations on a player's status and transfers that could improve the game. This development has brought a sort of sanity and stabilised the mobility of players in the European football labour market. Indeed, mobility projects of African footballers cannot only be linked to colonial and neocolonial ties; other elements may play also a role in this process, which is illustrated by the developed database. The concept of mobility offers footballers choice in the broader context of their career profession.

The majority of African players began their mobility from their communities of origin except those who left at pre-teen age to join families or continue their schooling and later became professional footballers. These chart the beginning of their domestic youth development through to becoming professionals in Europe where they experience mobility along their career paths. In Europe, African players' upward mobility is determined by their quality and performance with their clubs. Again, the majority usually experience upward mobility after their international development abroad (see Acheampong and Bouhaouala 2019) while a few must manage their downward mobility due to circumstance beyond their control.

Migration from Africa to Europe: description, analysis, definition, flows and dynamics

Studies on African migration have made significant progress from the strict focus on labour migration towards a more holistic approach to the local, national, and global levels (Mafukidze 2006, 103). Mafukidze argues that contemporary migration activity in Africa is internally focused but not mainly to other continents.

The opposite may be true because many African migrants have a strong belief that moving outside their continent can guarantee them better lives in the future. Their countries' poor economic conditions and weak structural measures impede their empowerment in the localities, and they therefore recognise a move abroad as a remedy to some of these problems.

This confirms a statement from an African migrant that 'c'est un fait, émigrer vers l'Europe est le rêve de beaucoup d'Africains. Mais les barriers entre notre enfer et votre paradis s'élèvent à présent jusqu'au ciel' (Bassong 2006).[11] The comment suggests that many Africans' dream of a successful life can be achieved by migrating to Europe which has a tendency to support their aspirations and ambitions. This illustrates how classical African migrants accept the challenges to forge ahead and migrate abroad. With this, some African migrants employ various strategies and means of dealing with pressures and restrictions in their bid to gain financial independence and individual freedom by seeking new opportunities, security, and a future as they overcome perilous routes while others can travel safely to Europe (König and de Regt 2010, 13). They identify migration abroad as something that can only support them to achieve their dream with some of the enumerated reasons related to their actions. Even though many migrants can testify that they migrated abroad to improve the living conditions of their families back home, it has increasingly been identified that this is not the only reason that individuals migrate (König and de Regt 2010, 6). There have been situations where some of them, such as women, seek their fortune in moving away from patriarchal family systems and try to realise their dreams to experience individual freedom (De Regt 2010). Also, pressures from family demands, unstable socio-political environment, and personal desires targeted at luxurious lifestyles can influence their migration abroad. There are those Africans who are bent on migrating by employing other means to get to their final destinations. Some African migrants even go to the extent of contracting loans to facilitate their movement overseas (see Büdel 2013).

Others crossed the Mediterranean Sea at different points and enter Europe long before the formation of the European Union. Things became tightened when the Schengen Agreement was finally enacted, opening the borders between countries in the European Union to encourage free movement of capitals, goods, and people (König and de Regt 2010). But the borders between Europe and other continents, in particular Africa, were reinforced (König and de Regt 2010), which made migration more complicated. This makes a move to Europe increasingly difficult for Africans with certain restrictions including getting a visa, reuniting with family, and others becoming more complicated and almost impossible. Yet, some Africans continue to explore migration opportunities with high risks via various illegal and legal means, all to satisfy their aspirations and ambitions. Others attempt to use options like crossing the Sahara Desert and engaging in other dangerous trips by boat to islands in the Mediterranean Sea and in the Atlantic Ocean (König and de Regt 2010). Despite the difficulties, Africans' presence and influence in Europe is undeniable (Akyeampong 2000; Grillo and Mazzucato 2008;

Segal 1995). Thus, there have been African traders, scholars, and professionals in Europe and their experiences have not always been connected to racism and discrimination (Blakely 1993). In the past two decades, the number of Africans travelling to Europe has continued to increase, yet this number is smaller in proportion compared to other groups after the Second World War. (Reliable statistics to support this are unavailable, but it is observable in relative terms.)

But today more Africans are eager to migrate abroad than before in modern history, particularly the young men and women driven by dreams, imagination, aspirations, and demands from families, relatives, and friends to make it abroad. Because of the kind of work migrants do, their families' relations at home and abroad, their future projects and the future of their children, as well as the elderly in the communities, are affected by their migration (König and de Regt 2010). This makes migration a collective project with the expected financial potentials which can support social welfare of families for the long term (de Vasconcellos and Dimeo 2009). Sometimes, what makes their migration special are the ways in which these migrants are forced to travel, often under perilous circumstances, and the resilience migrants show in dealing with unforeseen situations, tensions, and conflicts (König and de Regt 2010).

Yet, most African migrants are relatively well educated and come from moderate socioeconomic backgrounds, not from the lowest economic strata (De Haas 2006). Those with financial constraints most often contract loans or provide surety or collateral to enable them to secure funds to facilitate their migration abroad. Surprisingly, some families sell their properties or inheritance to support the migration of a family member, who wants to travel abroad. This clearly demonstrates that migration to Europe involves a considerable cost component which in many cases could be footed from contributions of 'extended' family or friends or others from the community. For such a project, migrants must be in good health, and they need to be embedded in viable transnational or other social networks in order to mobilise resources (including human, material, and social networks) and energy in their migratory processes (König and de Regt 2010; Acheampong 2018b). In all these circumstances, some migrants may face the challenge of dangers, particularly those who opt to cross the Sahara and Mediterranean, of which people are often unaware. The photos of Alfredo Bini display the harsh realities of the desert crossing and highlight the dangerous journey of African migrants *en route* to North Africa and Europe as evidence (see König and de Regt 2010). These do not even prevent or scare them, as they are determined to move abroad. This makes the journey fearsome and uncompromising, on the basis of the ordeals migrants must deal with or may be confronted with along their trajectories. Economic hardships, the collapse of educational systems, unstable socio-political environment, persistent poverty, high unemployment rates, the presence of repressive governments, agricultural reforms with disastrous consequences for rural areas and sometimes famines, natural disasters and others (König and de Regt 2010) all confirm strongly the existence of weak structural factors that rarely empower the young Africans who are desperate to experience survival. Some of these issues can influence many Africans' decision to migrate abroad where they can see a bright future for their lives.

A peculiar characteristic of African migration is the strong feeling towards immediate family and the responsibility associated, as diasporic Africans maintain ties with their home countries, peers, and families; these relationships (whether political, economic, social, or cultural) are often experienced as uneven since both sides (migrants and those who have stayed home) differ in their perceptions of reality out there in Europe (Akyeampong 2000). High expectations from family members play a special role in the diaspora and for one to flee from their kin can be a key motive for persons to migrate. For many Africans, '"Going 'abroad" … has been extended from the original conception of "overseas" to going outside one's homeland and country' (Akyeampong 2000, 186).

Furthermore, migrants from Africa have been likened to the notion of going to 'hustle' or seek one's fortune preferably in a country where one's efforts are not witnessed or supervised by one's kin (Akyeampong 2000). Thus, it puts a kind of social pressure on one's kin to explore the ways and means to succeed in the chosen overseas country. This is because, in many African settings, families, relatives, and the community recognise their support as an investment in the human capital of their kin or siblings and tend to expect returns in the future when successful or unsuccessful. Such support accordingly may help to strengthen the family or social bonding and maintain the intergenerational traits (Van der Meij and Darby 2014) which is the opposite in many Western countries. In African societies, many families are recognised as a homogeneous body of which the individual members share the same concept in their dreams even when they migrate abroad. This demonstrates a sense of recognition, feelings, and belongingness to family members and consequently, individuals are not expected to turn their back on them or ignore them when they become financially successful in their migration projects. The various supports, as little as it may be, can contribute to the social welfare of families or relatives or the community. Indirectly, it obliges migrants to reciprocate this action as ROI which is part of their culture. A person's refusal to support their family or relatives or the community is seen as an ungrateful act (Acheampong 2018a). This is because they think that they have also invested in their development through various means to get them to that level.

In many instances, African migrants who return successfully can leave a legacy in their communities and get decorated with special awards or recognition from the chiefs or/and local and national authorities. Some of these social and community rewards can inspire other migrants to do something in support of their local communities. This could explain why some migrants create hometown associations to support the cause of the larger society with their remittances including social financial assistance. African migrants' embeddedness is also demonstrated via the formation of school or community associations abroad, which often organise financial remittances, and other resources to facilitate the construction of projects like schools, hospitals, roads and the creation of other support organisations like charity foundations (Ozkul 2012).

The notion of hometown associations by migrants from Africa is a unique way for them to contribute their resources, efforts, and remittance to support the local community development. This is something professional players from Africa could adopt in order to help drive local development in their communities. In African settings, the concept of living abroad is often attributed to success and wealth creation and that puts considerable pressures on the individual migrants to succeed. This is the perception of many families or relatives or in the community, particularly those left behind in the localities, because they recognise Europe as a place for the individual to improve their life prospects not as they experience at back home.

Some of the reasons why immediate family and family members take active roles in the decision-making processes at home ('should one leave or not'), on the road ('who to turn to in times of despair?'), and in the country of migration ('does one stay in touch, get other members of the family over, or disappear from the family radar?'), (König and de Regt 2010) give a clear indication of how relevant social relations and networks support the migration activities of their people. Some of the above difficulties and challenges are encountered by many African migrants in their bid to move abroad.

Some African migrants develop and maintain multiple relations—with organisations, religious, and political bodies—that span borders. In Senegal for instance, membership of a religious group (Mouridiyya brotherhood) facilitates women's access to networks and gives them moral support (König and de Regt 2010) in their migratory paths. Others act, make decisions and feel concerns within a field of social relations that link together their countries of origin and their countries of settlement (Glick Schiller, Basch, and Blanc 1992, 9). This process promotes their networks of migration via the establishment of routes and transit places that support their move to their destination.

Families, relatives, and the community have high expectations from migrants in return for their contributions towards their migration process. These expectations do not consider whether the migrant has a job or not or what kind of work they do, but in the end, they are supposed to remit something back home. It is presumed that remitting something to families, relatives, and others in the communities will promote positive relationships back home. In some African countries like Senegal, migrant women often give back to the society which in their cultural settings is appreciated and engenders their reputation and image in the locality. In return, those women gain a new place in Senegalese society abroad (they spend their money and gain respect) and at home as well (König and de Regt 2010).

The Senegalese women's actions demonstrate that they are social entrepreneurs, able to indulge themselves, their children and their extended family with gifts; erasing an impression that they are often considered as domestic workers in many African communities (König and de Regt 2010). This shows their willingness to support and assist the people by giving back to the communities where they are embedded. Conversely, those migrants unable to give something back to the people at home may be tagged as ungrateful and this can create frictions and tensions among parents, immediate families, extended family, and others in their communities. This can be interpreted as a breach of obligations, trust, and reciprocity in relation to the latter's expectations since migrants have surrendered their greater part of involvement and interest in the societies of origin, which has been identified by social sciences to comprehend migration as a reciprocal process (Colic-Peisker 2002, 32).

It is yet to be identified whether African professional players experience some of these societal pressures in their migration project. This is because they seem to have a specific process connected to their migration project yet may have some similarities coming from the same African countries. In their studies, it was unclear what defines the specific patterns of migrants to South Africa (Adepoju 2006; Mafukidze 2006; IOM 2005a).

Patterns of migration too complex and inconsistent to conclude on a definition concerning their studies. The concept of migration applies to both football migrants and classical migrants at the same time, but their processes of migration may differ. Sometimes it becomes difficult to pinpoint any common characteristics applicable to all, since football migrants and classical migrants often transfer remittances to families, relatives, and the community in their countries of origin. But the reason for their actions may differ. According to Adepoju (2006) and Mafukidze (2006) for example, migrants to South Africa are attracted by assertive economic and relative political stability, including other resources that constitute the pull and push factors to that country, which can be the same for football migrants searching for professional survival abroad. However, the biggest difference is seen in the bureaucratic process of migration for both types of migrants because the ordinary migrants rarely get any assistance particularly in acquiring the necessary permits, but football migrants get all the necessary documentation from their prospective employers (clubs), sometimes in the course of their migration process to that country. This reflects the premium a football player may possess making him more valuable and attractive because of the internationalisation of the sport. Credit to the world football governing body, FIFA, for their role in introducing various institutional measures to streamline the football labour market.

Both Adepoju (2006) and Mafukidze (2006) argued that the notion of football migrants getting access to work permits is easier in the course of their professional career in that country. This is because the host country stands to benefit from frequent taxes and other indirect expenses that ordinary migrants can dodge paying. Again, professional players are easy to control and monitor since they have permanent work with the employer clubs. Thus, job opportunities favour football migrants as they are mostly assured of their work permit on arrival.

Analysis of the general migration of African migrants highlights the role of networks, families, and the expectations of their interests as they mobilise the various resources to facilitate their migration project. This demonstrates the investment in migrants' journey towards developing their human capital. Both families and migrant persons tend to maintain regular contact in order to strengthen their established relationships. The established connection with their families back home spans beyond while on the move abroad, which the study explains as transnationalism. The next section illustrates the concept of transnationalism in the context of African migrants.

Migration has intensified as a result of globalisation and new technologies that have contributed greatly to help migrants maintain contacts with their families, relatives, and others. This subsequently facilitates participation in their affairs back home in the communities of origin. The evolution of theories on transnationalism and the inception of a transnational structure has become an important aspect of the migratory practice, since transnationalism has persisted in the last decade in many studies on international migration. It has eased the flow of movement from one place to another, benefiting migrants who keep contact with their left-behinds both at home country and abroad.

Modern social sciences define 'transnationalism' as the processes by which migrants forge and sustain multi-stranded social relations that link together their societies of origin and settlement (see Lazăr 2011). This process is transnationalist in the sense that many migrants presently develop social fields which cut across geographic, cultural, and political borders (Basch, Glick Schiller and Szanton-Blanc 1994). Migrants' ability to develop such connections along their migratory trajectories not only expands their networks and social relations but also benefits them in their future endeavours.

Çaglar (2001) reports that transnationalism highlights how migrants construct and reconstitute their lives as simultaneously embedded in more than one society. Technological advancements have seen migrants from Russia, Poland, and Italy maintaining links with their countries, sending remittances, investing in businesses and visiting kin (Portes 2001, 183; Colic-Peisker 2002). This relationship also enables migrants to contribute and have knowledge about their economy, politics, culture, and social activities of their countries in various forms. It would be interesting to see how African professional players abroad utilise such mechanisms in their interaction with the community members.

Transnationalism also encompasses the sustained ties of persons, networks, and organisations across the borders, across multiple nation-states, ranging from simple to highly institutionalised forms (Faist 2000, 189). Yet, some theorists have advocated for the development of a network society, considering the technological advancements giving way to new patterns of social relations or at least strongly reinforcing the pre-existing tendencies (Remennick 2003, 371), while others trace people's cross-border activities and experiences of belonging that occur as economic, political, and social transactions across borders intensify (Portes *et al.* 1999).

Scholars' attention has also shifted to how migrants were able to sustain a connection with people, organisations, and institutions outside their borders after relocation in their migratory process. The term *simultaneous embeddedness* highlights one of the key ways in which migrants explore and settle into a new locale and concurrently maintain various social relationships that extend to other nation-states (Glick Schiller 2003; Itzigsohn 2000; Levitt and Glick

Schiller 2004). This permitted the analysis to move beyond conceptualisations of migrants as being *uprooted*, in favour of a perspective in which migrants 'travel along routes, back and forth across international borders, negotiating cultures and social systems' (Abdelhady 2006; Fouron and Glick Schiller 2001; Kearney 2004, 217–274 and Carter 2011, 25).

In sports labour migration, the focus has been on how sport migrants establish and maintain relationships and connections with multiple places using new technologies and social media, for example, with the studies of Agergaard and Botelho (2014) among others. Thus, it is through transnational and multiple deep connections that sports migrants can achieve and sustain their own mobilities (Agergaard and Ryba 2014). Migration within the same country can depict diversity rather than a unitary group of people having distinct personal and social endowments (Riccio 2001, 589). This shows how migrant footballers differ in characteristics no matter their socio-cultural backgrounds and cannot be expected to act in the same manner as they are unique individuals with different behaviour.

There are times that migrants may not necessarily have to be physically present at their home or host country yet can still communicate with their left-behinds. For instance, it is only possible for a migrant to be integrated to the degree that the integrationist host culture allows it (Robins and Aksoy 2001). Considering the case of African migrant players, their integration needs further investigation because some find it difficult to adapt to their new environment and that tends to affect their performance too. Usually, a migrant or a group is expected to be able to integrate well in all aspects including language skills and with an opportunity to explore their environments. There may be a situation where transnational priorities will be very different especially those marginalised migrants or groups (see Sampson 2003). In those instances, migrants may not be well integrated, hence, transnationalism which is predominantly cultural in character can emerge (Robins and Aksoy 2001; Carsten 2003; Hall 1990; Moorti 2003).

This development leads to the production and promulgation of cultural products and mindsets to produce transnational imaginaries capable of creating and sustaining new forms of transnational publics (Carstens 2003). In the past, researchers and politicians hardly considered the inclusion of migrants as part of the nation-state process but rather only emigrants that keep links with the home country and possibly other places or destinations lived in or visited. Scholarships on transnationalism have expressed multiple embeddedness of migrants in various context and societies (Glick Schiller, Basch, and Blanc-Szanton 1992). Studies on transnational migration have shown multiple embeddedness of migrant prospects that do not interfere with integration in the host society, nor limit their loyalty nor hinder their social mobility, nor their interaction with the local surroundings (Levitt, DeWind, and Vertovec 2003; Levitt and Jaworsky 2007). Yet some African players abroad experience reintegration difficulties in their new environment. With the social media and technology, some migrant players can still maintain connections with their countries of origin and with the settled country (Agergaard and Ryba 2014; Agergaard and Botelho 2014). This creates a kind of data bank for migrants as they get information from various countries' sources ranging from politics, culture, economy and society that can assist them to make appropriate decisions on their socioeconomic investment back home. In many African communities, this link shows the deep connections migrants have with their community members before their departure abroad and it suggests the concept of *embeddedness*. This concept explains how economic relations between individuals are situated within existing social relations, and thus, structured by these relations and the greater social structures of which those relations are a part (Granovetter 1985). Here, the individual player is considered as an embedded actor who exists in a set of relationships with others within their local surroundings, whose choices may affect their own choices as well. This explains how the choices of African players are not wholly determined by facts internal to their individual concepts and values but actions influenced by the observed and expected behaviours of others. Thus, African professional players in their migration and mobility abroad have had interactions with several people including teammates, friends, team staff, and management, and others with different backgrounds, and that can impact their behaviour as individuals (Acheampong 2018a).

African professional players are individual actors with different economic interests and they attach important meaning to their actions (Weber 1978 [1922) which are also embedded in concrete and on-going systems of social and cultural relations. Essentially, the probability of players' economic behaviour being influenced by significant others should be expected in their migration and mobility experience abroad, because players have surrounded themselves in community relationships that supported their migration process, straight from their humble beginning to leagues abroad. These transnational approaches provide an understanding of the active roles of individual migrants' ability to convert their migration dynamics of social embeddedness in several locations and across borders to their advantage.

To get a better understanding of transnationalism, analysis from various scholars provides some opportunities and challenges which have been outlined by IOM[12] concerning migrants. These are: Transnational migrants' contacts or networks developed along their paths can become vehicles for social and cultural exchanges between societies through, for example, the enrichment of arts, music, films, entertainment and cuisine, promotion of tourism, diffusion of alternative medicine, or exchanges at the level of education and research. Transnational exchanges can be economic in nature, including remittances as well as investment and trade in specialised goods and services sought by migrants in countries of destination from countries of origin, for instance.

Transnational migrants also manifest themselves in the transfer of ideas in the so-called *social remittances*.[13] Migrants can engage in social or political activism to raise awareness about their countries of origin in their host country, and they may advocate for the improved protection of human rights or raise funds to support communities in home countries. These contributions are of relevance in post-conflict reconstruction or following natural disasters, as is also the case with financial remittances. Migrants can also influence predominant ideas in the home and host societies in subtler ways, for instance, by spreading different views about social and political norms and practices in their countries of origin, or by creating a better understanding of different cultures in their societies of destination. Migrants and their families may experience their transnational existence as a source of personal enrichment and development. Generally, educational, professional, and lifestyle opportunities and language abilities can be enhanced. Conceptually, widening their horizons and the ability to tolerate and accept different cultures can be very rewarding for migrants. But different contexts need to be considered in tailoring migration policies to enhance the positive aspects of transnationalism for migrants, their families, and societies of origin and destination. This can be difficult, yet an alternative measure should be in place to help solve some of these issues in the future to minimise illegal migration globally. Beyond that, it would not be out of place for the authorities to reconsider enacting policy that can support their integration processes, particularly with African professional players before, during, and after their football career in those host countries. There are challenges at the individual and family level where several threats arise. Among them are;

(i) Family disruption due to the migration of the breadwinner or primary caregiver can be particularly acute. Separation of parents and children may give rise to psychosocial challenges and increase the vulnerability of those left behind in countries of origin. The elderly are left with additional care responsibilities and they may themselves need care. Family disruption can have wider social repercussions—with impacts felt differently by men and women and in many instances, women bear the brunt of the burden. In all these circumstances, it should also be recognised that family members often find new and creative ways to maintain and develop relationships across borders.
(ii) Migrants' access to pensions and health insurance can be limited or even denied because they are unable to transfer their accumulated benefits and entitlements when they move, despite having made contributions to these schemes.
(iii) Transnational experience may also result in loss of identity and belongingness for some individuals who are easily swayed off or become embedded in their new social environment. Issues may also arise within families, for instance when children feel an attachment to a different country than that of their parents. At a societal level, while migrants bring new ideas to their host countries, some migrant communities may hold on to lifestyles they associate with their places of origin. On occasion, they may do so even if the traditions in those places have since changed. This has raised concern in some destination countries about incompatible social or cultural practices, for example in terms of gender roles. In such cases, strong transnational ties may be detrimental, representing an inability or unwillingness to integrate into the new society. There are instances when migrants' transnational links can be interpreted as split loyalties. As a result, migrants and the intentions of their transnational activities may be regarded with suspicion in both home and host countries, sometimes even raising national security concerns (IOM 2010).

In sum, various explanations and contributions of transnationalism provide a platform to understand how migrants may choose to maintain connections with their left-behinds in the home country. This is applicable to conventional migrants like football players who also maintain a connection with their families, friends, and others in the community. Thus, the latter plays a significant role in the migration process. Alongside this they have also invested in migrants' development and human capital and it is relevant they sustain a positive social relationship to cement their bonding back home. All these points assist in analysing how African players' behaviour may differ from that of classical migrants from Africa toward their communities due to different migration processes. This contributes to ascertaining its effects on their relationships with their left-behinds in their countries of origin. In many African countries, family members, relatives, and others have the responsibility to invest their time, efforts, and resources into the migration process of their children or siblings abroad. When this happens, migrants have no option than to maintain regular contact with them. This development may have significant influence on migrants' decisions to invest or not in their countries of origin. The trend may be the same for African football migrants plying their trade in Europe. To understand their process of migration, the book provides insight into some rationales that can facilitate players' movement to league abroad.

Typologies of football migrants in the context of globalisation

Globalisation, media, and technological advancements had made migration far more diverse and enchanting for migrant groups and migrant profiles including categories of immigrants, refugees, and guest workers. This makes movements towards different parts of the world become easily accessible, much more quickly. Not only the movement to other parts of the globe but also the *sportisation* of the body to acquire characteristics and abilities to promote sporting performance (Dostie 1988, 225). The migration of footballers is more prominent due to the attractiveness of global football leading to sport participants moving across borders, nations, and continents to compete or undertake pre-season training. Sport, especially football, as an activity also creates the medium for the marketing of clubs internationally in all aspects of their endeavours.

These movements make players become more mobile in the course of their football profession. Beyond that, professional athletes from boxing, golf, tennis, athletics, etc., experience such mobility as they move and compete in their various fields of sports. Different mobility of sport athletes could be based on different forms of profiles of migrants as revealed by Bailey (2001). Bailey outlines three distinct forms:

1. short-distance versus long-distance moves,
2. forced (political) migration versus voluntary (economic) migration, and
3. short-term migration (as sojourners) versus long-term migration (settlers).

This book focuses on the types of sports labour migration which have some similarities to those outlined by Bailey (2001). Literature on various typologies for sport athletes has been recommended based on scientific research of male athletes migrating mainly to Anglo-American societies (Maguire 1999; Lanfranchi and Taylor 2001; Magee and Sugden 2002; Takahashi and Home 2004) including the specific case of African footballers to leagues in Europe and Asia (Poli 2010b). The studies of Maguire (1996) outlined five typologies of sports migrants as follows:

1. *pioneers*— those motivated by an almost evangelical zeal for the expansion of their sports;
2. *settlers*— those interested in subsequently staying in the host country;
3. *mercenaries*— those motivated by short-term gains;
4. *nomadic cosmopolitans*— those who want to experience other cultures and cities; and
5. *returnees*— those who aim to return home, an example to finish their career.

Analysis from various sports disciplines conducted by Maguire helped him to draw conclusions on the above typologies for sports migrants in general. This may apply to some of the African football talents in their search for a professional career abroad. Other scholars followed up on Maguire's study with an exact focus on the case of football players to develop or respond to his work. Among them are Lanfranchi and Taylor (2001), who presented a detailed historical survey and settled on three key types of football migrants which are:

1. *the settler,*
2. *the mercenary*, and
3. *the itinerant*—excluding, therefore 'pioneers', 'returnees' and 'nomadic cosmopolitans' as proposed by Maguire.

Lanfranchi and Taylor (2001) supported their argument based on structural and institutional factors that played a role to influence the movement of players by citing three main purposes: the economic crisis and national financial weakness, the offer of only semi-professional or unpaid amateur opportunities, and the attraction of lucrative contracts. Thus, they confirmed 'the motives of football migrants have mainly been economic' (Lanfranchi and Taylor 2001). Their conclusion can illustrate the motive behind some African footballers in searching for professional status abroad.

Also, Magee and Sugden (2002) developed Maguire's typology, outlining six types of migration observed in the English football league. These include:

1. *the mercenary*,
2. *the settler,*
3. *the nomadic cosmopolitans* (same as outlined by Maguire),
4. *the exiled*— those who move owing to political reasons, opted to leave their country and managed to keep their professional career abroad,

5. *the expelled*, applied to players who, due to a combination of behavioural problems and media exposure, are, in effect, forced to migrate to another country in order to play professionally; and
6. *the ambitionists*— that is further divided into three possible sub-types. First, there is a player who simply wants to have a professional football career (anywhere). Second, there is the player who moves to a specific country or club because he has a high preference for playing there, rather than somewhere else. Third, the ambitionist can be someone who wants to improve his career by moving to the league with the highest possible sporting level.

These scholars' concepts focused on the broader context of migrant types in the sports industry. However, there are some ambitionists (from Africa) who move as a result of better sporting facilities and methodological coaching or to become visible to the national team's handlers or managers. There are ambitionists who simply want to have an improved life in the future to support households, extended families, friends, and the community. This book hopes to substantiate some of these to explain some rationales for African players moving to play professional football abroad.

Migration of African footballers abroad in relation to the development of the typology revealed two additional types regarding the earlier studies on typologies of sports migration. We identified the following:

1. *duality*: those players who want to attain citizenship of the host country during their active professional career in addition to their national identity of their countries of origin.
2. *educational switch*: those sent abroad to continue their education and who ended up shifting to a professional career in football alongside obtaining an academic qualification.

In relation to previous studies of ambitionists' sub-types, Magee and Sugden (2002) identified how players are driven by the presence of modern sporting facilities that improve their quality while others are inspired by role models via watching foreign leagues on television in their home countries. Despite the economic and sporting ambitions influencing some football players' motive to relocate, particularly with male footballers, Agergaard, Botelho, and Tiesler (2014) identified some challenges in the typologies of sport labour migrants: first, existing typologies have failed to consider either the identified motivations of athletes' lived experience while playing abroad or the future prospects/outcomes of migration in a more encompassing description of migrant types; and second, lack of more detailed analysis of the various ways in which athletic migrants accommodate to their new environment while keeping connection with their countries of origin (transnational migration).

Agergaard, Botelho, and Tiesler (2014) suggest that the inclusion of *integration* with reference to settler's type shows the potential of football, providing a form of integration. The concept of integration particularly for African migrant players is a pressing issue because the majority find difficulties adapting to their new environment, which the existing studies have failed to identify. For instance, how a footballer can cope with life outside football, particularly changing clubs, family adaptation, relocation and other things as part of the work hazards they have handled along their career paths. This includes some difficulties professional footballers must grapple with, on the relocation of families, integration, and adaptation (Roderick 2012).

A collection of football biographies plus media interviews of migrant players like Didier Drogba from Ivory Coast (McShane 2008), Andriy Shevchenko from Ukraine (Shevchenko 2012), Eric Cantona from France (Auclair 2009), Ze Roberto from Brazil (Colonisio and Duque 2006), and Marta, female player from Brazil (Graciano 2009) provided a different dimension to the subject. Analysis of the lived experience of players overseas compiled by Rial revealed the *circular* international movement of players (moving from one club or country to another), which the players call 'the spin'. Many limit their social experience within the boundaries of the club with little interest and/or opportunity to interact with outside groups (Rial 2008).

International mobility of male footballers may be limited to the macro-level analysis emphasising the gains and losses for countries and clubs involved in the international market of football migration (Alvito 2007; Poli and Ravenel 2005). Economic, social, and political difficulties or hardships in the so-called underdeveloped parts of the world are identified as push components that influence individuals to migrate as opposed to the more advantageous pull elements in the so-called developed parts of the world (Maguire *et al.* 2002).

Studies from scholars on typologies of migration failed to consider origins or localities of people, particularly those from the underdeveloped and developing countries since some lack certain basic facilities and infrastructure, because players from those territories have a different 'ambitionist' perspective in migrating to seek a professional career abroad. From the typologies of migration, African players may exhibit different behaviours at each stage of their mobility trajectories in leagues abroad. This is essential because players need to consult with families, friends, networks, and the community to make decision on relocation abroad (see van der Meij and Darby 2017). Considering the football migrants' lived experiences and motives, it becomes difficult to understand how some of these social supports can influence their behaviour to invest their intellects, cultural and sporting capitals, and other resources to the benefits of their countries of origin in Africa.

The typologies of sports migrants provide a framework for ascertaining how they can play a role in affecting their behaviour to society. This concept of football migrants' types contributes to understanding the various rationales behind players' movement abroad during their migration projects. This again exposes migratory itineraries of African footballers regarding the different strategies they employ to facilitate their migration project. African players' migration projects cannot be defined simply, as they involve different actors and networks within and beyond their social environment. In understanding this, the book analyses the various actors and networks using economic sociology approaches to explain their roles in the process. The application of economic sociology approaches provides a generic solution to comprehend African footballers' migration process and its effects on their economic behaviour.

The migration of people has been part and parcel of the changing dynamics in the world. This has taken different perspectives, making it difficult to settle on a general definition of the migration process. In the context of the study, migration of African footballers is explained as the movement from the communities of origin to Europe. Yet, it recognises the intervention role of intermediaries who facilitate their migration process. This also contributed to explain the mobility of African footballers move within their host countries leagues.

Based on their relocation abroad, players maintain constant interaction with the families, clan, and the society in their countries of origin in order to strengthen and sustain their relationships as they stay far apart. Regular dialogue with the family members, relatives, friends, and the community are referred to as transnationalism of African footballers abroad. All the conceptualisations elaborated above provide insight into the discussions and analyses appertaining to African players' 'Give Back Behaviour' to their local communities.

African football migrants in Europe: new situation, difficulties, adaptation, social status and incomes

Despite setbacks in African football development, football talents and prospects are integral to the larger migration to Europe. African players' stay in the leagues abroad greatly increases their wages/salaries compared to what they used to receive back home in the domestic leagues or in other sectors of activities. In Europe, on the average, many African migrant players in the top tier leagues can earn between €15,000 and €100,000 or more as wages/salaries. Professional players may receive something in the range of €10,000–50,000 (for league one); €5,000–20,000 (for league two) and €2,000–10,000 (league three)[14] respectively. These economic earnings were calculated based on their average salaries/wages without bonuses and other expected incentives to players per their contracts. In the top elite European leagues, some high-profile players from Africa can earn more than €150,000 weekly.

Interestingly, most players' earnings compared to highly skilled African migrants like engineers, professors, medical doctors, etc. who may be earning between €7,000–20,000 are far better and mouthwatering. The earnings of African professional players tend to promote their social and economic status and national recognition in the communities.

Apart from the players' embeddedness, the community people expect to see the continuation of their existing relationship despite situational changes in status. That can go a long way to strengthen and cement their social bonding with their communities. The community might have played a role to facilitate their migration abroad in their humble search for a new professional opportunity. Here, we cannot ignore the interplay roles of families, relatives, friends, and others in diverse ways to enhance smooth departure abroad. This demonstrates the way talents and prospects are supported right from their beginning communities to achieve their professional football dream abroad.

Multiple embeddedness of migrants' prospects is anticipated since migration is not a straightforward journey. We provide an explanation of how African players' multiple embeddedness can influence their behaviour change via reconnecting to their local communities after becoming professional footballers. Beyond some factors that facilitate African players' migration to leagues abroad are the international football market dynamics that underpin the current systems and networks of the footballers' migration (Taylor 2007). This affects where players choose to go and where clubs scout for players due to the long-established colonial, cultural, linguistic, social and personal connections (Taylor 2007).

However, this pattern seems not to be the case considering the dynamics of the football industry where clubs have become business oriented, and footballers with their families, relatives, and agents need to decide on the best opportunities for them. This makes players become pivotal and recognised as cash cows for clubs and themselves. From the database analysis, African professional players joining leagues abroad skewed from the entire dominance of neocolonial perspectives towards the role of the new football market where talent's quality and performance are hugely rewarded. This is because African professional players have choices to control and manage their contractual rights, courtesy of the evolution of the European football that provides them with the freedom to do so. Moreover, it provides them with mobility opportunities in their circulation and movement to clubs and leagues abroad.

Studies by Poli, Ravenel, and Besson (2015) revealed a total of 18,660 foreign players from 194 origins in the 458 leagues from 183 countries situated in the existing confederations: Europe (UEFA), Asia (AFC), Africa (CAF), South America (CONMEBOL), North and Central America (CONCACAF) and Oceania (OFC). From Poli *et al.* (2015) the data analyses of Poli *et al.* (2015), there are 4,322 African players exported to foreign countries' leagues in world football representing 23.24 per cent. This confirms the rise of African professional players' migration to leagues abroad, courtesy of the football market shifting to Europe because of its financial resources and structural status (Poli 2007), together with the quality of play and other sociological facilitators (such as strong mediatisation, quality of life, social recognition, social status, etc.).This continues to attract football talents from Africa to the European leagues, which provides a lens for international football migration (Lanfranchi and Taylor 2001) with the number of African players representing the second highest after UEFA footballers (Poli *et al.* 2015). Yet, professional players' migration has been tied to general migratory patterns, and various countries in both Europe and Africa have been involved in different ways. For instance, countries like France, Belgium, or Italy serve as the core recipient (hosts) of African players from Senegal, Cameroon, or Ghana as the suppliers (donors) of talents. With the case of Ghana, it is difficult to trace the link with Italy.

The migration of footballers from Africa to Europe is based on certain factors that facilitate their movement to specific leagues. In general, what exactly informs the decisions of sports athletes' movement to a country may have different interpretations. The next section explains how African players can sustain their relations with the communities as they manoeuvred through various systems to become professionals in order to maintain their social ties in society.

Sustained relations with African communities of origin

The concept of this sustained relationship identifies the agency of African players ahead of other factors in their mobility abroad. It considers the mobility project as part of the broader processes of the new market of football, which begins from the communities. Through that, players get to know about some mobility opportunities abroad which inform their choices of where to begin their career. African players' mobility project includes but is not limited to opportunities to develop football skills, improve players' welfare, sustain an intergenerational trend, become a professional footballer; these are some of the factors that the new market of football offers them. Such elements support players' intention to exert their agency in managing their mobility projects. For instance, Alozie, a Nigerian international footballer who has spent over 11years in a Ukrainian league as his initial destination country narrated some reasons for seeking professional football opportunity abroad.

> I had good results but since the love for the game was just there so I wasn't really thinking of furthering my education rather finding ways of getting outside the country to seek greener pastures.[15]

Analysis of Alozie's statement showed that limited economic opportunities at home and his desire for a professional career abroad influenced his mobility choice. To a large extent, this made him discontinue his education and pursue a career in football abroad. He also remitted money to his family from his first professional contract because his family was not all that rich. But it was to make everybody more motivated for their support that something good has come out of his decision to play football. Hard work and family support paid off for him. This acknowledgement from the player to the family justifies the important role they played in his mobility project abroad (Van der Meij and Darby 2014). Alozie's remittance to his family supports the argument of Carter (2011) that family members are significant actors in the mobility of athletes, and the family can serve as a key unit for their mobility motivations and experiences, due to the active involvement of family members in his childhood development and in decision-making processes linked to his career path (Van der Meij and Darby 2014). It shows how African professional players are supported and encouraged by family members and their social relations because of the perceived potential future benefits that a professional career overseas might bring them (Van der Meij and Darby 2014, 22). Through the extended family intervention and support, Sadio Mané eventually moved from the village to the city to pursue his football journey abroad. He recalled;

> My uncle was a big help, but not the only one at the start …. When I moved to Dakar, I went to live with a family that I didn't even know! My family knew someone who knew them, and he took me to their house. They took me in, they took care of me and did everything to help me just worry about football until I left for Metz.[16]

Mané acknowledges the immense contribution of the family and relatives in supporting his professional career journey. In the beginning, he admitted that it was not easy leaving his family, but football was what he had chosen to play. The Liverpool star, who is also a graduate of street football, has since then managed to sustain that strong relationship with the family through technology and regular interaction on phone. The family's support from the initial football search has been sustained even after achieving his professional status abroad.

Despite different views from family members, agents and significant others, players are still able to make mobility decisions that can support their international football development. Here, the agency of players is paramount during such moments since they are at the receiving end and any wrong decisions made can jeopardise their own future. Still, African players are more receptive to mobility opportunities towards the new market of football that can support their future welfare and that of their families. Football opportunity abroad can influence young African talents who may decide to abandon schooling and focus fully on the sport as a profession. If this is not checked, it can breed a generation of poorly educated males keen to live the 'X-Way' by channelling their energies and attention toward a profession that is unlikely to reciprocate this devotion with employment and social mobility (Esson 2013, 91). Another player with over ten years of professional experience shared how he abandoned his college education in the USA to chase after his desired dream of professional football in Europe. Ayarna mentioned that, 'I was excited to move to Europe and play. I've always wanted to play in Europe, and I got the opportunity, and I took it.'[17]

The player's mobility choice of Europe has satisfied his professional dream because he has taken the opportunity to develop and improve his football skills there. The limited economic opportunities in their countries plus other conditions make African players recognise a professional career in Europe as a feasible way to secure a lifestyle characterised by wealth, conspicuous consumption, and considerable social status, one referred to by a Ghanaian youth as the 'X-Way'

(Esson 2013). This may entice young people to abandon school and take to football. But this can also affect their future when it becomes a habit among them. Some African players even abandoned their final year examinations to pursue a football career abroad. Abedi Pele Ayew, a former Ghanaian professional player and the youngest to win AFCON in 1982 with his national team narrated his experience as follows:

> I was then in my fourth year of college but because of that, I had to leave school. This is an interesting part. When the abroad club came for me, there was a group of people in the Real Tamale United FC who said, yes, because it was an opportunity for the club to make some money. The other group said no because he was too young, and we should hold on and protect him until the time is ripe. But who knows when the time is ripe, nobody knows? There were so many meetings and finally, Malik Yakubu, Aliu Mahama, B.A. Fuseini and others, who were all influential at that time, were in a dilemma. And this became a debate among them. We should allow him to stay on, make sure he is protected, and others were like, it was an opportunity for him because, we don't know tomorrow and maybe if this chance passes today, tomorrow we won't get it again. You know both sides have a case but, at the end those who said I should go succeeded because, I also came out and said though, education is good, writing my exams is good, my parents have never seen their son abroad before.[18]

From the player's narration, he made a mobility decision based on his family's future and later, became a breadwinner for them. Abedi became successful professionally and realised the need to reciprocate expectations from family members (Van der Meij and Darby 2014, 24). From his poor family background, he saw the mobility opportunity as a relief to their social welfare in the community. This mobility opportunity prevented him from writing his final college examination and he opted to pursue a profession in football abroad. What would have been the consequences for the player, if he had not been financially successful professionally? Well, he made the mobility choice towards the new market of football which eventually supported his desired professional dream abroad.

With two FIFA World Cup appearances (2006 and 2010), Paintsil explained how moving abroad accelerated his football development: 'I simply wanted to play abroad because of the quality of the game and, it doesn't matter where I'll start from because I wanted to play abroad.'[19] His mobility choices landed him in Europe, yet his lived experiences there have taught him many lessons that he would like to share with the young ones desperate to play abroad. He advises 'young African players to wait for their right mobility opportunity rather than to rush because sometimes, African players try to go to Europe at age 16 or 17, which to him is not necessary but the best age for them to move abroad should be around 21 or 22'.[20] In that case, players at that age can handle some of the challenges along their mobility paths abroad. African players interviewed admitted that having the opportunity is one thing and your ability to make appropriate mobility choice is another thing. But, in the end, a player should be satisfied with the choice made towards the new market of football in Europe.

The widespread presence and popularity of football in African communities has become a shared culture because they see a bright future from that, especially those who may achieve financial success professionally. African players admitted that their mobility abroad was brokered by football agents based on their choices and not limited only to the financial potentials but also the opportunity to play abroad. Some players interviewed moved to Europe by road through various routes connecting African countries with support from social relations and networks. They encountered a lot of problems along their adventurous journey, but they managed to reach Europe after spending some time in other leagues in Africa.

Others mentioned the barrier of language at their new place of work, however, they did not see it as an impediment to their mobility opportunity initially. Yet, it would be interesting to figure out what best explains how African players are supported with their integration regarding their new environments after their mobility abroad. Players admitted that the limited economic opportunities at home and neglect of their welfare, and a chance for development tend to influence their mobility choices towards the new market of football. George Ekeh recalled how he quit furthering his education to pursue a career in football:

> People who had completed university have no jobs and those graduates [are] loitering in the streets without jobs and that the future just looks bleak. The next tendency was to invest in something that one could see a better future from and that was football and that was how I got back to taking football seriously. And it is almost like the same path as every other African footballer's career who dream of ending in Europe as their solution.[21]

Ekeh realised the poor economic challenges of the country and opted for a professional career in football. His action could be similar to many African players who may see it as the only way to become a professional footballer abroad as truncating their education to chase after football. All in all, the factors favouring the new market of football include mobility opportunities abroad, developing football skills, becoming a professional footballer and a choice of league destination, future opportunities and promoting 'Give Back Behaviour' opportunities.

The nature of the globalised game has provided donor countries with the chance to dominate the offer of football talents in the international labour market. Particularly, African talents are still chasing a professional footballer status in Europe due to the weak structures and poor economic conditions and managerial issues in their countries. All these together had failed to empower its youths making them direct their energies to where they can find a better future to survive. Similar situations exist in the development of African football. These compelling situations have facilitated the movement of more African players to the European leagues in return for their contractual rights and service. Some statistics are provided in support of this migration trend of African footballers identified in the 30 professional leagues in 13 UEFA countries as at the 2012/2013 season. Figure 2.1 explains the distribution of players from the 44 African countries offering football talents to the host UEFA countries.

The figure explains the distribution of African players each country offers to the host countries in Europe. It shows the value assigned to each country in terms of the total number of foreign-based players in the 30 professional UEFA leagues. The first 15 donor countries from Africa to have more foreign-based players in the European leagues include Senegal (128), Cameroun (103), Nigeria (101), Cote d'Ivoire (91), Morocco (86), Ghana (84), Mali (50), Algeria (48), Cape Verde (42), Tunisia (40), Congo DR (40), Guinea (38), Guinea Bissau (24) Burkina Faso (24), and Congo (20). The same survey showed that more African talents are exported to the European leagues than South Americans. Figure 2.2 explains further.

From Figure 2.2, representation of foreign players exported to the 30 professional European leagues shows that Africa represents 7.17 per cent showing a greater migration to Europe than those from the South American territories representing 6.66 per cent. This study reaffirms the early work of Poli *et al.* (2015), which ranks the African continent as the second-best exporter of foreign players

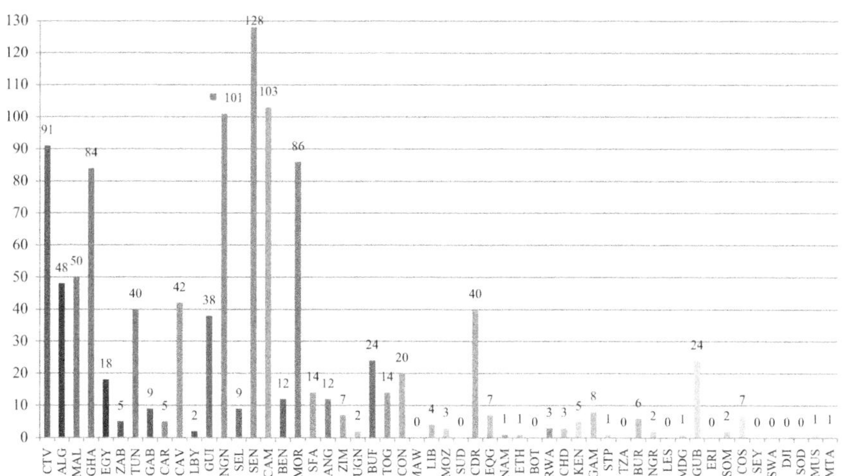

Figure 2.1 Number of professional footballers from each donor country as at 2012/13 season.

Key: Senegal (SEN); Cameroun (CAM); Nigeria (NGN); Cote D'Ivoire (CTV); Morocco (MOR); Ghana (GHA); Mali (MAL); Algeria (ALG); Cape Verde (CAV); Tunisia (TUN); Congo DR (CDR); Guinea (GUI); Guinea Bissau (GUB); Burkina Faso (BUF); Congo (CON); Egypt (EGY); South Africa (SFA); Togo (TOG); Benin (BEN); Angola (ANG); Gabon (GAB); Sierra Leone (SEL); Gambia (GAM); Zimbabwe (ZIM); Equatorial Guinea (EQG); Comoros (COS); Burundi (BUR); Zambia (ZAB); Central African Republic (CAR); Kenya (KEN); Mozambique (MOZ); Liberia (LIB); Rwanda (RWA); Chad (CHD); Libya (LBY); Uganda (UGN); Niger (NGR); Somalia (SOM); Namibia (NAM); Ethiopia (ETH); Sao Tome Principe (STP); Madagascar (MDG); Mauritius (MUS); Mauritania (MTA).

to UEFA. The total number of foreign-based players from Africa is classified according to CAF zoning and presented as per their percentages in the European leagues as illustrated in Table 2.2.

The majority of African professional players are from the Western zone followed by Northern and Central zones respectively. These three zones offer the bulk of professional players to the European leagues with the top five leagues hosting the majority because of its huge financial potentials, viewership and quality of play and football talents (Lanfranchi and Taylor 2001; Acheampong and Bouhaouala 2019). This supports what Poli and Rossi (2012) reported with the 'big five' European leagues commanding the major portion of the football market share representing 55 per cent of transfers in Europe. In short, the numbers from Africa may play a significant role in stabilising the football market in Europe. This same trend was observed from the players' entry leagues that chart the beginning of their professional career abroad. Table 2.3 is the database developed in support of this discussion on African players' migration.

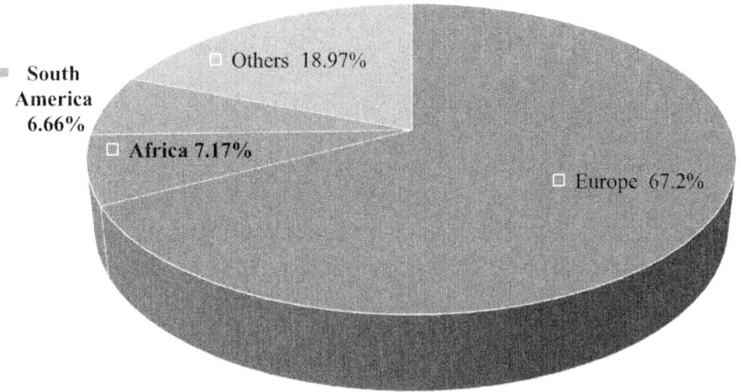

Figure 2.2 Professional players within the FIFA confederations division

Table 2.2 Classification of African players according to CAF zones in Europe leagues

CAF Zones	*West*	*North*	*Central*	*Southern*	*East*	*Total*
'Big five' league	318 (56.89%)	115 (20.57%)	97 (17.35%)	25 (4.47%)	4 (0.72%)	559
Other leagues	314 (59.81%)	79 (15.05%)	91 (17.33%)	26 (4.95%)	15 (2.86%)	525
	632 (58.30%)	194 (17.90%)	188 (17.34%)	51 (4.70%)	19 (1.75%)	1084

Table 2.3 African players' entry and the beginning of a professional career abroad

	C'TY	FRA	POR	OTH	BEL	ITA	ENG	SPA	GER	RUS	UKR	GRE	SWZ	TUR	NED	TOT
1	CTV	18	10	14	16	8	5	1		2			10	2	2	**88**
2	CAM	34	2	8	9	4	1	8	6		1	3	12	6	1	**95**
3	NGN	9	9	21	10	14	12	6	3	1	3	3	1	7	5	**104**
4	TOG	10		2	2						1			1		**16**
5	SEN	72	8	17	11	13	2	4	1			1	4	2		**135**
6	GHA	6	6	14	5	19	6	8	4			2	5	3	4	**82**
7	MAL	39	2	1	2						2					**46**
8	GUB	4	22													**26**
9	SFA		2	2	8	1	5			1					4	**23**
10	ALG	32	2	1	1	1	3	1	3				1			**45**
11	GAM			6	1			1	2				2			**12**
12	BUF	7	3	5	4	1	1		2			1				**24**
13	CAV	4	33					1						1	3	**42**
14	MOR	39		1	6	4	2	4	3			1	2		26	**88**
15	TUN	15	1		1	1		4	10		2		6	2	1	**43**
16	ZAB	1	4	1												**6**
17	ANG		6				1		1						2	**10**
18	CDR	9	1	1	13		4		5				5		1	**39**
19	BEN	9	1	2	1											**13**
20	GAB	9		1				1								**11**
21	GUI	18	1		7	3	1	1				1	2	1		**35**
22	SEL			3		1	1					1			1	**7**
23	EGY	2	1		1	1	3			1			1	1	1	**12**
24	LBY		1				1									**2**
25	LIB			1										2		**3**

(Continued)

	C'TY	*FRA*	*POR*	*OTH*	*BEL*	*ITA*	*ENG*	*SPA*	*GER*	*RUS*	*UKR*	*GRE*	*SWZ*	*TUR*	*NED*	*TOT*
26	MTA	1														**1**
27	MUS	1														**1**
28	CON	18						1	2				1			**22**
29	EQG	1						7								**8**
30	RWA				3											**3**
31	STP		1													**1**
32	MOZ		1													**1**
33	SOM					1	1									**2**
34	KEN			3	2											**5**
35	CHD				1					1			1			**3**
36	ZIM	1		1	2		1									**5**
37	CAR	6														**6**
38	BUR				5	1										**6**
39	NGR	2		1												**3**
40	UGN		1													**1**
41	MDG	1														**1**
42	COS	6														**6**
43	NAM								1							**1**
44	ETH				1											**1**
		374	118	106	112	73	50	48	43	6	9	13	53	28	51	**1084**

Authors (2014).

Table 2.3 shows the distribution of professional players from the 44 African countries absorbed by the leagues in Europe. It describes the beginning leagues of African players from the various professional leagues including those from Asia and America. This explains a different pattern from Figure 2.1. The first 15 donor countries from Africa are Senegal (135), Nigeria (104), Cameroon (95), Morocco (88), Cote d'Ivoire (88), Ghana (82), Mali (46), Algeria (45), Tunisia (43), Cape Verde (42), Congo Democratic Republic (39), Guinea (35), Guinea Bissau (26), Burkina Faso (24) and South Africa (23). Leagues in France dominate as the main recipient of African players followed by Portugal and Belgium. This confirms the earlier studies of Poli (2006) except for the Netherlands which has been overtaken by Portugal as the second-choice destination for Africa players. The francophone countries offer more players to France and Belgium, which are linked to colonial and language ties with their former colonisers besides other factors that are explained by the role of the European competitions and leagues.

This development follows the same trend as observed at the end of the 2012/2013 leagues season in the 13 UEFA countries. The observed patterns of African footballers' mobility follow this trend. First, movement from Africa to France, Belgium, Portugal and others (Nordic, Eastern Europe, and Asia), second, from the latter leagues to 'big five' European leagues, and third, movement from 'big five' leagues to minor (developing) and emergent leagues (Russia, Ukraine, USA, and Asia) where many often terminate their active professional career. Most of the players are from the West African nations representing over 55 per cent of the talents offer to leagues in Europe.

The following countries (Malawi, Sudan, Botswana, Tanzania, Lesotho, Eritrea, Seychelles, Swaziland, Djibouti and South Sudan) have no professional players in those leagues abroad probably due to the low level of their leagues on the African continent. Senegal has the highest number of African professional players with Nigeria having players in all the host leagues abroad, confirming the West African zone's superiority in football migration on the continent. The initial migration of African talents aids our understanding of the periodisation era, particularly the 1980s when the regulations on minors were not strictly enforced. It was also the same period that witnessed the rise in African players' migration after some youth national teams from Africa displayed raw talent at the FIFA Youth Tournament. In support, the statistics in Figure 2.3 were analysed using the ages at which African players began their professional career abroad.

Figure 2.3 focuses on the age categorisation of African players searching for the start of their professional career abroad. It included age 16–17 because the FIFA youth competition for male footballers started with U16 in 1985.[22] This was the first occurrence of the FIFA U16 World Championship held in Beijing, with the Nigeria team emerging as the gold medalist for Africa. Africa was represented by Nigeria, Congo, and Guinea (placed fourth). Football talents from Africa in the competitions were monitored and scouted for possible transfer to Europe, but it was not rampant until after the 1989 FIFA U16 World Competition in Scotland that saw the phenomenal display of raw talents from Africa and they became the

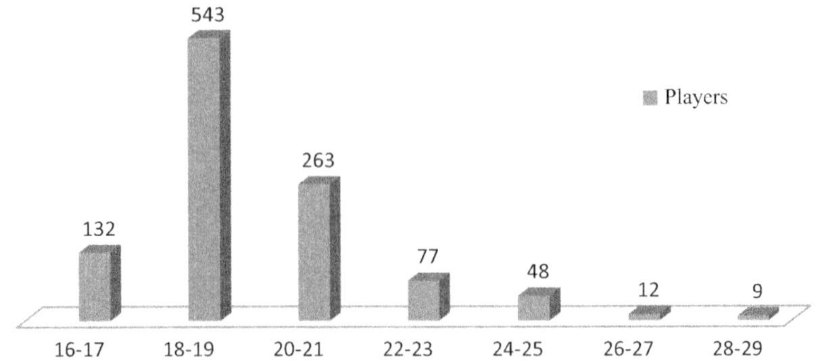

Figure 2.3 Age categorisation of African players towards entry leagues abroad (in late 1980s)

transfer targets of European clubs and leagues abroad as reported by Poli, Darby, Lanfranchi, and Taylor among other scholars (see Acheampong and Bouhaouala 2019). During this period, African players' international development was between age 16 and 19, and that forms the majority representing 62.26 per cent.

In the early 1990s, the migration of African footballers abroad intensified because they were regarded as a source of a talent pool, younger and much cheaper to buy and to speculate on, than the ones already established in the EU (Acheampong and Bouhaouala 2019). The activities of football agents or sports agencies deepened in the same period with foreign scouts turning their attention to Africa in search for cheaper and young talent, for the resale of their playing rights for a higher margin in Europe. This period also observed the exploitation of some African talents by the Global North (Poli 2006). Analysis from Figure 2.3 looks quite tricky and nonlinear as the majority of the players progressed steadily from 16–19 years, however, what happens afterwards is a bit alarming. Thus, after their peak at age 18–19 (50.1 per cent), there is a sharp drop in numbers. That tells us that European clubs hardly sign on African talent between age 23 and 27 for their international development. Apparently, this trend is not encouraging for African players' prospect and development because of their continuous decline that may have negative effects on the continent's game growth in the future.

The period from the 1990s to 2000s was also assessed using the age classifications of the African footballers as a follow-up to their early migration. Lapses in the regulations of minor players in the late 1980s greatly affected young players as some were exploited and dumped in the streets of Europe (Bennhold 2006). From Figure 2.4, data analysis indicates that 77.1 per cent of African players began their international development between the ages of 17 and 20, with most of them migrating to the French leagues. The expected peak performance for African players tends to reduce representing 18.5 per cent (21–24years) and this is quite disturbing for their performance progression trajectories. This situation is different from the

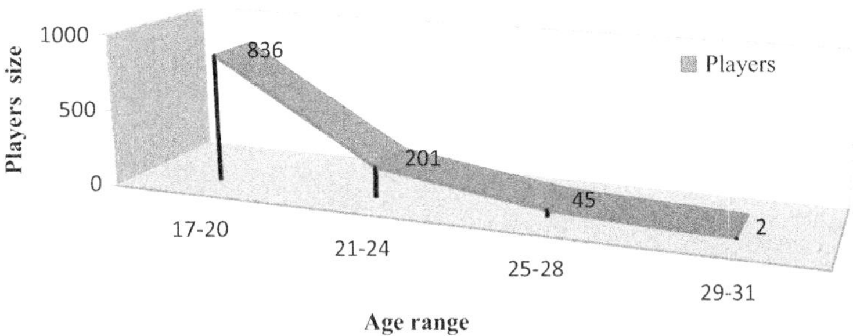

Figure 2.4 Age classifications of African players from the 1990s to 2000s

same professional footballers coming from Europe who participated in the UEFA Champions League according to the records (see Acheampong and Bouhaouala 2019). Thorough analysis indicates that the rate at which African footballers decline along their professional career abroad is unpleasant since they are expected to rather improve or maintain their performance between the ages of 25 and 28. This trend should be a concern for CAF if they really want to have a full impact on modern football management and development worldwide. From the database analysis, the representation of African players within the 30 professional leagues of 13 UEFA countries is displayed on the map according to CAF zoning of member associations (Figure 2.5). The map further shows the dominance of West African countries (indicated with the red arrows) offering more players to the professional leagues in Europe. This is followed by the Central and North Africans. In general, most of the professional players from Africa are found in the Western European leagues as displayed on the map.

Conclusion

Generally, explanation of the GBB is highlighted in the Africa context with specific reference given to social and economic interactions underlying players' economic behaviour in society. This is necessary because African players were attracted to the European leagues and competitions after its transformation, due to the professionalism and the structure of their leagues and its associated economic potentials. At the same period, African football evolved as their youth national teams participated in the FIFA World U-17 competitions. The displayed of raw talents allured intermediaries to Africa in search of the best football talent for the European football market. This provided a great opportunity for football talents to be developed and refined and led to the establishment of a strong relationship between Africa and Europe in the export of football talents, triggering the migration of best African football talents to the Global North due to limited opportunities for them to develop at home. The players' situation was likened to the classical migrant from Africa to Europe, who is obliged to reciprocate the

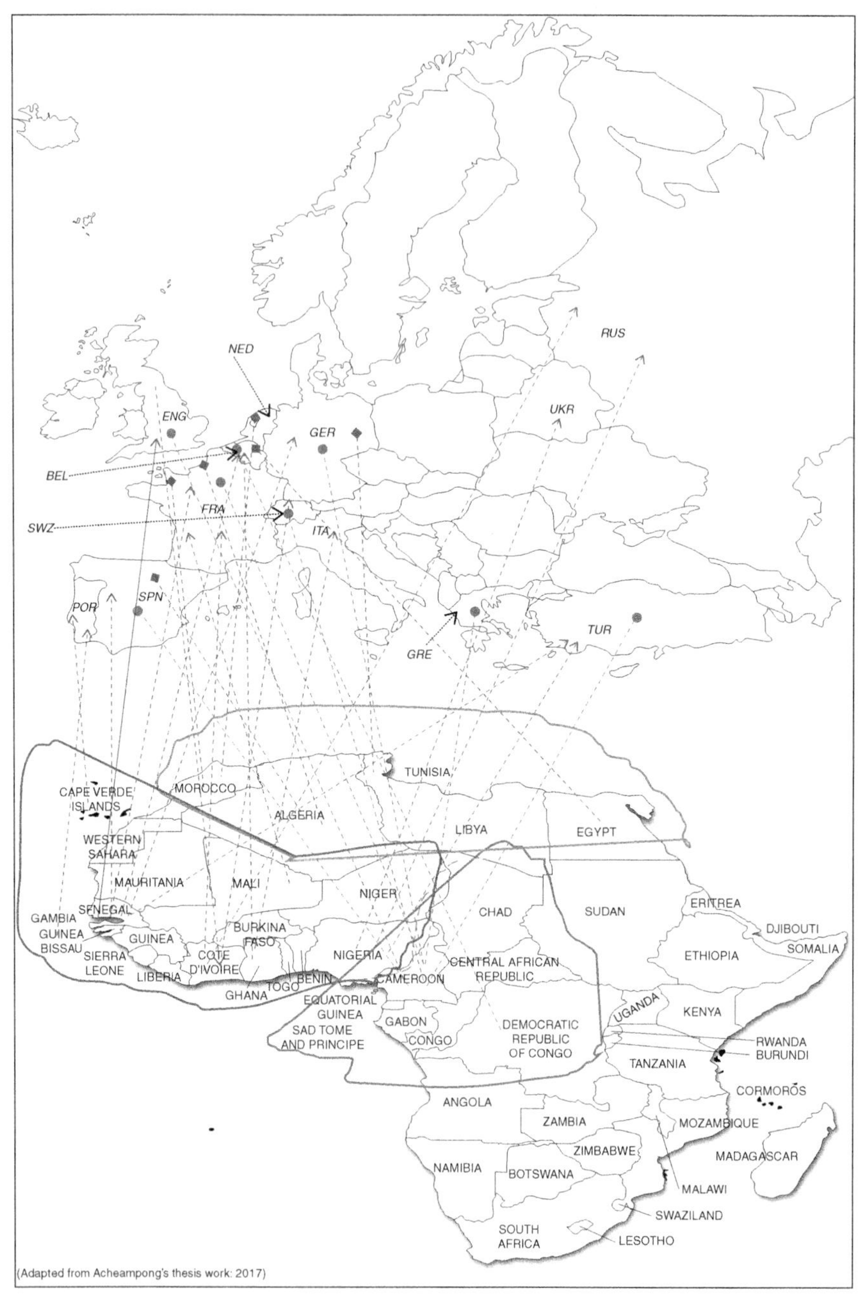

Figure 2.5 Destinations of African professional players in the 30 leagues of 13 UEFA countries

support invested in their migration projects. A peculiar characteristic of African migration is defined based on the strong feeling towards immediate family, relatives, friends, and the community, and with an associated responsibility. Furthermore, a thorough analysis of the typologies of football migrants led to the discovery of (1) *duality*: which involves players who attained citizenship of the host country during their active professional career in addition to their national identity, and (2) *educational switch*: those sent abroad to continue their education who completed it with a degree and a professional football career. The chapter also emphasised how African players manoeuvred within this international migration and mobility in spite of the challenges was discussed. Despite challenges, players still maintained a strong connection with their families, relatives, friends, and the communities. It is a reflection of the weak structures, poor economic conditions and managerial issues in their countries that African talents are lured to the European football market as they seek for a professional footballer status. An illustration of the subtleties of African players' migration and mobility in leagues abroad is given in the tables, figures and a map. This reaffirms previous studies (Darby 2014; Poli 2006; Poli, Ravenel and Besson 2015) on the persistent unceasing migration of African players to the Global North.

Notes

1. Deloitte annual report on football financial review
2. Report on the best paid professional footballers in the world (http://thekingmaker.me/200-best-paid-footballers-in-the-world-today/). [Accessed on 10 January 2016].
3. Pele (Edson Arantes do Nascimento), former Brazilian player. He received numerous prestigious honours and decorations including Brazil's Gold Medal, Knight Commander of the Order of the British Empire and Lifetime Achievement Award from BBC. (http://www.thefamouspeople.com/profiles/edison-arantes-do-nascimento-2544.php#deQI6frjuSMfDvCx.99). [Accessed on 30 September 2015].
4. Developed data on U16 and U17 FIFA World Cup competitions from its inception (http://www.fifa.com/u17worldcup/index.html. [Accessed on 20 October 2016].
5. Some achievements of African national teams at the Olympic Game [Football, Gold medalist (Nigeria-1996) and Bronze medal (Ghana-1992)].
6. Presentation on the "Influence of African Professional Players on AFCON tournaments" at the ACAPS congress in 2013, Grenoble, France by Acheampong, Bouhaouala, and Raspaud 2013.
7. Interview with Francis Oti-Akenteng (CAF technical study committee member/ Technical director of Ghana Football Association, FIFA/CAF grassroots coach instructor), in Ghana, on 8 October/2013.
8. http://trade.ec.europa.eu/doclib/docs/2006/december/tradoc_111588.pdf (Accessed on 7 October 2015).
9. We observed a consistent increase in migration of Africa players to leagues abroad from 1996 to 2015. This supports our findings on the subject. Presentation on the "Influence of African Professional Players on AFCON tournaments" at the ACAPS congress in 2013, Grenoble, France by Acheampong, Bouhaouala, and Raspaud 2013.
10. 'Pieds-Noirs' means 'Blackfoot' in English.

11. "Football 64", *Les Cahiers de l'Equipe*, trimestriel no. 19, Décembre 1963. Translation: It is a fact, migrants to Europe is a dream of many Africans. But the barriers between our hell and your paradise are presently rising to the sky.
12. IOM-International Organisation for Migration (2010).
13. The subject of social remittances at the second Intersessional workshop, *Societies and Identities: The Multifaceted Impact of Migration*, on 19–20 July 2010.
14. It was arrived at using the minimum and maximum wages/salaries of players in leagues of Spain, France, Germany, England, Italy and Switzerland.
15. Interview with Mike Alozie, on 10 December 2015.
16. Interview with Sadio Mané by Melissa Reddy, on 8 November 2016. (http://www. goal. com/ en/). [Accessed on 12 May 2018].
17. Interview with Reuben Ayarna, on 20 January 2016.
18. Interview with Abedi Pele Ayew, on 9 March 2016.
19. Interview with John Paintsil, on 13 July 2013.
20. Ibid.
21. Interview with George Ekeh, on 20 April 2016.
22. The FIFA under age tournament started with U16 http://www.fifa.com /u17worldcup / archive /chinapr 1985 /teams/index.html.

Bibliography

Abdelhady, D. 2006. 'Beyond home/host networks: Forms of solidarity among Lebanese immigrants in a global era', *Identities. Global Studies in Culture and Power* 13 (3): 427–454.

Acheampong, E. Y. 2017. 'Socioeconomic analysis of the Give Back Phenomenon: Professional footballers in Europe and their assistance to the communities of origin in Africa.' PhD diss., Université Grenoble Alpes, France.

Acheampong, E.Y. 2018a. 'How does professional football status challenge African players' behaviour?', *Soccer & Society Journal*. doi:10.1080/14660970.2018.1541797.

Acheampong, E.Y. 2018b. 'Giving back to society: evidence from African sports migrants', *Sport in Society*, doi:10.1080/17430437.2018.1551367.

Acheampong, E. Y. and Bouhaouala, M. 2019. 'African footballers' life cycles according to the analysis of transfer value along their career path: A case study of Ghanaian players', *Sport in Society –Cultures, Commerce, Media Politics*, doi:10.1080/17430437.2018.1551366.

Adepoju, A. 2006. *The Challenge of Labour Migration Flows between West Africa and the Maghreb*. Geneva, International Labour Office, Switzerland.

Agergaard, S. and Botelho, V. 2014. 'The way out? African players' migration to Scandinavian women's footbal', *Sport in Society: Cultures, Commerce, Media, Politics* 17 (4): 523–536, doi:10.1080/17430437.2013.815512.

Agergaard, S. and Ryba, T. 2014. 'Migration and career transitions in professional sports: Transnational athletic careers in psychological and sociological perspective', *Sociology of Sport Journal* 31: 228–247.

Agergaard, S. and Tiesler, N. C. 2014. *Women, Soccer and Transnational Migration*. Routledge.

Akyeampong, E. 2000. 'Africans in the diaspora: the diaspora and Africa', *African Affairs* 99: 183–215.

Alvito, M. 2007. 'Our piece of the pie: Brazilian football and globalization', *Soccer & Society* 8 (4): 524–544.

Auclair, P. 2009. *Cantona – The Rebel Who Would Be King*. London: Pan Books.

Auvray, Roland H. 1995. *Le Livre d'Or du football Pied-Noir et Nord-Africain*. Toulon: Les Presses du Midi.

Bailey, Adrian J. 2001. 'Turning transnational: Notes on the theorisation of international migration', *International Journal of Population Geography* 7: 413–428.

Bale, J. 2004. 'Three geographies of African footballer migration: Patterns, problems and postcoloniality.' In G. Armstrong and R. Giulianotti (eds), *Football in Africa: Conflict, Conciliation and Community* (229–246). Basingstoke and New York: Palgrave Macmillan.

Basch, L. G., Glick Schiller, N. and Szanton Blanc, C. 1994. *Nations Unbound: Transnational Projects, Postcolonial Predicaments and Deterritorialized Nation-states*. Switzerland: Gordon and Breach.

Bassong, L. 2006. *Comment immigrer en France en 20 leçons*. Paris: Max Milo.

Bennhold, K. 2006. 'Soccer dreams and reality', *International Herald Tribune* (www.iht.com). Paris.

Blakely, A. 1993. *Blacks in the Dutch World: The Evolution of Racial Imagery in a Modern Society*. Bloomington: Indiana University Press.

Büdel, M. 2013. 'An ethnographic view on African football migrants in Istanbul', Ankara Üniversitesi SBF Dergisi, *Cilt* 68 (1): 1–20.

Çaglar, A. 2001. 'Constraining metaphors and the trans nationalisation of spaces in Berlin', *Journal of Ethnic and Migration Studies* 27 (4): 601–613.

Carter T. F. 2011. *In Foreign Fields: The Politics and Experiences of Transnational Sport Migration*. London: Pluto Press.

Carter, T.F. 2014. 'On mobility and visibility in women's soccer: Theorising an alternative approach to sport migration.' In Sine Agergaard and Nina Clara Tiesler (eds), *Women, Soccer and Transnational Migration*. Abingdon, UK: Routledge.

Carstens, S. A. 2003. 'Constructing transnational identities? Mass media and the Malaysian Chinese audience', *Ethnic and Racial Studies* 26 (2): 321–344.

Cleveland, T. 2013. 'Following the ball: African soccer players, labour strategies and emigration across the Portuguese colonial Empire, 1949–1975', *Cadernos de Estudos Africanos* 26: 15–41.

Colic-Peisker, V. 2002. 'The process of community and identity building among Bosnian Muslims in Western Australia', *Mots Pluriels*, May 2002, available at http://www.arts.uwa.edu.au/Mots Pluriels.

Colonisio, C. and Duque, D. 2006. *Colhendo Frutos em Terra Seca*. São Paulo, Brazil: Editora Central Gospel.

Darby, P. 2007. 'Out of Africa: the exodus of African football talent to Europe', *Working USA: The Journal of Labour and Society* 10 (4): 443–456.

Darby, P. 2014. 'International football migration and Africa: Feet drain or feet exchange', *More than a Game, Sports, Society and Politics: Panorama Insights into Asian and European Affairs*, January 2014.

De Haas, H. 2006. 'Migration, remittances and regional development in Southern Morocco', *Geoforum* 37 (4): 565–580. doi:10.1016/j.geoforum.2005.11.007.

De Regt, M. 2010. 'Ways to come, ways to leave: Gender, mobility, and il/legality among Ethiopian domestic workers in Yemen', *Gender & Society* 24 (2): 237–260. doi/abs/10.1177/089124 3209360358.

Deloitte. 2008. *Annual Review of Football Finance*, Deloitte & Touch LLP Research Report.

De Melo, A. 2011. *Eusébio Enciclopedia*. Lisbon: Zebra Publicações.

De Vasconcellos Ribeiro, C. H. and Dimeo, P. 2009. 'The Experience of migration for Brazilian football players', *Sport in Society* 12 (6): 725–736.

Dostie, M. 1988. *Les corps investis* [The invested bodies]. Montreal, PQ: St-Martin.

Elliott, R. and Harris, J. (eds). 2015. *Football and Migration. Perspectives, Places, Players.* Abingdon and New York: Routledge.

Elliot, A., and Urry, J. 2010. *Mobile Lives: Self, Excess and Nature.* Abingdon, UK: Routledge.

Esson, J. 2013. 'A body and a dream at a vital conjuncture: Ghanaian Youth, uncertainty and the allure of football on football', *Geoforum*, 47: 84–92. https://dspace.lboro.ac.uk/dspace-jspui/bitstream/2134/17405/3/Geoforum.pdf.

Eugene Augustus 'Gusty' C., Jr. 2011. 'The African football development model', *African Governance and Economics, Naval War College.*

Faist, T. 2000. 'Transnationalisation in international migration: Implications for the study of citizenship and culture', *Ethnic and Racial Studies* 23 (2): 189–222.

Fouron, G. and Glick Schiller, N. 2001. 'All in the family: Gender, transnational migration, and the nation-state identities', *Global Studies in Culture and Power* 7 (4): 539–582.

Giulianotti, R. 2005. 'Playing an aerial game. The new political economy of soccer.' In J. Nauright and K. S. Schimmel (eds), *The Political Economy of Sport* (19–27). Basingstoke: Palgrave-Macmillan.

Glick Schiller, N. 2003. 'The centrality of ethnography in the study of transnational migration: Seeing the wetlands instead of the swamp.' In N. Foner (ed.), *American Arrivals. Santa Fe, NM: School of American Research*, 99–128.

Glick Schiller, N., Basch, L., and Blanc-Szanton, C. 1992. 'Towards a transnationalisation of migration: Race, class, ethnicity and nationalism reconsidered', *The Annals of the New York Academy of Sciences* 645: 1–24.

Graciano, D. 2009. *Você é mulher, Marta!*, Sao Paulo, Brazil: All Print Editora.

Granovetter, M. 1985. 'Economic action and social structure: The problem of Embeddedness', *American Journal of Sociology*, 91(November): 481–510.

Grillo, R., and Mazzucato, V. 2008. 'Africa-Europe: A double engagement', *Journal of Ethnic and Migration Studies* 34 (2): 175–198.

Hall, S. 1990. 'Cultural identity and diaspora.' In J. Rutherford (ed.), *Identity: Community, Culture, Difference* (222–239). London: Lawrence and Wishart.

IOM. 2005a. *Data and Research on Human Trafficking: A Global Survey.* Geneva.

IOM. 2010. *World Migration Report 2010.* https://www.iom.int/world-migration-report-2010.

Itzigsohn J. 2000. 'Immigration and the boundaries of citizenship: The institutions of immigrants' political transnationalism', *International Migration Review* 34 (4): 1126–1154.

Kearney, M. 2004. *Changing Fields of Anthropology: From Local to Global.* Lanham, MD: Rowman and Littlefield.

König, R. S. and De Regt, M. 2010. 'Family dynamics in transnational African migration to Europe: An introduction', *African and Black Diaspora: An International Journal* 3 (1): 1–15. doi:10.1080/17528630903368232.

Kunene, M. 2006. 'Winning the Cup but losing the plot. The troubled state of South Africa.' In S. Buhlungu, J. Daniel, R. Southall and J. Lutchman (eds), *State of the Nation: South Africa 2005–2006* (369–390). Cape Town: HSRC.

Lanfranchi, P., and Taylor, M. 2001. *Moving with the Ball. The Migration of Professional Footballers.* New York: Berg.

Lanfranchi, P. and Taylor, M. 2015. 'Mobility, migration and history. Football and early transnational networks.' In R. Elliott and J. Harris (eds), *Football and Migration. Perspectives, Places, Players* (3–20). Abingdon, New York: Routledge.

Lazăr, A. 2011. 'Transnational migration studies. Reframing sociological imagination and research', *Journal of Comparative Research in Anthropology and Sociology* 2 (2): 69–80.

Levitt, P. and Glick Schiller, N. 2004. 'Conceptualizing simultaneity: A transnational social field perspective on society', *International Migration Review* 38 (3): 1002–1039.

Levitt, P., DeWind, J., and Vertovec, S. 2003. 'International perspectives on transnational migration: An introduction', *International Migration Review* 37 (3): 565–575. doi:10.1111/j.1747-7379.2003.tb00150.

Levitt, P. and Jaworsky, B. N. 2007. 'Transnational migration studies: Past developments and future trends', *Annual Review of Sociology* 33 (7): 129–156. doi:10.1146/annurev.soc.33.040406.131816.

McShane, J. 2008. *Didier Drogba: Portrait of a Hero*. London: John Blake Publishers.

Mafukidze, J. 2006. 'A discussion of migration and migration patterns and flows in Africa.' In C. Cross, D. Gelderbolm, N. Roux, and J. Mafukidze (eds), *View on Migration in Sub-Saharan Africa*. Cape Town: HRSC Press.

Magee, J. and Sugden, J. 2002. 'The world at their feet: Professional football and international labour migration'. *Journal of Sport and Social Issues* 26 (4): 421–437.

Maguire J. 1996. 'Blade runners: Canadian migrants, ice hockey, and the global sports process', *Journal* of *Sport and Social Issues* 20 (3): 335–360.

Maguire, J. 1999. *Global Sport: Identities, Societies and Civilizations*. Cambridge: Polity Press.

Maguire, J., Jarvie, G., Mansfield, L., and Bradley, J. 2002. *Sport World: A Sociological Perspective*. Champaign, IL: Human Kinetics.

Moorti, S. 2003. 'Desperately seeking an identity: Diasporic cinema and the articulation of transnational kinship', *International Journal of Cultural Studies* 6 (3): 355–376.

Ozkul, D. 2012. 'Transnational migration research', *Sociopedia.isa*, doi:10.1177/205684601211.

Piraudeau, B. 2017. *Les migrations des footballeurs à l'heure de la mondialisation*. Paris: L'Harmattan.

Poli, R. 2005. 'The football players' trade as a global commodity chain: transnational networks from Africa to Europe.' In *The Workshop on Social Networks of Traders and Managers in Africa*, Iwalewa-Haus, Bayreuth, 4 November.

Poli, R. 2006. 'Africans' status in the European football players' labour market', *Soccer and Society* 7 (2–3): 278–291.

Poli, R. 2007. 'Transferts de footballeurs: la dérive de la marchandisation', *Finance & Bien Commun* 26: 40–47.

Poli, R. 2010a. 'Understanding globalization through football: the new international division of labour: migratory channels and transnational trade circuits', *International Review for the Sociology of Sport* 45 (3): 1–16.

Poli, R. 2010b. 'African migrants in Asian and European football: Hopes and realities', *Sport in Society* 13 (6): 1001–1011.

Poli, R. and Ravenel, L. 2005. 'Les frontières de la "libre" circulation dans le football européen. Vers une mondialisation des flux de joueurs?' *Espace Population Société* 2: 293–303.

Poli, R., Ravenel, L. and Besson, R. 2015. 'Exporting countries in world football', *CIES Football Observatory Monthly Report* no. 8: 1–10.

Poli, R., Ravenel, L. and Besson, R. 2016. 'Squad profile of the best performing national A-Teams', *CIES Football Observatory Monthly Report* Issue, 11 January.

Poli, R. and Rossi, G. 2012. *Football Agents in the Biggest Five European Markets. An empirical Research Report*. Neuchâtel: Centre International d'Etude du Sport (CIES).

Portes, A. 2001. 'Introduction: the debates and significance of immigrant transnationalism', *Global Networks* 1 (3): 181–193.

Portes, A., Guarnizo, L. E., and Landolt, P. 1999. 'Introduction: Pitfalls and promise of an emergent research field', *Ethnic and Racial Studies* 22 (2): 219–237.

Remennick, L. 2003. 'What does integration mean? Social insertion of Russian immigrants in Israel', *Journal of International Migration and Integration* 4 (1): 23–49.

Rial, C. 2014. 'Circulation, bubbles, returns: The mobility of Brazilians in the football system.' In R. Elliott and J. Harris (eds), *Football and Migration: Perspectives, Places, Players* (61–75). Abingdon: Routledge.

Riccio, B. 2001. 'From "ethnic group" to "transnational community"? Senegalese migrants' ambivalent experiences and multiple trajectories', *Journal of Ethnic and Migration Studies* 27 (4): 583–599.

Robins, K. and Aksoy, A. 2001. 'From spaces of identity to mental space: Lessons from Turkish-Cypriot cultural experience in Britain', *Journal of Ethnic and Migration Studies* 27 (4): 685–711.

Roderick, M. 2012. 'Domestic moves: An exploration of intra-national labour mobility in the working lives of professional footballers', *International Review for the Sociology of Sport* 48 (4): 387–404.

Sampson, Robert J. and Laub, John H. 2003. 'Life-course desisters? Trajectories of crime among delinquent boys followed to age 70', *Criminology* 41 (3): 302–334.

Segal, R. 1995. *The Black Diaspora*. London: Faber and Faber.

Shevchenko, A. 2012. 'Milan legend Andriy Shevchenko gave an interview to the Euro 2012', *Official Preview Magazine*. Online. Available at http://dailymilan.com/andriyshevchenko-euro-2012-interview/ [Accessed 9 July 2012]

Sloane, P. J. 1971. 'The economics of professional football: The football club as a utility maximiser', *Scottish Journal of Political Economy* 18 (2): 121–146.

Sugden, J. and Tomlinson, A.1998. *FIFA and the contest for World Football: Who Rules the People's Game?* London: Polity Press.

Takahashi, Yoshio, and Home, J. 2004. 'Japanese football players and the sport talent migration business.' In Wolfram Manzenreiter and John Horne (eds), *Business, Culture and the People's Game in China, Japan and South Korea* (69–86). London: Routledge.

Taylor, M. 2007. *The Association Game: A History of British Football*. Harlow, UK: Pearson Longman.

Urry, J. 2007. *Mobilities*. Cambridge: Polity Press.

Urry, J. 2010. 'Mobility.' In K. Hart, J-L.Laville and A. D. Cattani (eds), *The Human Economy: A World Citizen's Guide* (325–335). Cambridge: Polity Press.

Van der Meij, N., and Darby, P. 2014. 'No one will burden the sea and then never get any benefit: Family involvement in players' migration to football academies in Ghana.' In J. Harris and R. Elliot (eds), *Football and Migration* (159–179). Abingdon: Routledge.

Van der Meij, N. and Darby, P. 2017. 'Getting in the game and getting on the move: family, the intergenerational contract and internal migration into football academies in Ghana', *Sport in Society*, doi:10.1080/17430437.2017.1284807.

Weber, M. 1922. *Economy and Society: An Outline of Interpretive Sociology*, translated by Ephraim Fischoff *et al.*, 2 vols. Berkeley: University of California Press.

Weber, M. 1978. *Economy and Society*: 2 Volumes. Eds. G. Roth and C. Wittich, Berkeley: University of California Press.

Welch, F. 1970. 'Education in production', *Journal of Political Economy* 78: 35–59.

3

Theoretical approaches to Give Back Behaviour

Introduction

There is a form of giving back existing in some football clubs and football academies in Africa, but the underlying basis of the players' gesture is intricate and difficult to comprehend, because the give back phenomenon may be influenced by factors depending on the subjectivity of individuals based on their conceptions, values, objectives, and interests (Bouhaouala 1999, 2007). This shows the importance of the meaning attached to that particular social or economic behaviour in reference to society. The rationale of this chapter is to shed light on the contributions of theories and models that can assist in examining and analysing the arguments about African players' GBB to society. The section also combines multidisciplinary approaches to help develop a theoretical framework to aid our understanding of how players' GBB can reflect their economic rationality. We realised that the Give Back Behaviour is a complex notion and the application of economic sociology can create a balance to explain this thought in a holistic manner. In doing so, consideration was given to sociological, cultural, economic, and institutionalised networks' perspectives that may play a significant role in affecting the decision making of African players to society on their GBB. Altogether, this contributes to understanding the migration processes and the importance of their economic rationality. Lastly, the contributions of various theories and models supported the construction of a comprehensive socioeconomic model of the Give Back Behaviour that explains the logic of action of African players to society.

Give Back Behaviour: Social or economic phenomenon

The studies by Darby (2014) of African footballers abroad show that their earnings can drive local football development and support the social welfare of families and others back home through their socioeconomic initiatives and projects in the communities. These contributions by players are in different forms according to their interests, values, objectives, and conceptions (Acheampong 2017; Bouhaouala 1999, 2008). These social and economic contributions can be observed in the investment activities of players, which they offer to society through different ventures including those out of sport or in sport projects. Players' behaviour in social terms reflects the virtue of the subjective meaning they give their investments in the communities. This shows that the logic of players' action is inspired by their objectives, values, conceptions, and the interests they attach to their economic investment initiatives to the communities.

For instance, according to Darby, Right To Dream (RTD) Football Academy located in Old Akrade, Ghana operates other forms of giving back scheme which allow recruit trainees to support their communities through investment in social projects which may not align with their culture and social norms. Indeed RTD Academy is founded on a rational system of solidarity closer to Western rationality. RTD is registered as a European NGO in Ghana which uses 'credit' accumulation as the basis for their giving back scheme. Thus, recruit trainees are supposed to earn 'credits' through personal achievements in education and football, as well as involvement in community projects, foundations, and entrepreneurial activities in African contexts (Darby 2013, 50). The goal is to make people more responsible and to create a rational system of solidarity. Trainees are only asked to sign a declaration of 'give back' to support their communities and this may contradict their personal values, objectives, conceptions, or interests (Acheampong 2017; Bouhaouala 1999, 2008). To Bouhaouala (1999, 2008), individuals' values, objectives, conceptions, and interests must affect whatever socioeconomic support they prefer to offer society in their localities. In African settings, an individual providing economic non-economic investments to society must reflect their social values and norms, individual and collective objectives, conceptions shared with their social group or socioeconomic interests. In that sense, players would be in coherence with their cultural values and they would feel valued in their communities because they have been personally associated with the decision-making process that led to them offering such social and economic support to the community members. The RTD model insists on the responsibility and rationality of the individual whereas the African model of GBB refers to the respect for collective values and norms in terms of giving back behaviour.

For instance, after their participation in the 2014 FIFA Women's U-20 tournament, Dike, a Nigerian female footballer, returned all the allowances due to her back to the authorities, which she saw as patriotic and honourable, showing respect for her family, and for the social and national recognition for representing her country (Acheampong 2018b). Her decision made the Nigeria women's league boss (Dilichukwu) remark: 'She is a star and patriotic Nigerian who put service to her fatherland above money. The minister is aware, and we will push the act before the NFF so it can inspire many others.'[1] This social act of giving back to her country was applauded by many and recommended for the rest of the players to emulate.

Some African former professional footballers have supported in various capacities, all to contribute their quota to social initiatives to their communities and beyond (cf. Chapter 1, Give Back Behaviour is consubstantial to African migration). These former players' actions are not for economic gains or financial profit and were in line with their values and norms towards supporting a social course. In the end, their social and economic behaviour can be explained in reference to several types of rationalities as Max Weber demonstrated through his typology of social actions.

For instance, acquiring their communities' respect and national recognition are achieved through players' Give Back Behaviour to the community. This was revealed by female football migrants with African heritage in the Scandinavian women's leagues who described their professional achievement abroad as a way of gaining social respect and economic resources to climb the social ladder (Agergaard and Botelho 2014). In sum, the players' investments in different forms, either economic or non-economic, demonstrate the rationalities behind their behaviours oriented either to their cultural values, interests, objectives or conceptions that may further a good cause in society. It may also serve as an incentive to aspiring young players searching for a professional career abroad to follow this trend of giving back through their personal initiatives. This development if positively encouraged in societies can drive local improvement via individual personal investment contributions to the communities. Through this means, consistent support can be received and may become social and economic phenomena among community members since it also promotes their social identity and prestige.

Economic sociology — Weberian approach

Economic sociology perspectives provide a platform to assess the economic and non-economic behaviours of the players in a wider context. They help to reflect the principal facts identified by economics, in applying a radically different perspective and a unique type of institutional analysis (quoted by Parsons in Swedberg 1994, 65). On this basis sociologists believe that every economic behaviour exhibited by a person has a social component which is the case of African players after becoming professionals abroad. The various investment initiatives of players have an element of social contributions to society.

In Swedberg's (1994) assertion, every economic activity is fundamentally social. In this book we applied a contemporary economic sociology perspective, with a focus on Weberian methodology, which helps to understand the rationality behind individuals' course of actions and the important meaning a person gives to his/her subjective behaviour in relation to significant other subjectivities in society. This could be situated in the concepts of 'embeddedness' and 'the social construction of the economy' (Granovetter 1985).

The subject of economic sociology provides a heuristic tool in examining the rationalities behind African migrant players' interest towards the local communities they come from. In addition, the book draws inspiration from some studies including Bouhaouala's (1999, 2008) work on micro-mentalities of small and very small enterprises in the sports tourism sector. Bouhaouala concluded that the basis of individual decision making is influenced by the importance people ascribed to their values or conceptions or interests or objectives regarding their economic behaviour.

Again, it is essential to understand that economic sociologists accept rationality as a variable, not an assumption as economists assert. To illustrate the economists' view, Akerlof (1990) argues that the action of some individuals or groups may be more rational than others. This implies that a person who acts according to his/her values is not rational in terms of the economy model, which is the opposite of the economic sociology and sociology models, acknowledging rationality as a phenomenon to be explained not assumed. Economists claim that the '*meaning*' of economic action is obtained from the relation between given tastes, the prices and quantities of goods and services' (Smelser and Swedberg 2010), while Weber (1978 [1922]) admits that in sociology, it is historically developed and must be investigated empirically, and not simply based on assumptions and external situations. Further elaboration on the rationality of individuals as they make decisions in order to reflect their economic and non-economic behaviours is discussed below.

The concept of rationality and rational behaviour

The concept of rationality, according to Weber (1978 [1922]) examines the micro-perspective views of the individual within society. This explains the significant meaning a person assigns to their economic action (Weber 1978, 68). Thus, the notion of rationality contributes to understanding the real meaning behind the actions of individuals in society since a decision conceived by them does not exist in a vacuum but has an intended purpose to achieve a certain goal. For instance, an African player who decides to offer support to the local communities has a specific purpose to accomplish, which may reflect their personal values or conceptions or interest or objectives to the community (Bouhaouala 1999, 2007, 2008). This action can take various forms depending on individuals' subjectivity in relation to their economic behaviour.

Contemporarily, the advent of technological advancement and globalisation tends to influence people's economic action, often shifting outcomes of people's actions towards the specific beliefs and norms that may guide their everyday behaviour. This book considers the rationality concept as the subjective meaning a person apportions to his/her behaviour considering the behaviour of others who are oriented towards its course (Weber 1978). In a broader context, the notion of rationality provides a tool to appreciate when an action is deemed goal-oriented, value-oriented, traditional/cultural and affective/emotional by considering the importance a person attaches to such behaviours. That means social actions cannot be isolated. An explanation of Weber's categorisation of social action is also found in the theoretical approaches of this book which are outlined in four different ways.

1. A purposeful or goal-oriented rational action which involves making decisions based on the multiplicity of strategies to achieve outcomes that are economically viable to the individual. A player's decision is directed towards achieving certain purposeful desires to maximise returns or gains on investment.
2. Rational action may be value-oriented when the individual makes decisions using rational means to achieve goals or outcomes that are reflective of its value without considering the cost element. Players may adopt an effective means that cohere with their values to achieve their goals.
3. Traditional/cultural action occurs when social and economic behaviours are oriented towards customs and traditions not limited to habits and cultural norms. Simply, the outcomes and means of behaviour are instinctively fixed considering customs and traditions. For instance, a player sending regular remittance home or observing religious ritual can acquire cultural symbolism.
4. Affection/emotional action shows how individual decisions tend to reflect one's feelings in response to a certain situation at a point in time. This can result from social emotions, emotions generated by what may happen, emotions of love and disgust, etc. Players may determine their decision based on their passion or emotions. Here consideration is given to personal feelings of individual players that may influence their behaviour to give support or not.

The rationality theory provides a lens to analyse the complexity of African players' social and economic behaviours through their investment initiatives to society when they become professionals abroad.

Economic rationality

In economic theory, individual behaviour is economically rational when a person can make choice from a set of preferences and alternatives available to them to maximise their economic interest, because all economic behaviour hinges on human decisions or behaviour (Neva *et al.* 2014). Several scholars in economics have tried to use human behaviour and motivation to address the rationality of human action in social terms. This approach led to the development of the rationality principle or axiom which states that 'rational economic man maximises his utility.' (Some economists substitute 'self-interest,' or 'well-being' for 'utility'.) Indeed, this statement of self-interest or well-being is the *only* thing that can be identified with rational economic actors—and anything else is *irrational* (Neva *et al.* 2014, 146).

Economists believe that individuals should be free to choose their own goals, even if they are different from most people's choices. We can rule out a situation where people may choose reasonable goals and, in the end, engage in irrational behaviour that can drive them away from their achievement rather than towards it (Neva *et al.* 2014, 151). In this book, we focus on the rational behaviour of African professional players who make decisions by (1) choosing goals that are consistent with present and future welfare, and (2) pursuing those goals in a way that can rationally be assumed to lead to their achievement through their investment contributions to society (Neva *et al.* 2014, 151). Despite the players' rationale of supporting their local communities, there may be constraints including lack of information and limited resources that can have impacts on their socioeconomic behaviour. In this way, players can choose options that would meet their mobilised resources and satisfaction in supporting their investment initiatives to the local communities.

Perfect economic rationality to bounded rationality

According to Herbert Simon, it is difficult to have perfect economic rationality due to the constraints that can influence a person's decision and place a limit on information flow as well as the resources needed to achieve a particular goal. The way African players make decisions is thus dependent on their income resources and sporting capital which they can mobilise in order to achieve their goals for the local communities. Simon (1978) outlines how rational behaviour can be affected. That is, meliorating —'defined as starting from the present level of well-being and then taking an opportunity to do better', African players' humble beginning from their local communities before becoming professionals abroad tend to have an influence on their behaviour as some see themselves as 'different human being' (Acheampong 2018a). This is because their level of social and economic status has changed which may challenge their behaviour in society as well. Thus, the players view each situational change choice as a success in terms of their previous experience (Neva *et al.* 2014). Players' progress in their football career by achieving professional status abroad cannot be related to their beginning experience where they struggled with limited facilities, no proper training gear, etc. amidst looking for opportunities to showcase their talents at home.

A thorough analysis of all the situations presents a general concept that the proposition that 'people make choices among somewhat arbitrary subset of all possible options is due to limits on information, time, or cognitive abilities' bounded rationality' (Neva *et al.* 2014, 152). Thus, the individual may prefer to settle on the 'best' decision that would get them close to their intended goals concerning the choices or options available to them in contributing to the societal cause.

Human capital theory vs gift and counter-gift theory

The human capital theory explains the importance of skills, abilities, and knowledge acquired through education and training that influences the future income earnings of the investment made in an individual (Becker 1993). This theory does not exist in a vacuum since financial and other resources are needed to make it functional for the development of the individual. In that sense, the main responsibility shifts from individuals to parents, family members or households or guardian right from early childhood to adolescent and finally adulthood.

Analysis of human capital concept, that is, investment in human capital goes with costs which are borne by parents, family members, or households or relatives in the near or far terms and with the expectation that they would have accrued benefits in future. The costs of adding to the individual human capital can be classified into three main levels as outlined by Becker (1993):

1. *Out-of-pocket or direct expenses* to include tuition costs and expenditure on books and other supplies. For a football player with talent, direct and indirect expenses occur in their education and training including sports kits, training gears, etc. which involve costs. Admission into some football academies is initiated by families, relatives, and the community for the talented kids through the payment of fees to enable them to be enrolled. Others join juvenile teams or a colts' team where they do not have to pay any specific fees, but some contributions are made for their travelling to play other teams away from their communities.

   As well, some parents, family members, and relatives occasionally borrow money to finance their children's football practice in those established football academies. This is becoming a common norm in many African countries where structured football academies operate. In the past, playing in colts' teams was perceived as leisure but now it is pursued as part of the speculative strategy in the hope of making a profit (Esson 2015), because local clubs and football academies in both the amateur and semi-professional leagues are now turning their attention to the development of football talents in order to transfer players to Europe, the Middle East, and Asia (Esson 2016). Such an opportunity associated with football enables families including the extended family and others in the community to assume the responsibility of providing proper care for their talent to benefit from playing abroad. Thus, investing in their children's human capital through football training makes them more productive for the future.
2. *Foregone earnings* are another source of cost because, during the investment period, it is usually impossible to work throughout the whole year or at least not a full-time all year. This shows that parents, families or relatives might have to take some time off their work or busy schedule to spend time with their children at football training as well as providing their social needs where necessary.
3. *Psychic losses* are a third of cost incurred because learning is often difficult and tedious. Parents experience a sense of loss after being unable to achieve their projected target, which makes it unreliable. Taking responsibility for their children's human capital development in football activities can lead to some parents not meeting their anticipated goals along their career path.

Like workers, the investment in their education and training are expected to yield returns in the form of higher future earnings, increased job satisfaction over a lifetime, and a greater appreciation of non-market activities and interests.

Considering the worker's goal, families, relatives, and the community investment in the individual talent through direct or out-of-pocket expenses are focused towards their development. Eventually, this investment approach prepares a person for a lifetime with the expected benefits supposed to be enjoyed by all parties concerned. This can be achieved when the individual develops well enough to become a useful and better person in the community. This means putting a huge responsibility on families or households catering for their developmental and other social needs that would facilitate their growth in the future. Young people's development goes beyond the provision of education alone. From the onset, families and others in the community have accepted education as the only means for their wards to be successful in life at the neglect of their sporting talents that must be developed alongside.

In theory, every child is supposed to have access to basic formal education, but this is not always the case. More importantly, investment in child education provides a solid foundation for his/her lifetime benefits. At the same time, children/young boys who have talent must be identified and developed, yet this is somehow ignored in various communities. In African communities, parents, relatives or households are obliged to take charge of their children's/siblings' upbringing which is their core mandate in order to produce better individuals for the benefit of society. Thus, families or households and the community have a huge responsibility to invest in the individual's capabilities by offering direct or indirect financial support through education and training. These investments support the individual's appropriate development in their localities. This scenario is very common in many African communities whereby it is the sole responsibility of families including the extended family, relatives and societies are obliged to ensure proper development of an individual through training and education in their communities. But the advent of cultural proliferation and poor economic hardships can limit such supports to individuals. Despite the lack of basic amenities in some communities, by convention, parents, families, or households must ensure that their children/young boys have access to basic formal education. This basic formal education is expected to provide children/young boys with a sort of foundation to better their lives in the future. This is their fundamental human right as stipulated in the UNESCO mission on Education.[2] Apart from some of the remote villages where children rarely have access to good educational facilities, they also lack qualified teachers or personnel to support their progress academically.

All these means of support from parents, families, or households or relatives are determined by direct expenses or out-of-pocket expenses. Sometimes the latter may skip work or important assignments in the name of attending to their children's development through the various sacrifices, like skipping or undertaking additional jobs in order to raise enough funds for their child's care and development. All those investments raised from other sources are supposed to help develop and nurture the individual to become productive in the future. That is why it may be necessary for a successful African professional player to consider improving the living conditions of their families, relatives, and the community in return for the support they have received regarding their upbringing in the communities. Indirectly, the family's benefits may be recognised as the return on investments (ROI) from the individual player's development from their childhood to adulthood.

Even though African football players in their migratory process maintain a link with their families, relatives and other people in the communities, it is also a way of strengthening the family bonding. This may compensate for the knowledge and skills provided (by childhood experiences) as an investment to have increased a player's lifetime earnings in their career after they become professionals abroad. These investments in the footballer may take different forms from different parents, families, relatives and the communities because of their social status, group norms and rules, yet the expected returns may vary accordingly, which should have a positive effect on them. The direct expenses or out-of-pocket money (including tuition/training costs, expenditure on equipment and other suppliers), foregone earnings (because it is usually impossible to work throughout your lifetime-taking days off work, forfeiting additional work hours among others), and psychic losses (which often make learning difficult and tedious). All these constitute a specific cost of investment in the individual (professional player) to have accelerated his professional status of reaching that height in his career. For instance, Darby (2014) noted that an African professional player who can play in Europe can achieve considerable financial rewards though a small proportion of their earnings from professional football, their earning power not only facilitates luxuriant lifestyles both during and after their careers but also allows them to support extended families in their country of origin.

Beyond that, intergenerational reciprocity is often at the centre of the process as some families, parents, and relatives strongly support their talented sibling's quest to develop into a professional player (Van der Meij and Darby 2014). This is important because some family members, relatives or households and the family as a key unit assign so much prominence to the development of their child's talents pending the expected returns in the future. It is not unusual to see families or households or relatives making decisions for their children's career especially in the African settings.

This is linked to the past, where parents or families and relatives accepted *only* education as a means for a person to be successful in life hence all resources were committed to producing scholars, copying the European way of ascribing social success to education alone. Thus, most African parents consider 'education as a privilege that they view as important for becoming "somebody", defined as a person of status and respect, somebody who is responsible, matured, independent, knowledgeable and capable of taking care of others in the future' (Langevang 2008). In many African communities, strong social values about education are indispensable (Van der Meij and Darby 2014), continuing to guide parents, family members, and the community as they support the training of children in spite of financial constraints. It supports the footballers' concept that education is the best gift one can give to their child/children because no one can take the acquired knowledge away from them and in the end, they will earn a living from it.

For instance, in Ghana, there was a series of state policies after independence linked education directly to development and this saw education as crucial in terms of social mobility in the minds of parents and other older family members (Esson 2013). That is why, for example, some family members and relatives frown on children taking to football rather than education. This perception still exists though some prefer their children to combine both school and football. Indeed, parents or families or relatives have understood something called 'talent', which is natural and when not properly nurtured and developed can produce a difficulty for one's social and personal situation in the future (e.g. unemployment). This sporting talent needs to be managed, particularly in the case of football so that it can benefit the individual's social and personal development. The game of football has become truly globalised not to mention its economic potentials for the best talents, should one become successful abroad. Thus, families or parents can subscribe to both football and school because the two complement each other. One stands to gain if successful in football or can switch to education should the football career fail, so that the child does not necessarily lose anything but would have something to rely on in the future. Furthermore, the individual footballer having a professional career abroad benefits from the new environment as one acquires skills, knowledge and technical acumen (tactics) through the training and education offered to impact on their performance. This can also lead to an increase in their economic value in the transfer marketplace and future earnings with their club. A reflection of the end-products from parents' or families' upbringing and support from childhood to adolescent and adulthood create that opportunity for the player in leagues abroad.

Parents or families or relatives' contributions and support, both tangible and intangible, provide individuals with the necessary tools to have better lives in the future. According to Marcel Mauss's gift theory, the gift leads to a counter-gift everywhere as cultural norms and social rules impose it. In contrast, Gary Becker's human capital theory recognises it as an investment that should be paid back when they become successful through ROI. These two models of analysis are behind two different conceptions of human behaviour in the frame of social and economic relationships. This can influence individuals' behaviour when they become successful footballers professionally and financially successful in life.

In sum, education, assistance and care provided by parents, families, relatives and the community, may be seen on one hand as a gift or investment, and on the other hand, as central in the footballers' training and migration process to Europe. In the two visions, footballers are identified as social or economic actors who give back to their community depending on their rationality, based on economic or social reasoning. This also contributes to social support and economic investment processes in preparing young footballers for a professional career. Thus during their training processes, support or investment in young players may represent a social or an economic approach depending on the model of analysis used and the subjectivity of footballers themselves. These sorts of support or investments can oblige footballers to give back with reference to the counter-gift or ROI or other forms when they become successful along their career path. Indeed, individuals learned norms and cultural values in the communities of origin and they may adopt other rational reasoning through their socialisation process and education either by acculturation or after spending many years abroad. This is because they are also embedded in different communities and social groups (Granovetter 1985).

Social and cultural limits for the economic rationality

Economic rationality according to Weber (1978, 68) is concerned with 'any peaceful exercise of an actor's control over resources which in its main impulse is oriented toward an Economic end'. This explains that a football player may feel satisfied after contributing to a good cause in society from their relatively scarce resources and with limited options available to them. The player as a social actor can be economically rational or non-rational based on the significance he allots to his action. Here, economic action refers to a *conscious* reference to meaning by the player or may involve values, traditions (culture), and affection (Brubaker 1984; Swedberg 1998; Weber 1978, 24–25).

For Weber, 'an economic action is "social" insofar as its subjective meaning takes account of the behaviours of others and is thereby oriented in its course' (Weber 1978, 4). Thus, the individual actor can be influenced in his action by considering the behaviour of significant others in society as they make economic decisions. This shows that the behaviour of players could be influenced based on their subjectivity and their relationship within the society and the community. In that sense, goals, interests, social rules and cultural norms of the community can affect the behaviours of players in their giving back action to provide socioeconomic support and investments in the communities.

Zukin and DiMaggio (1990) reported how economic behaviour is culturally entrenched and this makes culture set limits on economic rationality. These cultural norms and values may limit economic rationality because of the ideologies, beliefs, norms or customs of the community, which can have ripple effects on African migrant players' choices in terms of their socioeconomic projects to their local communities. DiMaggio (1994) went on to explain that culture provides the categories and understandings that enable us to engage in economic activity. Another school of thought on culture treats economic action as critically distinct from culture but emphasises the ways that norms and conventions constrain the individual's free pursuit of self-interest (DiMaggio 1994, 28). All the distinctive views suggest that culture may play a certain role to influence the social and economic behaviour of footballers especially those born and bred in a particular locale because of their shared values and norms, which are embedded in the community. An example can be seen in the communal labour activities such as general cleaning of hospitals, schools, community centres among others.

Cultural embeddedness advances the role of shared collective understandings in shaping economic means and ends, making its influence on economic action undeniable as the strongest among the types of embeddedness proposed by Zukin and DiMaggio (1990). Also, culture may influence people's economic action and there is a tendency for others to avoid those systems of shared meaning which can be attributed to acculturation because of globalisation and new technological advancements. But in many African communities like the villages, it is difficult for a person to influence the inhabitants' cultural values, norms, taboos, and customs due to the significant meaning they attach to their culture. Some of these cultural elements are identified as measures to inculcate good values, discipline, and control that may help to shape and reshape behaviours of their people. With time, these cultural elements become part and parcel of those people and have a high chance of affecting the goals and means of their economic actions.

However, it is questionable whether that assertion can be totally accepted for rural— urban migration, urban— rural migration and transnational migration. Yet, culture permeates almost everything that we do and the ability to observe its effects on social and economic initiatives can be quite difficult in some situations. As contended by Swidler (1986), the effect of culture on economic action cannot be understood as deriving from the cultural determination of ends or goals. But we are persuaded to believe this 'because of the intuitive credibility in our own culture of the assumption that all action is ultimately governed by some means-ends schema' (Swidler 1986, 274). Swidler reports that culture rather provides 'cultural components that are used to build strategies of action' (Swidler 1986, 273). Thus, an action or behaviour should not be explained by reference to values (or interests) but rather based on the cultural competence of actors, which is manifested in culturally shaped skills, habits, and styles. These *strategies of action* help to organise action into relatively stable and enduring patterns which can prevail even if goals change (Hamilton and Biggart 1992, 182). Some scholars identify culture as a 'toolkit' from which actors select differing pieces for constructing lines of action (see Mead in Doyle 1984). In unsettled periods, the role of culture in shaping strategies becomes more direct. Culture in the form of ideologies then shapes action in a highly conscious way and reduces the contingencies inherent in the situation (Swidler 1986, 280).

Understanding the economic rationality behind some African migrant players' giving back behaviour could have a significant cultural influence considering where their career started from and their embeddedness in the communities. For instance, it may be expected that the majority of professional players have deep connections with their social environment where they grew up playing in the streets or inter-street competitions or travelling several kilometres to play with other villages and towns. Thus, the humble beginning of individuals from their communities before their departure abroad is important for African footballers searching for a professional opportunity abroad (Acheampong 2018a).

The cultural aspects of African migrant players can be observed through their various economic actions and social interactions, as a result of the impact of social forces on their behaviour in various contexts (e.g. Akerlof 1980; Austen-Smith and Fryer 2005; Becker and Murphy 2000; Bernheim 1994). African players' cultural reasoning can also be seen in their social relations and networks that facilitate their migration and mobility to leagues abroad. This cultural embeddedness can drive players' social and economic initiatives to society.

Social relation and social embeddedness theory

Granovetter (1985, 1990) reported that social embeddedness influences the economic action of an actor, which is situated in the networks of interpersonal relations and the structure of the overall network of relations, or 'economic rationality is "embedded" within social relationships' (Granovetter 2005). Simply, social actors cannot exist in a vacuum rather within the relational, institutional, and cultural context and therefore cannot be seen as atomised decision-makers maximising their own interests (Granovetter 2005). Actors must consider significant others in their choice of actions, yet their prime interest may supersede other personal interests. For example, regarding societies, sociologists, anthropologists, political scientists, and historians reaffirmed the place of economic behaviour as completely embedded in social relations. Thus, social embeddedness has a role to impact on the decision making of others as they are part of their social environment of abode.

Mark Granovetter argues that economic action considers individual choice, which is importantly refracted by social relations within the environment. For Granovetter (1985), social embeddedness incorporates networks of social interaction in which an action takes place. Here, Granovetter identified a large distinction between rational actor models of the social world, where the actor makes a choice within a thin set of context-independent decision rules and the social actor models that highlight how the actor is largely driven by a context-defined set of scripts he/she makes a choice from. Granovetter (1985) went on to explain how economists interpret *social influences* as a process by which actors acquire customs, habits or norms which are followed mechanically and automatically, irrespective of their bearing on a rational choice. Beyond that, Granovetter framed a more fluid and relational conception of the actor, while the pragmatist theories of the actor (Abbott 1993; Gross 2009; Joas 1997) report that the actor's choices emerge from a flow of interactions and shifting relations with others.

The scholars' concept aligns with the position of Granovetter (1985) but does not remove the importance and agency of the actor because the actor still reacts and responds to their social relations surrounding him or her; however, actions are established and refracted through the consciousness, beliefs, and purposes of the individual. For instance, the migration of African players could not have been possible without the support of families, relatives, footballers' networks, and the community. They continue to play a significant role in mobilising human, material, and social resources that contribute to their professional journey abroad. These contributions from society may have gone to enhance their relationships with them (Acheampong 2017). Indeed, this deep-rooted social relationship might have a greater likelihood of influencing players' economic action to society.

This explains the imperative role of social relations and networks which individual actors can rarely ignore in the environment where they function. It makes the idea of an embedded actor different from the idea of an atomised actor as the individual's choices and actions are generated, in part anyway, by the actions and expected behaviour of other actors (Granovetter 1985). This made Granovetter admit that, in the relational concept, the embedded actor exists in a set of relationships with other actors whose choices affect his or her own choices as well. This aids our understanding that the choices actors make are influenced by the observed and expected behaviour of others, and not simply based on the domains of individual deliberation and beliefs (Granovetter 1985). Thus, the importance an individual commits to his or her actions seems to be rooted in a process of social relations that he/she may be part of.

The concept of social embeddedness extends to the role of concrete personal relations and structures (or networks) of such relations in building trust and avoiding malfeasance (Granovetter 1985, 490). To Granovetter, *trust* is an important component in developing social relations and social networks as one progresses in life. The notion of trust and the theory of the actor play a significant role in facilitating our understanding of social behaviour in a broader context. At best, the individual's choice of action may consider the expected choices of others in order to appreciate how concrete social relations are critical to their actions. This shows that African players' integration, social relations, and networks in the community can affect their economic rationality in terms of the 'Give Back Behaviour' to society. Players are embedded in social networks of football comprising the community, scouts, clubs, football academies, football administrators, and local managers (see Esson 2016).

As contended by Polanyi (1982), a society should make decisions based on economic interests rather than being embedded in social relationships. Polanyi's theory presents an interesting argument; however, Granovetter's (1985) provides a broad perspective that fits into the context of the giving back phenomenon in order to understand the economic rationality of African professional players through their various socioeconomic initiatives to support and assist their communities. Understanding how African players incorporate their values, conceptions, objectives, and interests into the needs of society and community can explain the social embeddedness effects to their communities. This indicates how African players are deeply rooted in their communities of origin which strengthens their social relationships along their career paths, since developing a positive relationship help improve one's social resources in life (Laumann and Pappi 1976).

The players' relationships with their social groups are often observed through the transfer of remittances, sporting capital, and other resources to families, relatives, and community members as they maintain social ties with them in their migratory process. It will be interesting to examine how the interplay of these elements of integration, social relations, and social networks of African players influence their economic rationality with their Give Back Behaviour.

The concept of embeddedness provided an essential component often used by economic sociologists to make a clear distinction in understanding the economic behaviours of individuals (Granovetter 1985; Zukin and DiMaggio 1990). This makes embeddedness encompass the social structural, cultural, political, and mental processes of decision making in economic and social contexts, showing how connected the actor is with his or her social environment. In sum, African players are embedded in their local communities of abode where they adhered to cultural values, customs, norms, and taboos which form an integral part of the community. This shows that their social relations and networks are embedded in their culture and social norms and may influence their economic rationality to society via their socioeconomic investment initiatives.

Institutionalised networks theory

North (1991) acknowledges that institutions are humanly devised constraints that shape political, economic, and social interaction. Without institutions, there would be anarchy and uncontrolled violence in society. The institutional framework has provided incentives in human exchange, which consist of both informal constraints (sanctions, taboos, customs, traditions, and codes of conduct) and formal rules (constitutions, laws, property rights). Throughout history, institutions have been devised by human beings to create order and reduce uncertainty in exchange (North 1991). This explains the reason behind specific times for international players' transfers as regulated by FIFA. We should not lose sight of the fact that the European football market provides an opportunity for African talents to secure a professional contract and start a new journey in their football career.

Institutional changes have affected the way societies evolve through connecting the past with the present and the future, and provide a key understanding of historical change (North 1991). This has led to the globalised world promoting easy movement across continents. That is why FIFA has put in place rules and regulations (formal constraints) to stabilise and bring sanity to the international transfers market. These institutions help to regulate the system and offer the opportunity for clubs and players to make the best choices in their endeavours. All these rules and regulations are measures to streamline the football market activities and promote the game's uncertainty.

Clubs not only benefit from international transfers but also professional players having the ability to control their movements within the football market because of decisions in the 'Bosman ruling'[3] in 1995 which has contributed to intensifying the migration of international players across borders, nations, and continents. These institutions provide incentives that have transformed the structures of professional clubs and the shaping and reshaping of the football market towards growth, yet there may be traces of some unethical and governance issues. Some clubs have taken advantage of the system by using the informal institution to lure or commit footballers in order to acquire their playing rights. Some clubs have mandated scouts, agents, sporting directors, former and current footballers to act as recruitment referrals (Agergaard and Tiesler 2014) in getting the playing rights of best talents for them.

The evolution of the football market has provided intermediaries with an opportunity to scout, recruit, negotiate, manage, and connect with other agents or sporting agencies. To ensure a fair play environment, it calls for the proper enforcement of institutions (together with technological approach) to improve on how transactions are done in the labour market. The literature on institutions and transactions might have provided efficient solutions to remedy issues of the organisation in a competitive framework (Williamson 1975, 1985). Relating to football, the regulatory framework enacted by FIFA has helped to bring sanity to the football market, attracting the best international players to rich clubs and prestigious leagues (Darby 2014). This has also attracted investors to acquire shares in clubs' ownership. Some of these FIFA regulations in the game have stimulated player movements, clubs, agents, and the football market, all to reduce problems and ensure smooth functioning of the system.

With the institutionalised networks, the best talents from Africa can move and play professionally in leagues abroad. Migration of African footballers started with the merchants who docked on the coast of Africa and continued through the colonial era, to the post-colonial phase, and then the electronic colonisation pioneered by transnational media (Onwumechili and Akinde 2014, 7). These illustrative processes brought their own specialisation and division of labour at the various levels of activity or operation. Yet, FIFA's frequent revision of its regulations after the post-colonial period has improved the football labour market for players and stakeholders of the game. The movement of players has been possible with the supportive activity of network facilitators such as licensed agents, scouts, sports agencies, and club officials to spread across the globe through a partnership where they could not have operated previously (Poli and Rossi 2012). The development in the football arena has changed the trends with the defined roles of intermediaries including licensed agents and other parties to bring sanity and stability into the market. In the football market, a system of exchange provides an incentive for actors or parties to invest their time, efforts, and resources like knowledge and skills in order to improve upon their activities and sporting visibility. All these together help to enhance the economic and social interactions for clubs and other stakeholders of the game working within the ambit of the laws and regulations of FIFA.

Apart from the formal regulations such as laws, the immediate sources of decision interactions are guided by mostly informal rules that include the code of conducts, norms of behaviour, and conventions (North 1991) that ensure fair play and soundness. Yet, it would be difficult for the FIFA laws to create equality among clubs since less financed clubs can never get to the standard of rich clubs. Informal rules like the conventions, norms, etc., form part of the cultural heritage that enables people to socially transmit information. Through those informal constraints, some African players can manoeuvre around to move abroad in pursuit of their professional dream. That is, they play a crucial role in facilitating the migration process of many African professional players abroad due to their humble beginning from the communities (Acheampong 2017). Such informal rules also promote social connections situated in 'friends-of-friends' networks involving colleagues, former and current players, especially serving as important tools for passing information about mobility destinations and employment opportunities (Bale 1991). This has been a major contributor to many African players' mobility and circulation in leagues abroad.

Similarly, Elliott and Maguire reported that sometimes migrants use 'bridgeheads' and Meyer (2001) went on to explain how those who have experienced mobility are actively involved in mobilising additional movement through their own interdependent networks (Elliott and Maguire 2011, 104). The significance of people getting more connected through social relations and networks is that it helps to facilitate their interests and actions. In some players' migration, information is gathered from community people through their social relations supporting their migration project abroad by road via some borders of African countries, then to Europe. In African settings, the family tree is quite limitless and consists of the extended family which often encompasses the so-called 'good' people as part of the nucleus family. Culture has been an essential part of society and how it is sustained and continued from the present to the future serves as an important legacy for generations to come. In the same vein, it ensures that the community people are guided by the informal constraints (social norms, customs, taboos, and values), which contribute to shape and reshape their way of life (as it reflects in the giving back of players' behaviour) and social networks.

In African communities, people are governed by a delicate balance of power and should not be taken for granted because each person has been constantly involved in securing his own position in situations where he had to show his good intentions. This is especially the case in the villages and towns where the informal rules are the order of the day and spearheaded by the chiefs as head or leader of those specific territories. That makes the usage of customs appear to be flexible and fluid given that judgement on whether or not someone has done rightly varies from case to case (Colson 1974). In most cases, the informal rules are applicable to the individual being judged and not the crime.

Considering these conditions, flouting of generally accepted standards is tantamount to a claim of illegitimate power and becomes part of the evidence against the person (Colson 1974, 59). In the African context, cultural values and norms (informal institutions) are real and show how certain communities applied them to streamline the behaviours of their people. That society which refuses to grow could be deviant where primitive institutions still exist, and innovations and technology are threats to the group survival.

In brief, the literature tends to provide the direction and form of economic actions that individuals and institutions are identified with, considering the basic institutional framework of customs, religious precepts, and formal rules (and the effectiveness of enforcement). Similarly, some scholars have described the development of a network society as shrouded in the 'new technologies that have created a new pattern of social relations to the existing ones' (Remennick 2003). This is experienced in various ways as migrant players have constant deliberations with families, relatives, and the community via visual and audio communication gadgets, all to maintain a constant connection with their left-behinds. North (1991) recognises institutions as 'personalistic' relationships which are still a significant tool for political and economic exchanges. The evolution of FIFA's institutional framework has produced significant growth in the football industry in terms of player transfer issues and the football market dynamics.

This book explores how some elements of institutions influence social behaviour or economic rationality of African players in their communities. Dequech (1998, 2002) outlined at least three characteristics of institutions that have a greater chance of influencing economic rationality or social behaviour of individuals.

1. The *restrictive function* of institutions clarifies how roles can influence the economic behaviour of people. This has been accepted and re-emphasised by neoclassical economists and many new institutional economists.
2. The *cognitive function* of institutions, which is related to the (strictly) cognitive aspects of culture. It involves the information institutions provide to the individual including effects of the likely action of other people. It explains the very perception that people have of reality, that is observed in the way people select, organise, and interpret information. This is something common among the media people who have a strong influence on the dissemination of information. Some of their comments tend to put social pressure on celebrities including professional footballers.
3. Institutions perform the third function through their *influence* on the ends that people pursue. It is likened to the value-oriented aspect of culture and identified how culture inspires values.

From the analysis of Dequech (1998, 2002), institutions influence emotions, values, and interests that guide social behaviour or economic rationality of people. These three types of institutions confirm how they can have an influence on the decision making of African players in relation to their 'GBB' to the communities. For the purpose of this book, we focused on the cognitive and social behaviour or economic rationality of African players and how it influences their socioeconomic behaviour through their investment initiatives. Thus, institutions can affect individuals' social behaviour by considering others in the pursuit of their economic interests.

In organisations and communities, institutions are essential in shaping and promoting orderliness as well as defining organisational culture. This defines the unique cultures of many African countries where institutions may hold different views. In some communities, the young ones are expected to respect their elders as well as giving them a helping hand whenever they are in need without hesitation. Ethically, a person who refuses to support the elderly in the locality gives himself/herself a bad image or is seen as disrespecting their culture, which the community people frown upon. Cultural values and norms are non-negotiable in some African communities. Some of these cultural values and norms are to guide African players because they are supposed to respect their culture, no matter the social status they might have achieved.

Through culture, some players can establish networks or social relations that create an opportunity for them to move abroad, because the cultural values and beliefs of the community tend to strengthen and sustain positive social relationships (Laumann and Pappi 1976) that facilitate some players' migration abroad. Those established networks or social relations developed by their family members, relatives, and friends within the locality also play a significant role to facilitate migration projects abroad.

Indeed, no African player can move to any European club or league without the appropriate documentation as enacted in the transfer regulations of FIFA, otherwise it becomes illegal. This illegality aspect of the migration of some African players has attracted scholars' attention as football trafficking or young talent exploitation (Ali 2008; Darby *et al.* 2007; Haynes 2008; McDougall 2010; Poli 2010; Rawlinson 2009; Scherrens 2007; Sparre 2007). That can lead to having an adverse risk for the Africa continent as their future leaders have drifted overseas. Based on this, it is appropriate for the community leaders and chiefs to collaborate in handling this unabated migration canker. This emerging trend continues to be worrisome for the community because they stand to lose their football talents and see prospects going to waste. For some scholars, this migratory practice is creating a tragic legacy of homeless young boys across major European cities (Bennhold 2006; McDougall 2008). But this book focuses on those African players who migrated through legal means.

The institutionalised networks strongly support the activities of the intermediaries acting informally as network facilitators, supporting mobility (within the leagues) and the regulatory framework of the football market, all to ensure healthy competition and stability in the football industry. These institutions' processes extend to member associations of African countries where these professional players' careers began in their domestic leagues, clubs, football academies, the juvenile team (Colts), community teams, and corporate leagues. Some of these informal leagues undoubtedly create opportunities for the best talents to be exposed to the European football market. Others get into those teams through social relations and later become visible to authorities and sometimes those who matter in the game (Agergaard and Engh 2013). Similarly, Carter (2014) reported how coaches and club officials collaborate to develop young players with certain skills through their own formal connections within global soccer and suggest to higher authorities that an individual may be a prospective footballer. This approach reflects how some professional players from Africa were able to be developed through such processes and later had the chance to feature for any category of their national teams through networks of coaches and friends at all levels.

Certainly, social relations and networks are embedded in societal culture and are the reason why Zukin and DiMaggio (1990) propose that it can influence

African players' economic behaviour in their communities' support through the 'Give Back Behaviour'. This is because the culture of African players is mostly situated in both *embeddedness and institutionalised networks*. That tends to have consequences on the individual player's economic rationality in their choices of investment initiatives for the community.

Family, extended family, the community, scouts, agents, clubs officials, and sports agencies as human resources play a crucial role in the migration processes of the African players abroad. These interrelated connections facilitate a successful migration of African players to leagues abroad. In the end, the various contributions from family, extended family, the community, scouts, agents, and clubs officials have a strong influence on players' decision making in giving something back to their communities. This provides an insight into how African players are supported in their migratory projects abroad and its effects on their GBB to the larger society.

A key issue explored here is the social rationality concept that determines African footballers' 'Give Back Behaviour'. In doing so, the book relies on the Weberian concept of social action as a methodology in analysing the contributions of the various theoretical models connected to the research.

In a nutshell, these theoretical models were derived from the economic sociology approaches that provide a clue to understanding the economic rationality of African players 'Give Back Behaviour' to their countries of origin. These include human capital theory—which analyses how individuals are equipped with the necessary skills and knowledge through education and training to make them become productive economically. This is identified with the economic approach. The embeddedness concept provides the individual with a wealth of social relations and networks that enhance their integration in the communities and beyond. This determines the sociological approach that facilitates their economic and non-economic activities in society.

In African communities, individuals are guided by cultural values, norms, and custom that shape and reshape their actions in the locales. This is the reason why culture affects individuals' economic rationality. Culture involves formal and informal constraints that constitute institutions. These institutions create an integrated web that improves individuals' social viability in the social system. Individuals mobilise the various social relations and networks to their advantage through the integration of the institutionalised networks. Together, these contribute to understanding the effects they have on African players in relation to their GBB via their socioeconomic investments to society. The institutionalised networks help to understand the socioeconomic approach adopted by the players in managing their migration and mobility abroad. These theories help to identify some indicators or variables that were incorporated into the players' interviews guide for the analysis grid.

Socioeconomic model of Give Back Behaviour

The socioeconomic model of GBB shows clearly how African players' subjective dimension can have a strong influence on their giving back behaviour. This behaviour is identified through the values and norms they share with the community which create a porous boundary between them, but also through their interests and the social networks to which they belong. The players recognise the immense contributions and support they have received from different people towards their development and migration process abroad and this contributes to explaining the importance African professional players ascribe to their actions (including values or conceptions or objectives or interest) regarding their investments, efforts, time, finances and other resources that define their 'Give Back Behaviour' to their communities of origin.

The rationalities of African players are determined through their economic and non-economic activities in the larger society. Players' 'Give Back Behaviour' is influenced by their values (economic, social, norms or cultural, professional) or conceptions (work, economic, future, sport, social and reintegration) or objectives (economic, social, solidarity, professional or cultural) or interest (social, economic, professional, solidarity). African players' decision making is situated in Weber's (1978) typologies of social action, which determine their rational purpose or goals—oriented towards creating investment opportunities and making profit to maintain a family's future; the value-oriented aspect is often towards social or rational projects, not for profits but in reference to their values; traditional action which obliges them to transfer regular remittances to families, friend and others (under the influence of customs and norms); and emotional or affective action observed through donations to charity, orphanage homes, awarding scholarships to needy students, etc. (oriented towards one's feelings/emotion in a certain situation). Again, the players' decisions are observed from their socioeconomic behaviour via their 'Give Back Behaviour'. This is reinforced by the study of Darby (2014) that apart from some players transferring direct remittances to their people, a few high-profile players like Samuel Eto'o, Michael Essien, Didier Drogba, Stephen Appiah and Emmanuel Adebayor are engaged in charitable work and philanthropic activities, which allow them to 'give back' and contribute to various causes in Africa.

The social pressure from the communities (often spearheaded by the media) cannot be ignored as they have influenced some players' decisions to give something back to society. Others' behaviour is seen through their emotion or passion to undertake certain social projects in the communities. In a broader context, those actions of players connote the importance they commit to such social activity which determines their rationality in supporting society. There are times when players' social activity and behaviour reflect their deep connections to society, situated in their cultural norms and values. In sum, the economic rationality of African players demonstrates the individual sense of significance they give to their behaviour while incorporating other views which should not overshadow their preference in supporting society. This also confirms players' behaviour reproducing their values or conceptions or objectives or interest to the local communities. A thorough analysis (Figure 3.1) indicates that African players' 'Give Back Behaviour' to families, relatives, communities, societies, and grassroots clubs

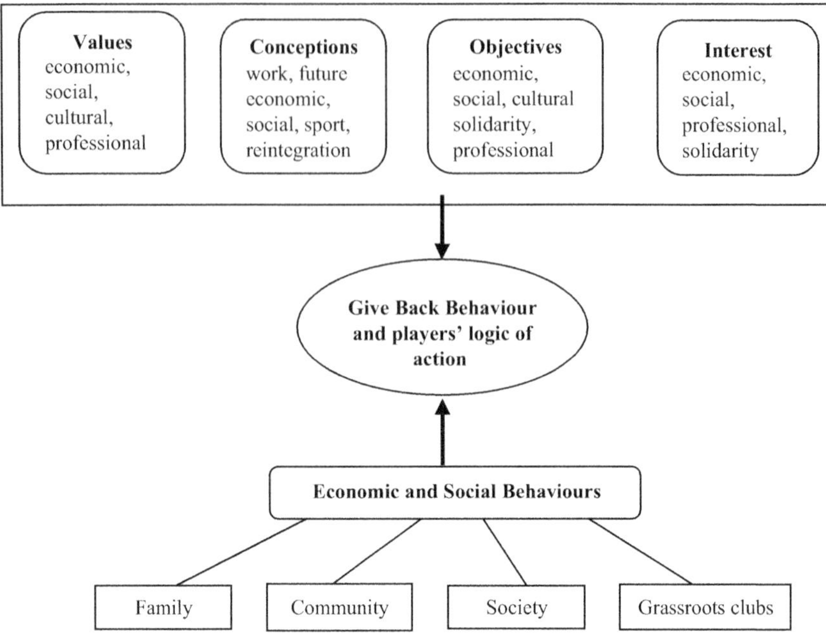

Figure 3.1 Socioeconomic model of Give Back Behaviour.
Source: Application of micro-mentality analysis model of Malek Bouhaouala (1999).

through the various socioeconomic investment initiatives is based on either their values or objectives or conceptions or interests. This exactly reveals the rationality that determines their behaviour to society. In this book, we not only focus on African players' investment initiatives to society (Acheampong 2018b) but also analyse the rationality of their socioeconomic behaviour to the communities. That is to say, whether their economic behaviour is determined by the return on investments (ROI) or norms and cultural values or social and cultural embeddedness or the integration of the institutionalised networks or the economic interest to invest in their countries of origin. The contributions of theoretical models provided a tool to develop interview questions explained in the next section.

Conclusion

We relied on an economic sociology approach to set the tone for understanding how the players' GBB can be explored because it provides diverse angles to explaining Africa players' giving back attitude in a holistic function. The engagement of multidisciplinary approaches including the use of Weberian concepts on social action (economic rationality) supported the development of the socioeconomic model of African players' Give Back Behaviour framework. Analysis of the theories and models employed apparently showed how African players' economic behaviour can be determined based on economic, cultural, social, and institutionalised networks, which reflect the significant meaning they give to their socioeconomic contributions to society. The developed framework illustrates how African players' Give Back Behaviour considers the contributions of significant others (family, community, grassroots clubs, society) in relation to their values, objectives, conceptions, and interests, which influence their socioeconomic investments in their countries of origin. This is as a result of the various contributions they have received and enjoyed from the family, community, grassroots, clubs, and society before and during the migration projects. The socioeconomic framework arrived at explains how the GBB of players and logic of action are influenced by their subjectivity (values, conceptions, objectives or interests) to reflect their distinct economic and social behaviour to societal cause in the communities.

Notes

1. Galleria News on 5 November 2014. http://gallerianews.com/courtney-dike-rejects-7000-world-cup- bonus/. [Accessed on 15 October 2015].
2. UNESCO mission on education which stipulates that every child must have access to basic formal education.
3. This was a vital decision on the free movement of labour among the EU Member States which had heavily impacted on the transfers of footballers within the EU territories. Its freed players at the end of a contract without any transfer fees being paid to their former club.

Bibliography

Abbott, B. 1993. 'A pragmatic account of the definiteness effect in existential sentence', *Journal of Pragmatics* 19: 39–55.

Acheampong, E. Y. 2017. 'Socioeconomic analysis of the Give Back Phenomenon: Professional footballers in Europe and their assistance to the communities of origin in Africa.' PhD diss., Université Grenoble Alpes, France.

Acheampong, E.Y. 2018a. 'How does professional football status challenge African players' behaviour?', *Soccer & Society*, doi:10.1080/14660970.2018.1541797.

Acheampong, E.Y. 2018b. 'Giving back to society: evidence from African sports migrants', *Sport in Society*, doi:10.1080/17430437.2018.1551367.

Agergaard, S. and Botelho, V. 2014. 'The way out? African players' migration to Scandinavian women's football', *Sport in Society: Cultures, Commerce, Media, Politics* 17 (4): 523–536, doi:10.1080/17430437.2013.815512

Agergaard, S. and Huagaa Engh, M. 2013. 'Producing mobility through locality and visibility. Developing a transnational perspective on sport labour migration', *International Review for the Sociology of Sport* 23 (1): 1–20. doi:10.1177/1012690213509994.

Agergaard, S. and Tiesler, N. Clara. 2014. *Women, Soccer and Transnational Migration*. Routledge.

Akerlof, G. A. 1980. 'A theory of social custom of which unemployment may be one consequence', *The Quarterly Journal of Economics* 94 (4): 749–775.

Akerlof, G.A. 1990. 'Interview.' In Richard Swedberg (ed.), *Economics and Sociology* (61–78). Princeton, NJ: Princeton University Press.

Ali, S. 2008. 'Play the game: Football's trafficking in third world athletes.' Available at: http://www.playthegame.org/news/detailed/footballs-trafficking-in-third-world-athletes 1255.html [Accessed 8 November 2009].

Austen-Smith, D. and Fryer, Roland G. 2005. 'An economic analysis of "Acting white"', *The Quarterly Journal of Economics* 120 (2): 551–583.

Bale, J. 1991. *The Brawn Drain: Foreign Student-Athletes in American Universities*. Urbana, IL: University of Illinois Press.

Becker, S. G. 1993. *Human Capital: A Theoretical and Empirical Analysis with Special Reference to Education*, 3rd edition. Chicago: University of Chicago Press.

Becker, G. S. and Murphy, K. M. 2000. *Social Economics: Market Behaviours in a Social Environment*. Cambridge, MA: Harvard University Press.

Bennhold, K. 2006. 'Soccer dreams and reality', *International Herald Tribune* (www.iht.com). Paris.

Bernheim, B. Douglas. 1994. 'A theory of conformity', *Journal of Political Economy* 102 (5): 841–877.

Bouhaouala, M. 1999. 'Micro-mentalités et logiques d'actions des dirigeants des petites entreprises du tourisme sportif: contribution à une sociologie économique du sport.' Thèse de Doctorat de l'Université Joseph Fourier Grenoble 1.

Bouhaouala, M. 2007. 'Micro-mentalités et logiques d'action des entrepreneurs dirigeants de petites entreprises', *Revue Internationale PME*, 20: 2.

Bouhaouala, M. 2008. *Management de la petite entreprise des loisirs sportifs, une approche socio-économique*. Bruxelles: De Boeck Université, Collection New Management.

Brubaker, R. 1984. *The Limits of Rationality*. London: George Allen and Unwin.

Carter, T.F. 2014. 'On mobility and visibility in women's soccer: Theorising an alternative approach to sport migration.' In Sine Agergaard and Nina Clara Tiesler (eds), *Women, Soccer and Transnational Migration* (161–174). Abingdon: Routledge.

Colson, Elizabeth F. 1974. 'Tradition and Contract: The Problem of Order.' Lectures presented at the University of Rochester, New York. Chicago: Aldine.

Darby, P. 2013. 'Moving players, traversing perspectives: Global value chains, production networks and Ghanaian football labour migration', *Geoforum* 50: 43–53. http://dx.doi.org/10.1016 /j.geoforum.2013.06.009.

Darby, P. 2014. 'International football migration and Africa: Feet drain or feet exchange', *More than a Game, Sports, Society and Politics: Panorama Insights into Asian and European Affairs*, January 2014.

Darby, P., Akindes, G., and Kirwin, M. 2007. 'Football academies and the migration of African football labour to Europe', *Journal of Sport and Social Issues* 31 (2): 143–161. doi:10.1177/0193723507300481.

Dequech, D. 1998. 'Rationality and institutions under uncertainty.' PhD diss., University of Cambridge.

Dequech, D. 2002. 'The demarcation between the "Old" and the "New" Institutional Economics: Recent complications', *Journal of Economic Issues* 36 (2): 565–572.

DiMaggio, P. 1994. 'Culture and economy.' In Neil Smelser and Richard Swedberg (eds), *Handbook of Economic Sociology* (27–57). Princeton, NJ: Princeton University Press.

Doyle, E. McCarthy.1984. 'Toward a sociology of the physical world: George Herbert Mead on physical objects', *Studies in Symbolic Interaction*, 5: 105–121.

Elliott, R. and Maguire. J. 2011. "Net-gains: Informal recruiting, Canadian players and British professional ice hockey.' In J. Maguire and M. Falcous (eds), *Sport and Migration: Border, Boundaries and Crossings* (102–111). London: Routledge.

Esson, J. 2013. 'A body and a dream at a vital conjuncture: Ghanaian youth, uncertainty and the allure of football', *Geoforum*, 47: 84–92. https://dspace.lboro.ac.uk/dspace-jspui/bitstream/2134/17405/3/Geoforum.pdf.

Esson, J. 2015. 'Escape to victory: Development, youth entrepreneurship and the migration of Ghanaian footballers', *Geoforum; Journal of Physical, Human, and Regional Geosciences* 64: 47–55. doi:10.1016/j. geoforum.2015.06.005.

Esson, J. 2016. 'Football as a vehicle for development: Lessons from male Ghanaian youth.' In N. Ansell, N. Klocker and T. Skelton (eds), *Geographies of Global Issues: Change and Threat*, Berlin: Springer.

Granovetter, M. 1985. 'Economic action and social structure: The problem of Embeddedness', *American Journal of Sociology* 91 (3): 481–510. doi:10.1086/228311.

Granovetter, M. 1990. 'The old and the new old economic sociology: A history and an agenda.' In Roger Friedland and A. F. Robertson (eds), *Beyond the Marketplace: Rethinking Economy and Society* (89–112). New York: Aldine de Gruyter.

Granovetter, M. 2005. 'The impact of social structure on economic outcomes', *Journal of Economic Perspectives* 19: 33–50.

Gross, N. 2009. 'A pragmatist theory of social mechanisms', *American Sociological Review* 74 (3): 358–379.

Hamilton, Gary C. and Biggart, Nicole W. 1992. 'The Western bias of neoclassical economics: On the limits of a firm-based theory to explain business networks.' In Robert Eccles and Nitin Nohria (eds), *Networks and Organisations* (471–490). Harvard Business School Press.

Haynes, J. 2008. 'Football trafficking–the new slave trade', *Modern Ghana News*. Available at: http://www.modernghana.com/print/159436/2/football-trafficking-the-new-slavetrade.html [Accessed 6 September 2010].

Joas, H. 1997. *Pragmatism and Social Theory*. Chicago and London: The University of Chicago Press.

Langevang, T. 2008. 'We are managing! Uncertain paths to respectable adulthoods in Accra, Ghana', *Geoforum* 39: 2039–2047. doi:10.1016/j.geoforum.2008.09.003.

Laumann, E. O. and Pappi, F. U. 1976. *Networks of Collective Action: A Perspective on Community Influence Systems*. New York: Academic Press.

McDougall, D. 2008. 'The scandal of Africa's trafficked players', *The Observer*. Available at: http://www.guardian.co.uk/football/2008/jan/06/newsstory.sport4 [Accessed 13 January 2008].

McDougall, D. 2010. 'Traffickers exploit Africa's soccer dream.' *The Sun*, June 1.

Meyer, J-B. 2001. 'Network approach versus brain drain: Lessons from the diaspora', *International Migration* 39 (5): 91–110.

Neva, R. G., Harris, J. M., Nelson, J., Roach, B., Torras, M., Ackerman, F. and Weisskopf, T. E. 2014. *Microeconomics in Context*. 3rd edition (145–157). Armonk, New York/London, England: M.E. Sharpe Publishers.

North, Douglass C. 1991. 'Institutions', *The Journal of Economic Perspectives* 5 (1): 97–112.

Onwumechili, C. and Akinde, G. (eds) 2014. *Identity and Nation in African Football: Fans, Community and Clubs*. Global Culture and Sport Series. Palgrave Macmillan.

Polanyi, K. 1982. 'The economy as instituted process.' In M. Granovetter and R. Swedberg (eds), *The Sociology of Economic Life* (29–51). Boulder, CO: Westview.

Poli, R. 2010. 'African migrants in Asian and European football: Hopes and realities', *Sport in Society: Cultures, Commerce, Media, Politics* 13 (6): 1001–1011. doi:10.1080/17430437.2010.491269.

Poli, R. and Rossi, G. 2012. *Football Agents in the Biggest Five European Markets. An Empirical Research Report*. Neuchâtel: Centre International d'Etude du Sport (CIES).

Rawlinson, K. 2009. 'Mbvoumin: Make no mistake; this is trafficking of young people', *The Independent*. Available at: http://www.independent.co.uk/sport/football/european/mbvoumin-make-no-mistakethis-is-trafficking-of-young-people-1789345.html [Accessed 8 November 2010].

Remennick, L. 2003. 'What does integration mean? Social insertion of Russian immigrants in Israel', *Journal of International Migration and Integration* 4 (1): 23–49.

Scherrens, J. 2007. 'The muscle drain of African football players to Europe: Trade or trafficking?' Master's Thesis, Karl-Franzens University of Graz.

Simon, Herbert A. 1978. 'Rationality as process and as product of thought', *American Economic Review, American Economic Association* 68 (2): 1–16.

Smelser, N. J. and Swedberg, R. 2010. *The Handbook of Economic Sociology*. 2nd edition, Princeton, NJ: Princeton University Press.

Sparre, K. 2007. 'Prevention programme proposed to stop football trafficking', *Play the Game*. http://www.playthegame.org/news/detailed/prevention-programme-proposed-to-stop-foot ball-trafficking-1417.html.

Swedberg, R. 1994. 'Markets as social structures.' In Neil J. Smelser and Richard Swedberg (eds), *The Handbook of Economic Sociology* (255–282). New York: Russell Sage Foundation; Princeton, NJ: Princeton University Press.

Swedberg R. 1998. *Max Weber and the Idea of Economic Sociology*. Princeton, NJ: Princeton University Press.

Swidler, A. 1986. 'Culture in action: Symbols and strategies', *American Sociological Review* 51: 273–286. doi:10.2307/2095521.

UNESCO and Education: Everyone has the right to Education. UNESDOC Digital Library. (http://en.unesco.org/themes/education-21st-century).

Van der Meij, N. and Darby, P. 2014. 'No one will burden the sea and then never get any benefit: Family involvement in players' migration to football academies in Ghana.' In J. Harris and R. Elliot (eds), *Football and Migration* (159–179). Abingdon: Routledge.

Weber, M. 1978 [1922]. *Economy and Society: An Outline of Interpretive Sociology*, translated by Ephraim Fischoff *et al.*, 2 vols. Berkeley: University of California Press.

Williamson, O.E. 1975. *Markets and Hierarchies: Analysis and Antitrust Implications*. New York: Free Press.

Williamson, O. E. 1985. *The Economic Institutions of Capitalism*. New York: Free Press.

Zukin, S. and DiMaggio P. 1990. 'Introduction.' In Sharon Zukin and Paul DiMaggio (eds), *Structures of Capital. The Social Organization of the Economy* (1–36). Cambridge: Cambridge University Press.

4

Methodological approaches to Give Back Behaviour

Introduction

In understanding the complexity of the influences on players' GBB, this chapter looks at the collection of data through survey and observation to explain clearly the concept. We applied the methodology of social sciences research to gather the data required to analyse the subject matter. Various sub-themes were derived from the literature which supported the development of our analysis grid or table. Selecting a qualitative approach provided us with the opportunity to have face-to-face interactions with the participants. This also contributed to acquiring the relevant information from the players in relation to the GBB to society.

Using methodology in social sciences research we were able to solicit the information needed to explain and analyse the GBB of players and address this phenomenon. In socioeconomic theory, the analysis models and methodology are often constructed *ad hoc* in coherence with the main question and the hypothesis. In our case, the question concerns the analysis of professional footballers' Give Back Behaviours in a socioeconomic perspective. This defended the idea that the GBB can be based on different rationalities and may refer to economic and sociological factors, both at the micro and macro level of analysis. This certainly presents a methodological conflict between holism and individualism. Going beyond this theoretical obstacle, we mobilised the Weberian methodological contribution, which introduces an intermediate meso level of analysis.

The theoretical framework supported in constructing the analysis grid, out of which structured interviews were generated to understand the logic of actions of African players in terms of their Give Back Behaviour to society. At the same time, all ethical issues were considered to help produce a reliable and viable study. The theoretical framework contributed to extracting the various indicators in constructing the analysis grid (details in the subsequent section, 'Analysis grid'). This captured all aspects of the players' career trajectory from their communities to leagues abroad. This is essential because it created the opportunity to obtain information that was directly connected and related to the real situation of African players (Burns and Grove 2009). Also, the views of former African professional players were captured; even though some ended their career before 2008, it was very important for the study. In gathering the required responses from the players, the authors constructed an analysis table with the various indicators extracted from the literature to develop structured interviews and informal conversations—interviews with the participants.

Max Weber demonstrated the approach based on the ideal-types which makes it possible to articulate micro and macro levels, individualistic and collective factors, economic and/or non-economic parameters. In this perspective, the GBB may be based on economic and/or social rationality, individual and/or collective logic, interests and/or values, etc. The literature review provided some theories and models to help explain the rationalities behind socioeconomic individuals' behaviours.

The aim of this chapter is to employ the social action theory of Weber (1978 [1922]) as a methodological contribution to examine and analyse African footballers' GBB according to their economic and non-economic actions to society. Weberian theory provides insight into how valuable the decisions of African players are, regarding their economic investment and social initiatives to society. This supports understanding their GBB which may have different connotations regarding their contributions to families, relatives, friends, and the community. The subsequent sections focus on how relevant data was gathered, materials and methods used for data collection and analysis, and interview questions derived from the analysis table, and a brief social background of high-profile players interviewed and a summary of the chapter.

Data collection and methods

Data was collected from documents of African players both at home and abroad to understand the process of their migration, mobility to leagues, and their GBB. To gain an insight into the study both quantitative and qualitative approaches were used to analyse the decision making of the players.

Source

Statistics gathered included the analysis of relevant documents from secondary data and autobiographies and biographies of some African migrant players. The literature review from the various sources contributed to developing an extensive database with the needed indicators or variables to design and construct the analysis grid. With the quantitative aspect, data was collected from academic materials, articles, newspapers, magazines, sports and clubs' websites, players' personal sites, federations, the FIFA website, international transfer records and national teams' sites to develop a comprehensive database of African players abroad. This also included players' profiles, national team, domestic clubs, beginning leagues in Africa and Europe, town or city, youth club, country of origin, current and previous clubs in Europe, transfer market value, and wages/salaries, image right, socioeconomic projects, stay in leagues abroad and other criteria.

African players included former footballers who left at pre-teen to join family members or relatives abroad to continue with their education or for relocation purposes and reconnected to their roots and invested in the local communities (Acheampong 2018b). The beginning leagues of the players were traced from the late 1980s until the 2012/2013 season, which also determined the entry and end of some players' careers in the 30 UEFA professional leagues. These African players drawn from the professional leagues in Europe were based on the quality and represented the best 13 UEFA leagues ranking in the season of 2012/13 and 2013/2014. The top elite Leagues of England (Premier, championship and League One), Spain (Primera, Segunda and Segunda A), Germany (Bundesliga 1 and 2, Liga 1), Italy (Serie A, Serie B and Lega Pro), and Switzerland (Super League, Challenge league and Liga 1) were considered because of their professionalism, but Ukraine has only one professional league and the following have two top Elite Leagues—France, Turkey, Greece, the Netherlands, Belgium, Portugal, and Russia.

The 'top five' European leagues of Spain, England, Germany, Italy and France engrossed many of the African players because of their huge economic potentials and sporting success of clubs with their global viewership. Autobiographies and biographies of some African players were consulted. Other sources of information complemented the extensive interviews from the former and current professional players that provided the necessary information for the research questions.

Statistic— Descriptive analysis:

In the construction of the database, materials were collected from the early part of 2012 to September 2018. Statistics cover African professional players from the 56 members associations affiliated to CAF but only 44 have players in the 30 professional European leagues studied. Twelve African countries had none of their players in the 30 professional European leagues studied. The selection has been defined to cover the 30 professional leagues based on the need to include a satisfactory number of players in the survey. The study looked at the years players have spent playing professional football abroad which spans from 1–20 years per the study's timeframe. This provided information on the longest stay and the player with most mobility in leagues.

The research considered the mobility of players in different leagues with the highest of 14 movements across nine different UEFA countries. A few players stayed in a particular UEFA league for less than 11 years. The research provided essential insight into the domestic clubs' development of players, before their movement and the pattern of mobility exhibited abroad. Despite the amount of details covered, the research was limited because a large sample of African players' mobility could not capture the entire 55 UEFA countries though some moved to the lower leagues in Europe.

Both current and former players' views were captured due to their different migration experiences. Statistics on the age range favour most players having less than 12 years of professional experience abroad (83.86 per cent). The database analysis included those players who began their professional journey from the leagues of Asia, Gulf and South America.

Materials and methods

The data analysis explained how professional footballers from Africa make decisions with their socioeconomic investment initiatives to support their local communities. We used a qualitative method including a data set and individual in-depth interviews (Kvale and Brinkmann 2015). This contributed to utilising different interviewing strategies that enabled African players to provide answers to exact questions and generated insights and understanding by promoting narration (Witzel 2000). Indeed, qualitative methods are useful for studying a phenomenon in its natural setting through a theoretical lens (Creswell 2007). The book focuses more on the qualitative survey with structured and semi-interviews and observations to analyse the economic behaviour of African players to society.

In sum, data on African players in the 30 professional leagues abroad were gathered and analysed in the early part of 2013 through to September 2018. The developed database on African players ended in May 2013 and included their profiles, football itineraries, transfers, leagues' mobility, etc. African players were traced from their beginning leagues overseas until the 2012/2013 season and the same time determined the end of some players' active career in the 30 European leagues. It also showed the entry of new African players into their leagues. Here, African professional players included those who left for Europe at pre-teen from their communities of origin to either join families or relatives or on a social visit or to continue with their education and ended up becoming footballers.

Interviewees arbitrarily selected played in the following leagues in Europe: England, Spain, Germany, Italy, Switzerland, France, Turkey, Greece, the Netherlands, Belgium, Portugal, Ukraine, Russia and Nordic countries. The majority of African players were hosted by the top five European leagues, noted for their mammoth economic potentials, the sporting success of their clubs and the global viewership they commanded.

The book concentrates on understanding the Give Back Behaviour of African players after they migrated and achieved professional status abroad. Weber's concepts provided a basis to understand the rationality of the players' Give Back Behaviour and how they value their actions to society. Former players' inclusion was important because of their vast mobility abroad and post-career transition experiences. Interviewees provided interesting revelations about some of the things that influence African players' Give Back Behaviour between their humble beginning in the communities and becoming professional abroad (Acheampong 2018a). The interviews were taped or recorded, transcribed with the consent of the participants and processed using the techniques of qualitative content analysis (Mayring 2007).

Interviewing of African players started from June 2013 to February 2019, but it was difficult to cover all participants due to their clubs' busy schedules and the unavailability of their services. Also, it was difficult getting African players to share their experiences on their football career path and some simply refused to be interviewed due to reasons that are best known to them. Interviewees were between the ages of 19 and 55 and have experienced different mobility along their career paths abroad. They represent different generations of African professional players who had featured for their national teams, either the home country or abroad, in the age categories in international competitions and with varying social backgrounds and levels of education.

Interviewees explained their migration process, itinerary, mobility and how professional football status influenced Give Back Behaviour to the countries of origin. Autobiographies and biographies of Didier Drogba, Jay-Jay Okocha and Fabrice Muamba were critically analysed to enhance the book's discussions.

Analysis Grid

The analysis grid was derived from theoretical approaches and results of other studies from the literature. This supported identifying some characteristics or variables to construct the interview guidelines. It was based on the economic, sociological, cultural, and socioeconomic parameters as extracted from the theoretical model contributions. This is presented in table 4.1.

Profiles of African footballers interviewed

This section highlights the social background of African professional players interviewed according to their career trajectories and achievements in Africa and abroad. It also considers players' beginning leagues abroad to their end of club career and those actively playing.

1. **Abedi Ayew Pele** (born in 1964): One of the first African players who made history with French Club of Olympique Marseille after winning the UEFA champions league trophy in 1993. He was awarded the African player of the century by IFFHS (International Federation of Football History and Statistics). He won African footballer of the year award for three consecutive years and played professional football for over 18 years in six foreign countries. He is the youngest player at age 17 to have won a gold medal in the 1982 AFCON tournament. He was former captain of Ghana senior national team (Black Stars) until his retirement from active football in 2000. His interview took place at his residence in East Legon, Accra-Ghana on 9 March 2016.
2. **Anthony Yeboah** (born in 1966): One of the finest strikers for Ghana and Africa who is noted for scoring spectacular goals. He played for Ghana national senior team (Black Stars) several times until his retirement from active football in 2002. He is always remembered in Germany for his role in fighting

Table 4.1 Analysis grid used for the players' interviews

Sub-theme	*Characteristics/Criteria*	*Questions*	*Observations*
Career path	aim, previous club, current club, years spent, success, difficulties, memorable moments (understanding the evolution)	Could you talk about your aims before and after becoming a professional, your difficulties, successes and memorable moments?	What was your motive for becoming a professional player?
Football and sport profile	training, position, other sport, duration/length of stay	Could you talk about your football background?	Did you do other sport apart from football?
Sociological and economic activity	evolution of economic situations (revenue, investment, salary, wages, remittance, etc.)	How do you invest your football money?	What did you do with your first contract money?
Social profile	education, parents' profession, family, siblings, ethnicity, city or town, village, religion, local dialect, beginning of football, attitude of parents and household	When, where, and how did you begin to play football and what were the attitudes of parents and family?	What support did you receive from your family?
Link with the community and country of origin	travel, regular visits, financial aid, remittances, contract, network, commitment to national assignments, social, cultural and economic capital	What is your relationship with the community and country of origin?	What kind of support did you receive from the locality or community people?
Professional itinerary	Europe, another country, country choice, agents, scouts, officials, media influence, transnational media, family aid and support, networks support.	What informed your choice of country to start your career there?	How did you relate with your team colleagues or mates or what was your relationship with your teammates and staff?
		Could tell us how you were able to join the club and who facilitated your move to Europe?	
		Did you have anybody briefing or orienting you before your departure abroad?	
	orientation prior to moving abroad, choice of country		Were you fortunate to have former players or people orienting you before moving abroad?

Traditional motive (cultural, social)	remittance, hospitals, schools, community health centre, playing grounds, church, water pump facility, sport pitch, toilet facility, sporting facility,		What exactly influenced you to invest in those social and economic projects?
Individual motive (value oriented or emotional)	financial support, charity foundation, needy support.	Could you explain what drives you to undertake projects in the communities?	
Objectives and interest	football academies, sporting facilities, transport business, management of clubs, real estate, manufacturing, factory, entertainment and music promotion, schools, credit facility, Treasury bills, bonds, etc.		
Opinions or views on country and Africa	lifestyle, people and Africa	What is your general view of the life of your country people and Africa?	General view of the life of your country people and Africa as a whole
Socioeconomic profile	revenue/wages/salary/transfers	Could talk about how your revenue evolves as you change clubs? (Evolution of your salaries during transfers)	Do you have a fair idea about your salary increases?
Socioeconomic commitment	charity foundation, schools, scholarship schemes, health centre remittance, hospitals, training & vocational centres, playing grounds, needy support.	Could you mention some of the social and economic projects you have done in your country of origin?	What is your reason for investing in those types of socioeconomic projects?
Engagement of experts/ professionals	individual /business groups/ partners/ associations environmental	What role did other professionals play in your projects?	Did you have other people managing your investment while playing?
Socioeconomic prospects	actual and future projects	Could you talk about your short or medium and long-term projects?	What are your short, medium and long-term future plans?
Reflections (lessons and experiences) in Europe	feedback on your experience abroad	Could you share your experience in general on football?	What lessons can we learn from your experiences abroad?

racism as an ambassador. He played over 14 years of professional football in three different foreign countries. He granted the interview in his office at one of his magnificent hostel buildings in Dansoman, a suburb of Accra, Ghana on 10 August 2015.

3. **Charles Kwablah Akunnor** (born in 1974): He was a former Ghanaian international footballer who spent most of his professional career in the German leagues and has coached some Premier league clubs in Ghana. He played professional football for over 16 years in two different foreign countries and had the privilege to captain the Ghana national team, Black Stars, during his active playing time in 2008. His interview took place at his residence in East Legon, Accra-Ghana on 1 September 2015.
4. **Marcel Desailly** (born in 1968): He is a Ghanaian-born footballer who opted to play for France's national team and has since reconnected to his country of birth, Ghana, where he has established some businesses. He won the FIFA World Cup title with France in 1998. He won two UEFA champions league titles with French Club of Olympique Marseille in 1993 and AC Milan in 1994. He played professionally in four different countries. Currently, he manages his own businesses in Ghana and abroad as an entrepreneur. He played professional football for over 19 years and his first interview took place in his office in Accra, Ghana at Lizzy Sports Complex on 14 June 2013. His second interview was on the telephone when he was on transit in Schiphol airport, Amsterdam, on 17 May 2016.
5. **Samuel Eto'o** (born in 1981): He is the most decorated African player of all time having won the best player award four times. He scored over 100 goals with Barcelona and was the former captain for the Indomitable Lions of Cameroon. He had made history with his national teams as a youth player and with European clubs in the UEFA Champions League. He won three UEFA champions league titles with Barcelona in 2006, 2009 and with Inter Milan in 2010. He has played professional football for over 20 years in seven different countries abroad and is still active with Qatar SC (2018/2019 season). His interview took place in Guinea after he inaugurated a new Sports Training Centre. He granted an exclusive interview to BAH Abdoulaye, a correspondent for Africa Top Sport.com on 24 March 2013.
6. **Asamoah Gyan** (born in 1985): Currently, the captain of Ghana national senior team and among the first 10 Best Paid footballers in the world published by Matt Hamilton in an article 'In Football/Business of Sport.'[1] He is now the all-time highest goal scorer for Africa in FIFA World Cup competitions. He has played professional football for over 16 years in seven different foreign countries and is an active player of Kayserispor in Turkey. The interview took place both on television and radio on 20 May 2015 and 26 November 2015 concerning his football career path, which was recorded and transcribed for the study.
7. **Stephen Appiah** (born in 1980): He was the former captain of Ghana national senior team (Black Stars) and is always remembered for his role in qualifying

his country for its historic first FIFA World Cup in 2006. He achieved the same feat in 2010 for the second time. He played professional football for over 16 years in three different overseas countries and is adored for his humanitarian activities in Ghana and Africa. His interview took place at Lizzy Sports Complex, Accra, Ghana on one of his routine gym training sessions on 10 July 2013.

8. **Jean-Claude Mbvoumin** (born in 1973): He was a former Cameroonian international footballer who played over 11 years of professional football in France. Some of his youthful national teammates' generation players were the late Marc-Vivien Foe, Rigobert Song, Jay-Jay Okocha among the rest. His European football experience led him to establish the 'Foot Solidaire' (Association Culture Foot Solidaire–CFS) with the humanitarian action towards young players who are recruited or trafficked in Africa. He was interviewed on the telephone from his 'Foot Solidaire' office in Paris, France on 7 October 2015.
9. **Augustine Ahinful** (born in 1974): He was a former Ghanaian international footballer who played over 15 years of professional football in five different foreign countries. He has been actively involved in the Ghana Football Association activities as a member of the technical committee for the past six years and management member for the national U20 team, a board member of the Professional Football Association of Ghana (PFAG). His interview took place at his residence in East Legon, Accra-Ghana on 11 August 2015.
10. **Bouna Coundoul** (born in 1982): He is a Senegalese international footballer with over ten years of professional football in four different foreign countries. He received All New York City Goalkeeper of the Year award from his beginning league and holds of a degree in Information Science and Policy from the United States. His interview took place when the Senegalese senior national team was camping at the Lizzy Sports Complex, Accra-Ghana on 14 July 2013.
11. **Nii Odartey Lamptey** (born in 1974): He was predicted by the Pelé from Brazil as his replacement after his exploits during the FIFA U17 World Cup in 1991 ahead of Alessandro Del Pedro and other future stars as he won the Player of the Tournament Award. This made him a superstar as a teenager and he played professional football for over 17 years in ten different foreign countries. He played in all the categories of Ghana national youth teams through to the senior team. Currently, he is a football licensed coach and a director of GlowLamp Football Academy and School Complex in Ghana. His interview took place at his residence in Spintex, Accra, 100 metres from his Educational Complex in Ghana on 26 April 2015. His second interview was on 8 August 2015.
12. **Seyi George Olofinjana** (born in 1980): He is a Nigerian international footballer with over 12 years of professional football experience in two different foreign countries. He is one of the African players with a master's degree in Project Management, in addition to his chemical engineering degree.

He won two gold medals with the Nigerian national team in AFCON competitions. He was interviewed on the telephone from his residence in England on 17 January 2016.

13. **Prince Ikpe Epong** (born in 1978): He was a former Nigerian international who played over 18 years of professional football in 12 different foreign countries before his retirement in 2012. He is known in Nigeria as the most travelled Nigerian player in their history after playing with several clubs in different countries. He was interviewed on the telephone from his residence in Sweden on 9 December 2015.
14. **Michael Chidi Alozie** (born in 1986): He is a Nigerian international football player with over 15 years of professional football experience in four different overseas countries and is still playing actively in Slovakia. He also benefitted from the advice of a former Nigerian international (Julius) in the area of investments that made him described the former professional footballer as 'super professional'. He was interviewed on telephone from his residence in Ukraine on 10 December 2015.
15. **Anthony Kofi Annan** (born in 1986): He is a Ghanaian international footballer with over 12 years of professional football experience in five different countries abroad and playing actively in Finland. He has won several league titles with his clubs abroad. He was a former member of the Ghana national senior team that won a silver medal in AFCON 2010. He was interviewed on the telephone from his residence in Europe on 13 April 2016.
16. **Noah Chivuta** (born in 1983): He is a Zambian international footballer with over 14 years of professional football in three different countries overseas and still playing actively. He played for five different clubs in the same league abroad. He was a member of the Zambia national senior team that won a gold medal in AFCON 2012. His interview took place on telephone from his residence abroad on 23 April 2016.
17. **Reuben Ayarna** (born in 1985): He is a Ghanaian international footballer with over 13 years of professional experience in two different countries abroad. He has individual honours to his credit at the club level and is still playing actively abroad. He was interviewed on the telephone from his residence in Europe on 20 January 2016.
18. **Sam Ayorinde** (born in 1974): He was a former Nigerian international who played over 14 years of professional football in 14 different clubs in nine different countries abroad before his retirement in 2008. He played for the Nigerian senior national team and started his professional football journey by road through some African countries without an agent. His interview was on the telephone from his residence in Sweden on 8 December 2015.
19. **Emmanuel Eboué** (born in 1983): He is an Ivorian international footballer with over 14 years of professional experience in three different countries abroad. He won some trophies with his previous clubs abroad. He has played in five AFCON tournaments and two World Cups for his country. His interview took place at the Lizzy Sports Complex, Accra on 14 June 2013 while

on holiday in Ghana. His career ended abruptly due to his divorce and bad investments that were made under his former wife's control and he became a pauper and homeless abroad.

20. **John Paintsil** (born in 1981): He is a Ghanaian international footballer with over 13 years of professional experience in three different countries abroad. He has achieved individual honours at both club and national levels. John has participated in two FIFA World Cup competitions in 2006 and 2010 and won a bronze medal in AFCON 2008. His interview took place at the Lizzy Sports Complex, Accra, Ghana on 13 July 2013 during his personal training session. He is now a licensed football coach after ending his career in 2016.
21. **Isaac Cofie** (born in 1991): He is a Ghanaian international footballer with over eight years of professional experience in two different European countries. Still playing actively, he has also featured for his country's senior national team. He has spent most of his playing career in the Italian league. He was interviewed on the telephone from his residence abroad on 22 January 2016.
22. **Samuel Bangura** (born in 1995): He is a Sierra Leone international footballer with over four years of professional experience in two different countries abroad. He is a member of his country's senior national team and still plays actively in Europe. He combined football with schooling in Europe after relocation with his parents. His interview took place on the telephone from his residence in England on 6 January 2016.
23. **Michael Anaba** (born in 1993): He is a Ghanaian international footballer with over four years of professional experience in two different overseas countries. He won a bronze medal at the FIFA World Cup U-20 competition in 2013. He still playing actively in Europe and was interviewed on the telephone from his residence in Spain on 7 December 2015.
24. **Stéphane Badji** (born in 1990): He is a Senegalese international footballer with over seven years of professional experience in three different foreign countries. He is an active member of Senegal's senior national team. Stéphane played for the Senegalese national U-23 team in the Summer Olympics in 2012 and is still playing actively in Europe. He was interviewed during the Senegalese national team camping in Accra, Ghana at the Lizzy Sports Complex on 14 July 2013.
25. **Samuel Owusu** (born in 1996): He is a Ghanaian international footballer with over four years of professional experience abroad. Samuel still plays actively in Europe and is yet to have his debut for the senior national team. His interview was conducted on the telephone from his residence abroad on 22 December 2015.
26. **Lumor Agbenyenu** (born in 1996): He is a Ghanaian international footballer with over three years of professional experience in two different countries abroad. He has featured for Ghana national U-20 team and is now a key member of the senior national team, and still playing actively abroad. He was interviewed on the telephone from his residence in Portugal on 10 January 2016.

27. **Gideon Baah** (born in 1991): He is a Ghanaian international footballer with over five years of professional experience in three different foreign countries. He has been a member of his country's senior national team for some time and actively playing professional abroad. He has achieved both individual and club honours. He has a diploma from the Polytechnic University in Ghana. His interview took place at the Lizzy Sports complex, Accra-Ghana on 5 December 2013.
28. **Yaw Yeboah** (born in 1997): He is a Ghanaian international footballer with over four years of professional experience in four different foreign countries. He still plays actively and has featured for his country's U-20 team and the senior national team. He was the best African Youth Player at the African U-20 tournament in 2015. He was voted the best player at the Gothia Cup in 2014 with the U-17 category. He was interviewed on the telephone from his residence in France on 26 March 2016.
29. **Ibrahim Ayew** (born in 1988): He is a Ghanaian international footballer with over seven years of professional experience abroad in two different foreign countries. He was a member of the Ghana senior national team that reached the quarter-finals stage of the FIFA World Cup in 2010. He won a silver medal at the CHAN tournament in 2009. He is the first son of player 1 and his interview took place at the Lizzy Sports Complex, Accra-Ghana on 30 July 2013.
30. **Richard Gadze** (born in 1994): He is a Ghanaian international footballer with over three years of professional experience in four different foreign countries. He has featured for his country's national U-23 team and currently, playing active football in Europe. He holds a diploma in Marketing from the Accra Polytechnic University in Ghana. He was interviewed on the telephone from his residence in Europe on 9 April 2016.
31. **George Ekeh** (born in 1980): He was a former Nigerian international footballer with over 13 years of professional experience in five different countries abroad before retiring in 2015. He decided to discontinue his education and stuck to only football. He was interviewed on the telephone from his residence in Sweden on 20 April 2016.
32. **Zakaria Isa Sukura** (born in 1996): He is a Togolese international footballer with over four years of professional experience in one country and still playing actively abroad. He is yet to receive his national team invitation. He was interviewed on the telephone from his residence abroad on 22 December 2015.
33. **Edema Fuludu** (born in 1970): He was a former Nigerian international footballer with over three years of professional experience in Turkey before his retirement in 2012. He holds a master's degree in Sports Management and is currently involved in football administration. He was a member of the Nigerian AFCON winning squad in 1994. His interview took place in Lagos city, Nigeria on 20 February 2018.

34. **Mohamed Salah** (born in 1992): Egyptian international footballer with over six years of professional experience in three different European countries and actively playing. In 2012, he won the CAF Most Promising African Talent of the Year award. He also came third in the 2018 Best FIFA Men's Player award. He won the Premier League Golden Boot award in 2018 after scoring 32 goals in 36 league games. He has won the CAF African Footballer of the Year Award twice in 2017 and 2018, and the BBC African Footballer award in the same years. He was interviewed by James Masters and Becky Anderson on CNN, on 24 April 2018.
35. **Victor Wanyama** (born in 1991). He is a Kenyan international footballer with over ten years of professional experience in three different countries overseas and actively playing. He is from a sporting family and won some clubs' laurels along his professional career. He was recorded on Kwesé Sports TV Show on 23 August 2017 during an interview when he spoke about his football career path.
36. **Sadio Mané** (born in 1992): Senegalese international footballer with over eight years of professional experience in three different European countries and still playing active football. He won the Liverpool FC Player of the Year Award in the 2016/2017 season and other laurels with his previous clubs abroad. He was a member of the Senegalese Olympic Team in 2012 and captained the senior national team at the FIFA World Cup 2018 in Russia. His interview was extracted from the goal.com when he shared his football career story with Melissa Reddy on 8 November 2016.
37. **Rabiu Mohammed Alhassan** (born in 1989): He was a member of the Ghana national U-20 team that won the first African trophy in the FIFA Youth Tournament in Egypt in 2009. He has over 11 years of professional experience in four different European countries and is now recovering from an injury after a year of treatment. He was a member of the Ghana senior national team until his unfortunate injury situation. His interview took place in Accra on 2 February 2019 as he accompanied his mentor boys for trials at the University of Ghana football pitch.

Conclusion

The chapter began by exploring ways of gathering appropriate data to explain the GBB of African players to society. Application of methodology in social sciences was chosen to have effective responses to the interview questions. Data was collected from various sources including documents of African players both at home and abroad to understand the process of their migration, mobility to leagues and their GBB to society. It provided information on the level of leagues where these Africa players are plying/plied their trade. The majority of the players have played/are playing in the top five leagues in Europe namely English Premiership, Bundesliga, Spanish Liga, Serie A and the French Ligue 1, which offer considerable economic earnings. These professional players from Africa were scattered across 30 professional UEFA leagues in 13 UEFA countries. Players were arbitrarily selected covering the elite European leagues. These African players have been playing/played in UEFA leagues and competitions for periods of over a year to 20 years. They were aged between 19 and 55 at the time of their interview. The interview session lasted over five years from the period of June 2013 to February 2019 and included high-profile players like Abedi Pele, Samuel Eto'o, Stephen Appiah, Marcel Desailly, Emmanuel Eboué, Jean-Claude Mbvoumin, Asamoah Gyan, Bouna Coudoul, Tony Yeboah, Mohamed Salah, Victor Wanyama, etc. In all,37 professional players from Africa were interviewed who shared their candid views on their various economic and non-economic contributions to society. From their humble beginnings in the communities to becoming professional footballers (Acheampong 2018b), and how that affects their GBB to society, featured prominently in the interview discussions. Participants' views were taped or recorded, transcribed with their consent and processed using the techniques of qualitative content analysis of Mayring (2007). The analysis grid supported extracting characteristics or variables that enhanced the interview quality in generating individual in-depth interviews (Kvale and Brinkmann 2015). All these together contributed to enrich the text discussions and explained the rationality behind the players' GBB to society.

Note

1. A write-up on the best paid professional footballers in the world as of 2015. http://thekingmaker.me/200-best-paid-footballers-in-the-world-today/[Accessed on 10 January 2016].

Bibliography

Acheampong, E.Y. 2018a. 'How does professional football status challenge African players' behaviour?', *Soccer & Society*, doi:10.1080/14660970.2018.1541797.

Acheampong, E.Y. 2018b. 'Giving back to society: evidence from African sports migrants', *Sport in Society*, doi:10.1080/17430437.2018.1551367.

Burns, N. and Grove, S. K. 2009. *The Practice of Nursing Research: Appraisal, Synthesis and Generation of Evidence*. Maryland Heights, MI: Saunders Elsevier.

Creswell, W.J. 2007. *Qualitative Inquiry and Research – Choosing Among Five Approaches*. Thousand Oaks, CA: Sage Publications.

Kvale, S., and Brinkmann, S. 2015. *Interviews – Learning the Craft of Qualitative Research Interviewing*. 3rd edition. Thousand Oaks, CA: Sage Publications.

Mayring, P. 2007. 'On Generalization in Qualitatively Oriented Research', *Forum: Qualitative Social Research* 8 (3): 1–9.

Weber, M. 1978 [1922]. *Economy and Society: An Outline of Interpretive Sociology*, translated by Ephraim Fischoff *et al.*, 2vols. Berkeley: University of California Press.

Witzel, A.2000. 'The Problem-Centered Interview', *Forum Qualitative Social Research* 1 (1): Art.22.

5

Street football, periodisation, and migration itineraries and strategies

Introduction

For over two decades, some scholars including Büdel (2013), Darby (2002, 2010, 2014), Lanfranchi and Taylor (2001), Poli (2006a, 2006b) among others have written on the migration of African players to the Global North leagues in search of survival for their professional dreams. They assigned various reasons not only limited to economic potentials but also lack of professionalism and insensitivity to players' welfare. We sought to explain some of the processes African players have to endure in their struggling to reach the top leagues in Europe from their communities of origin. Despite some challenges, the players have to go through, at the end some progress from the street football and inter-street competitions to become professional footballers. The aim of this chapter is to further illuminate how the street football activities catapult African players to achieve their professional footballer dreams abroad with the support of their families, relatives, friends, social groups, and the communities. The involvement of the latter in their football migration project has a propensity to influence their GBB to society.

We start by explaining how young boys enjoy playing street football with their social groups within the communities which eventually lands some of them in the big stadiums in Europe before describing the periodisation of African football within three distinct periods: the 1980s, 1990s and 2000s. Here, the focus is on the evolution of African football and its society in coherence with the European football market transformation, to engross the best football talents from Africa. A migratory process involving the itineraries and strategies of players is analysed via the various contributions of families, relatives, friends, and the communities. This provides an understanding of the model of African player itineraries with pertinent theories and their potential effects on their GBB. Finally, we conclude with a summary that enlightens our readers on the clear process of African players to achieve a reputation as a professional footballer abroad in order to discuss and construct their migratory typology.

From the African street football to the big stadiums in Europe

In view of the lack of infrastructure such as football facilities and clubs, street football plays a major role in promoting and developing football in African countries. Indeed, football games are easily improvised in the streets near young boys' homes. It also exposes and makes young boys visible to football enthusiasts or fans who sometimes support them by sending those with talent and potentials to football nursery grounds (academies, colts' teams, etc.) to be refined and developed. In many instances, young African players experience this kind of support especially those from low-income communities. A typical example is the case of C. K. Akunnor, a former captain of Ghana Black Stars' team and the 'first black' captain for the VfL Wolfsburg FC. Akunnor explained how some 'wild' football fans spotted him in the community and decided to support with the development of his talent via various contributions.

> I moved to stay with some guys who were crazy about the game in Tema City. They were friends, not family members. These guys saw my potentials and decided to help me by accommodating me. These guys were the people we now called scouts but, in those days, it wasn't like that.[1]

Akunnor was from poor family background and through street football with his friends in the neighbourhoods got scouted to Hearts Babies Colts' team in the city of Tema, Ghana, where football was much more promoted and organised. Thereafter he had the chance to join local clubs like Okwahu United FC and Ashgold SC. While playing for Ashgold, he was scouted for the Ghana national U-20 team. Within the same period, he had an invitation to the senior national team where he met high-profile players like Abedi Pele, Anthony Yeboah among others. His social networks established from the beginning played a significant role in getting him to those local football clubs. Through the exposure at the senior national team, he attracted foreign agents who facilitated his move to Europe. Indeed, the majority of African players admitted that their football careers started from the streets in the 'native' communities at an early age of five years or thereabout (Acheampong 2017). According to the players, street football is a preconditional social activity towards exposing their football talents and prospects to the communities (Acheampong 2017). Similarly, Eto'o, an accomplished professional player who has won every trophy in Europe and Africa except the senior world cup, is convinced that one day Africa can win the world cup, but they must have the solid foundation in order to achieve that. He recalled:

> We have a lot of luck because our moms made us have some talent while Europeans learn football at football academies. However, we go to the streets to find ourselves in big stadiums. I say Congratulations to all the children of Africa.[2]

Eto'o admits that for Africa to be able to win the world cup, they need to have strong foundations for grassroots football development and even without that, its football talents are seen in the big stadiums in Europe. Thus, if the social activity of football from the streets is able to support them to play in top leagues abroad, then when structures are improved on the continent, Africa can achieve that dream. He said, 'I think that if the level of African football increases, we will have more chance of having an African team in the future as world champion and this is my wish.'

In the 'native' communities, football is a social activity and helps to promote integration of social groups in the communities. Víctor Wanyama shared his experience on how street football supported his aspirations; 'we used to play in the streets with "bare feet" and the pitches weren't so good, but it was also a good experience. Sometimes we walked like 10 kilometres to just go play with other guys.'[3] Indeed, all these footballing activities are often organised by football enthusiasts or fans to enable them to assess the talents and potentials of young boys from other communities and that of their localities as well. This gesture promotes integration of social groups and drives them away from indulging in social vices.

Some young African boys are inspired by role models either from Africa or Europe depending on their style of play, fame, commitment level among other qualities. Such inspiration boosted Liverpool FC attacker and the 'PFA Player of the Year for 2018' in the Premiership, Mo Salah, when he was a kid. This is further explained in the context. Mo Salah's ambition was to play like those excellent players he admired and therefore he worked hard towards achieving that goal. As a graduate from the street football, he followed his passion and progressed to an academy before finding himself in the prestigious clubs and rich leagues abroad (Darby 2010). Interestingly, other African kids in the communities may take after him as their role model looking at his exploits for clubs and country.

In African communities, some boys play anywhere barefoot, legs caked in red dirt, playing the game with an old ball or one made of recycled materials, on an uneven dirt pitch and with pieces of rock or rubber containers as goalposts (Van der Meij and Darby 2014). All these street football activities including area tournaments provided boys with some confidence that supported them to perform anywhere they have space to play. For instance, Jay Okocha on a social visit to Germany had the opportunity to train with a team and afterwards, he was offered a contract due to his talent (Orr 2007).

In sum, from the street football, some boys either moved to football academies or received invitations to national teams or played in local leagues or international tournaments before they were able to secure contracts to play in big leagues abroad. Young boys' passion for street football tends to support their professional football dreams abroad. The street football replaces the football structures, in that it played a central role in the process of players' professionalisation and evolution of African football. However, the ways and means players get to the big leagues in Europe are elaborated and juxtaposed starting from this point of evolution of African football and the growth of the European football markets. This process of professionalisation which starts from African streets to terminate in European professional clubs highlights one specific evolution including a process of migration we termed as 'Periodisation' of the professional football evolution.

Periodisation of African football evolution

We identified one periodisation of African football within three distinct periods: the 1980s, 1990s and 2000s. These periods represent the shifting perspectives about the professional opportunities available in European and African football and the evolution of social structures. A clear shift in how football evolved regarding each period: from a social activity to creating socioeconomic opportunities and professional activity. Overlaps were identified but these did not affect the periods regarding some players beginning and ending their professional career abroad.

The controversial vision of football (the 1980s): Football vs. school

> We had two stones for goalposts and played four against four. Sometimes, something sharp would cut your feet, but we played through our wounds and didn't even think about them. We just loved to play.[4]

In many African communities, football is played anywhere provided children found space and round objects like a ball. Boys play at people's backyards, verandahs or a piece of land lying bare to have fun. Others even walk some kilometres to play against other guys after school or on weekends. Playing football is part of their social activity. Annan, with 67 caps for his national team (Black Stars of Ghana) explained how his football career started:

> I started in my area where we used to play football with friends in the neighbourhood. It was mostly at the backyard of people's houses with boys in the area like the street football stuff because there was no 'colts' football.[5]

The Colts'[6] system did not exist and young boys within the locales played sometimes through their wounds because they loved to play, and football was socially inclusive. Other interviewees shared the same experience and it was a practice in the 1980s. Some young boys could walk over 5 km to play football with other social groups from different towns. Football then constituted a special inclusive social activity for young people. The social activity leads to the economic or social alternative which is another social role that we assign to football in Africa. Incidentally, it kept young people active, improved their social relations and served as a strategy for integration into their community. Annan's narration confirmed this:

> Mum was like we should make sure that we take our studies seriously, yet we could play football alongside. She only got annoyed when you refused to do

> your house chores. All the same, she knew our dad was a footballer, and that she wasn't against us playing football at all.[7]

In schools, boys played football because it was part of extracurricular activities over which parents have less control. Street football was seen by some adults, parents, and community members as a waste of time and they did not encourage their young boys either. They were against children playing football at the expense of their schooling. Interviewees admitted that as Prince Ikpe explained:

> In those days, the 1980s and 1990s, you don't dare say you want to play football even your neighbours will laugh at you, people will mock you. I knew a lot of friends that by the time we go to play football and come back, they have to sneak in or wash very well before they go home otherwise, they get serious beatings. In Africa, people saw football players to be hooligans, cowards, uneducated. So, playing football, it was like you are 'jobless', you don't have a future, no plan, no career ambition.[8]

To most parents, football was not a socially endorsed activity and seemed to be the trade of visionless people. Football ranked low on the socioeconomic matrix and little was known about professionalism. In this context, a few boys got scouted and integrated into teams, thanks to some football enthusiasts or fans via their personal and social relations, and networks. C. K Akunnor, a former international and currently the head coach for Kumasi Asante Kotoko in Ghana explained how he got scouted as a young boy in the neighbourhood. Thus, 'I was a young boy playing for fun. We used to meet as community boys to play in the area. I was spotted by someone who took me to Tema, the industrial city of Ghana.'[9]

Contrary to the perception of parents and society, all the interviewees admitted that football indeed extended their social integration and group dynamics. They prevented their boys from playing football but encouraged them to concentrate on formal education. Football supposedly was for 'lazy' boys, which in some African countries is termed '*kobolo*'.[10] This term had existed since the 1960s, for example, Wilberforce Mfum, a former Ghanaian international and one of the prolific strikers in the 1960s on the Africa continent, and part of the early wave of African football migrants to the North American Soccer League (NASL), in 1968 recalled how the society perceived football players: 'As people who were only interested in football-*kobolo*.'[11] Boys who played football were presumed to be from deprived areas and/or low-income communities. Mbvoumin recalled:

> In Cameroun, that time a football player was sometimes from a very poor home and it was an activity for bad guys who are unsuccessful in life. Football was not a good example or model for the youth because of the kind of perception people had at that time.[12]

Undeniably, football was not considered by parents as a way of social advancement. After the decolonisation, African families adopted the European model of social growth through education as a supreme model to follow. In Europe, football was not an attractive professional activity, it was considered a popular social activity that sociologically identified workers' classes and immigrants, for instance, those from the Eastern European countries. Again, football players had to adopt different approaches to their social activity. With over 18 years of professional experience abroad, Prince Ikpe recalled:

> There were times people were murmuring and gossiping about me in the street that, he was a hopeless guy always football, football. So, it became obvious that sometimes I had to put my football shoes in a 'polybag' pretending to buy something in the market or coming from the market, but my football shoes will be rather inside.[13]

In the 1980s, football was prickly and generally difficult among African societies because it did not create social advancement let alone provided incomes for footballers. It was rather considered a social activity for young people and lower social categories. However, its social role as an inclusive activity in young groups was appreciated among younger generations and affected the development of football talents.

In totality, football players were passionate and behaved as craftsmen or self-made men who explored the unknown ways of becoming footballers. Some of their approaches were achieved through social negotiation, social activity of football and the resilient strategies that emerged from the various street football experiences and events. The wrong perception of football gradually waned after the growth of the football economy in Europe. This also coincided with the performance of African teams at the FIFA youth and senior competitions in the early 1990s which shifted the direction of African football.

The 1990s: football structures, international competitions and socioeconomic opportunities

The social vision of football improved with the UEFA leagues' evolution which attracted rich sponsors, brought media attention to the game and increased broadcasting rights. The economic growth and the labour market rules changed in European football, which was perceived as a positive shift in African societies. The performances of African national teams (both youth and senior teams) contributed to this shift in perspective and engrossed considerable viewership across the African continent, which enhanced the image of footballers who became national heroes. This was accompanied by the growth of formal and informal institutions (e.g. football academies, scouts, and intermediaries) recruiting players for the European labour market. As Sam Ayorinde recalled:

> Football started to change people's perception in Africa after the FIFA World Cup in the USA in 1994 when Nigeria performed so well in that tournament.

> Then people began to get an idea but still, it was not rampant. That was when scouts began to come to Nigeria from Europe. Though, I was very good at other sports and could have represented Nigeria in all. But I quit handball because it was dividing my attention from football.[14]

Football began to open up new economic opportunities for Africans. New social status with a professional career was recognised by all. Some activities of football in the 1980s were carried over to this period too. At the same period, there was a little upgrading of sporting facilities with the organisation of tournaments in the communities, which became a norm. Through the live broadcasting of international competitions and UEFA leagues, young boys began to pick role models or mentors after watching such games. This was exactly the case of Mo Salah as he was fascinated by the skills of his role models. He specified:

> I first fell in love with football when I was a kid, around seven or eight years old. I remember watching the Champions League all the time and then trying to be like the Brazilian Ronaldo, Zidane and Totti when playing out in the street with my friends. I loved those kinds of players, players who played with magic.[15]

The exposure of the UEFA leagues and competitions on the African continent stimulated young boys' interest as they tried to emulate their role models that might be quite difficult but, in the end, challenged them to pursue their professional football dreams. Concurrently, tournaments were often organised to select the best young talents for foreign agents. This shows how African football has been organised around recruitment structures and training in readiness for the European football market. These structures provided a guarantee for families as they considered young players' schooling as well. After the African teams' success at the FIFA World U-17 championship (Ghana 1991, 1995, and Nigeria 1993) foreign agents flooded the continent to recruit footballers to the European football market (Darby 2007). Football was recognised by the schools as a positive type of Physical Education. Sport in secondary schools and colleges was quite competitive and served as a ground for unearthing talents. Through secondary schools and universities, some earned an invitation to their national teams. Edema was a member of the Nigeria national team that qualified their country for the first World Cup in 1994 narrated how he got selected.

> They saw me as a schoolboy footballer but with a lion's heart. I became the young tireless midfielder in the Nigeria League… In 1991, I played my first senior national team match against Burkina Faso.[16]

Edema got invited to train with the senior national team and had his debut in 1991. This exposure hurled him to Turkey where his professional career began in 1992. He finally became the 'breadwinner' for his family and supported them financially as well as sponsoring his siblings' educational expenses. Parents and families accepted for their young boys to play football on the condition that clubs took charge of their school fees. Mbvoumin narrated how he was permitted to play for his locale youth team after they agreed to pay for his school fees.

> I was in school then … and my family didn't approve of me to play football. As I was a very good player, my team Yaoundé was paying my school fees, buying books and everything for me. Later, my family accepted that I can play football because my team was helping with my schooling.[17]

This shifted the perception of parents that football could create positive conditions for professional and social success. Young players' breakthrough was boosted when the media began to focus their attention on the exploits of some African players who were earning a lot of money in Europe. This new development gradually changed the perception of African societies with the emergence of pay-tv and live telecast of international matches and leagues across some countries featuring African players. Also, the deregulation of the European football labour market (cf. Bosman ruling in 1995)[18] provided the professional clubs with an advantage to attract highly skilled players (Acheampong 2017; Darby 2007; Skogvang 2008). The trend intensified significantly in the midpoint of the decade with an estimated 350 Africans playing in Europe (Gleeson 1996). This migration pattern vigorously accelerated and as of 1998, 481 foreign-based players had participated in the AFCON tournaments (Acheampong 2017).

Afro-European football structures located on the African continent reassured parents and families who associated schooling with football. Fathers of ex-footballers succeeded in convincing their wives to allow their sons to play football due to the family traits. This phenomenon is the opposite of the 1980s period, as mothers and fathers' position on football reversed. Here, mothers still have emotional rationality and fathers are formal, based on their interest. Interviewees admitted that they were asked to take their schooling seriously while playing football alongside.

Families and football structures played an important role in deciding whether children could combine football and schooling. Upper social groups continually believe strongly in a link between schooling and social success (Acheampong 2017). With them, social success is not limited only to high incomes but also social status and social recognition which are important. The socioeconomic benefits of football became evident for parents, family members, and the community because some started to support young boys with training kits or sports gear and enrolling them in football academies. In the 1990s, African players in Europe behaved like entrepreneurs since they knew how to mobilise football structures, getting into national teams and making effective use of their environmental resources to achieve their ambitions. Players employed both emerging and deliberate strategies (Mintzberg and Waters 1985) that made them visible to the European football market. Through these strategies, some were exploited abroad due to lack of basic education. For instance, Nii Odartey Lamptey described how he was cheated by football agents for over five years, simply, because he could not read, write and understand whatever documents he was presented with to sign:

> Some agents cheated me because I couldn't write and read; so, I did not want other kids to go through this experience that is why I decided to use my football money to set up a school in Ghana. Football gave me something so, I decided to give back as I said, education was a problem for me, and I have learnt a lot as a professional footballer.[19]

This justifies parents' and families' strong value of formal basic education as a necessity for all children, showing that a link between education and football was relevant for those with talents and who wanted to go further as professional footballers. In the early 2000s, the Senegalese senior national team's historic appearance at the FIFA World Cup in Japan saw them exhibiting a phenomenal performance to the dismay of the pundits. The exhilarating performance catapulted them to the first quarter-finals of their first appearance at the World Cup event and that made a strong case for African players. The fact that a profession in football could provide socioeconomic benefits for the players, families, and the community, meant that football was accepted as a professional activity.

The 2000s: huge financial rewards, social recognition and family support improved

Football development in Europe was transformed as the marketing and professionalism gained prominence. The media rights, clubs' budgets and the international investments in the game rapidly increased the football economy during the 2000s. Abedi Pele recalled how the game suddenly changed.

> We were enjoying it and having fun but to see that such a thing (game) can turn to be the most lucrative business in the world is what amazes me, something I started, like a joke became the most unique, powerful, influential business in the world that when you speak people listen, when you talk you inspire millions of people, it's really incredible.[20]

Transformation of the football economy continues to improve the socioeconomic status of African players beyond their communities. This contributed to promoting European football as a pathway to success among young men in Africa (Poli 2010). Between 2000 and 2010, 1,279 foreign-based players had participated in AFCON tournaments (Acheampong 2017). The number was more than twice that in the 1990s showing an astronomical growth. Here, players are recognised as social change agents in societies. Parents and family members have become more enlightened about professional football than before. As Ayarna puts it:

> Now, every parent is open-minded so you can do everything but back in the days, schooling was the only way you could be successful. Every parent wanted their kids to go to school but now they watch football, other sports, and see what is going on around the world that everybody could be successful anyway not just school. I don't blame them or hold them responsible for, it was just that culture back then so, they had to do what to make their son a better person.[21]

The professional dimension of the sport provides hope for parents, family members, communities, and nations that football can make their children financially successful and better persons, to the extent that, some parents might sell their properties to support sons' professional career abroad. From Togo, Zakaria narrated: 'My mum supported me to enter the football profession by selling her house to support me when I told her I had gotten a chance to play in Serbia.'[22] This is how powerful football had become: that it could influence some parents to trade their properties for providing a professional activity for their children. In their studies, Van der Meij and Darby (2014) reported how family members and relatives were at the centre of the decision-making process for their son regarding which football academy he could join. In some cases, family members, friends, and lovers of football accompany their siblings or nephews in search of a place for them to showcase their talent to organisers of competitions. Sadio Mane narrated how his uncle trekked with him to attend such trial outs in the city.

> I left my city to go to the capital with my uncle, and there were trials on. We went to them and there were lots of boys being tested and getting organised into teams. I will never forget this, and it is funny now, but when I went to try out there was an older man that looked at me like I was in the wrong place.[23]

Through some of these trial outs, he got scouted into Generation Foot academy in the city of Dakar that boasts of alumni players like Diafra Sakho and Papiss Cisse. Sadio was also inspired by his role models and heroes of the Senegal World Cup squad in 2002 when they reached the quarter-finals and he could not imagine himself becoming one of them in the future. And after 16 years, he led his country to their second world cup event in Russia and they could not qualify from the group stages. He is now a player at the Liverpool FC, and this has transformed his life, that of the family and friends as a high-profile professional in Africa and Europe.

In the end, his success has translated all the support received back home into a long-term financial reward for their families, friends, and the community. This has provided an incentive for players and the community to look for migration opportunities as identified by Van der Meij and Darby. Interviewees admitted the immense contributions of their parents, families, and community members to their professional project.

The exploits of African players abroad served as an inspiration for scattered football academies in Africa (Darby 2002). Societal interest increased because football can provide strong economic opportunities and high social position. Parents and communities have unified young players' strategies toward a professional career by providing them with social and material support. Families' vision changed and they adopted rational strategies as they could anticipate a better future from football. The investment in players became significant as they developed their human capital through formal training in football academies. Formal structures in African football provided a platform for preparing young people and integrating them into society through a job opportunity. The 2000s brought a new model of African footballers who behaved like managers, using the resources of their families and football structures rationally to achieve their professional aspirations.

In short, we observed a periodisation in African football based on social, economic, and football structures' evolution. The first period described the role of the informal organisation of football and the opposition between football and school. Footballers had to behave as craftsmen and explore emerging strategies to become professionals in Europe. In the second period, football evolved with its economic and social growth, and formal structures emerged. Families and communities accepted this shift and participated in players' migration strategies. New structures for training, selecting and recruiting on the African continent provided the football players with the chance to explore and imagine new deliberate strategies. Based on the expected return on investment, players and families started to take risks and adopted an entrepreneurial logic. The third period presented characteristics of a rational and well-organised market of football with stimulating socioeconomic conditions for professionals in leagues abroad. The resources and opportunities are well identified by players and their families. Marketing of football is enhanced and players became good managers of their career with a better image to negotiate and promote their economic worth. As well, this authority shifted from players to clubs as they identified quality players with marketing dexterity and value in order to balance or improve their financial books. Footballers behaved as managers who plan to optimise their career and secure their migration process.

In conclusion, the section enlightens us on the professionalisation strategies and resources players mobilised in the context of the evolution of the European football market. The periodisation of African football adds knowledge to African footballers' strategies and opens prospects for further research. What should we envisage from the new period based on the current and future development of the professional football market worldwide? From this, it would be interesting for researchers to consider the evolution of women's football in the framework of female African professionalisation. Table 5.1 gives a summary of the shifting perspectives of African football evolution in the context of the economic growth of European football.

Table 5.1 Summary of the social and economic evolution of Africa football

Period	*Vision*	*Structures*	*Social role*	*Strategy*	*Logics of players*
The 1980s	Controversial: school vs. football	Informal with social groups, e.g. inter-street football competitions	Social integration, social leisure, social activity	Emerging	Craft approach: explored their social environment
The 1990s	Football structures, international competitions and socioeconomic opportunity	Formal and informal institutions. e.g. football academies, non-affiliated teams, colts, etc.	Social integration, professional and semi-professional activity	Emerging and deliberate	Entrepreneurial approach: professional opportunity.
The 2000s	Huge financial rewards, social recognition and family support improved	Improved formal and informal structures plus partnerships. e.g. Afro-European football academies, federation academies, etc.	Social status, national recognition, social mediatisation, social obligation, etc.	Deliberate	Managerial approach: increasing their financial resources and social recognition

Migratory process: Itineraries and strategies typology

African young footballers with a passion for football always dream of becoming successful professional footballers when they can move and play in leagues abroad. Yet, getting to play professionally abroad is often not as easy as people may anticipate. Moving to pursue a football career in Europe involves planning carefully to avoid being stranded or wasting the resources invested in the migration project. Sam Ayorinde shared his experiences on the road in searching for a professional footballer status abroad. He recalled:

> The transport in between the borders, they don't go every day because they said they have the bandits .... There were a lot of traders from Senegal and Mali that comes to Lagos to buy stuff so everybody gathers in this place from Monday till Thursday, then they have a long entourage with military guys in front, middle and at the back to guide us across the desert. So, I had to wait for these few days to get there. From Mali... I continued to Senegal. I got to Senegal then I started to get scared because you meet a lot of people that have been stranded on the way trying to do exactly what I was going to do.[24]

Eventually, the player was stuck in Tunisia and started to make contacts with friends both local and abroad to see how best they could help him get to his final destination in Europe. Sam's adventurous journey came to a pause in Tunisia where he had the opportunity to join Stade Tunisien FC after showing his football pictures and magazines, which convinced the club management to offer him a year contract. After a season in Tunis, he continued his professional football aspirations and explained how he finally landed in Europe.

> I played in Tunisia for one season and then I still wanted to continue my journey to Europe. So, I met an agent through Fred Odegbami's brother. He was a legend in Nigeria and introduced me to a football agent and through him, I went to Austria, Sturm Graz FC... I was not 18 years yet and so, I was loaned out to a lower division team because of my age.[25]

While others were struggling on the road to Europe, some got scouted from the local leagues and national teams which paved the way for their professional career abroad. Another successful professional African player with two FIFA World Cup appearances for Ghana and the first captain to qualify his country for two successive world cup events in 2006 and 2010, Appiah described how he finally landed in Europe: Appiah recalled:

> After a domestic league match, I saw this white man (agent) with one of our team officials and I was invited to join. There, I was told that there is a team in Italy which was interested in me so they think that I have to go to Italy ... because I was doing magic for the team so I didn't want to travel outside. Because

> I was enjoying the support of the Hearts of Oak SC fans ... So, I travelled with the white man (agent) and there my professional career started.[26]

Appiah with 16 years of professional experience abroad got scouted from a Colts' team to Accra Hearts of Oak SC in the Ghana Premier League. He was introduced to a football agent through the social network of his club officials after they watched him play a league match. Although the player was not keen to travel, he could not resist either because of his poor family background. In Europe, he passed his trials and was signed on by Udinese Calcio in Italy.

Through football, some players had the opportunity to study abroad. Still playing actively in Europe, Ayarna described the way it all happened as he moved overseas. From the street football, he was scouted by the officials of the U-14 team of Liberty Professionals FC based in Accra, the capital of Ghana, where Michael Essien, Asamoah Gyan, Sulley Muntari, Paintsil and others played. At the club's junior side, his former coach introduced him to his friends in the States who came to Ghana and watched him play some games. As Ayarna puts it: 'I played two games while they watched. They said we want you to come and play for us in the States. There was no involvement of an agent, but it was only my former coach's friends.'[27] Ayarna had the chance through the social network of his former coach at the Liberty Professionals FC and that propelled him to the States where he schooled alongside playing football. Similarly, the former Senegalese goalie, Coundoul, with 28 caps for his national team, explained how he moved to the US.

> I left Senegal when I was 13 years and went to America, New York City. I went there to get my education. To me, the most important for a football player, you need to get an education, so I went to America to finish my education and after that, I was drafted into the MLS.[28]

In African communities, education is key to an adapted social success and that is one of the main reasons parents and families were seriously against their young boys taking to football in the 1980s. Studying abroad offers children the best conditions to be educated. Schooling abroad supported the player to graduate with an academic degree alongside their football professional career.

The embeddedness in viable transnational or social networks tends to facilitate the migration aspirations of young boys even when on a social visit abroad. As earlier noted, in the case of Jay-Jay Okocha (Orr 2007), like any African boy, he played street football for fun and leisure. Okocha had nine appearances at the FIFA World for Nigeria national team and was a member of the 1994 AFCON winning team and twice voted the BBC African Player of the Year in 2003 and 2004. He explained how his quick social visit transformed his professional career in Europe.

> It was all quite amazing ... It never occurred to me that I was old enough to be on my own and start my own career. But I realised I had a big opportunity in front of me and knew that I didn't want to let it go. I knew I had to... grab the chance I'd been given.[29]

Okocha benefited from his brother's social relations that provided him with an opportunity to visit Germany. This transformed his football aspirations after he got signed on by Borussia Neunkirchen, a third division team in Germany. The concept of significant others played a role in securing a team for Okocha who only had to prove his talent and potential. Through the intervention of his senior brother, Yaw Yeboah was spotted, nurtured and refined at a football academy. The parents knew of their boy's talent but did not know how he could be supported and developed until the arrival of his senior brother at the village. The senior brother took him from the village to a town and enrolled him in a school. Yaw Yeboah, a Ghanaian international with over four years of professional experience described the sudden change in his football career after participating in the schools and colleges regional competition.

> I was selected from my school to join the district team where I became the captain of the football team and ended up in the regional team for the Brong Ahafo. After the regional tournament, there was this scout from Right to Dream Academy (RTD) called Joe who approached me after seeing my performance…. I left within that month to the academy to do trials there for almost 3 months. Afterwards, they told me I had been picked for the academy and was very happy. From there I stayed in the RTD academy for almost 3 to 4 years.[30]

He still plays for Manchester City FC but is on loan to Spanish side Real Oviedo and was (on loan) the best player of the AFCON U-20 in 2015. Yaw passed through the schools and colleges system to the regional team, then to one of the best-resourced football academies (RTD) on the African continent which exposed him internationally (winning the best U-17 player award at the Gothia Cup tournament, Sweden in 2014). He has since become a member of the Ghana senior national team. The RTD academy transformed his dream by improving his education and football training which ultimately took him to Europe.

In sum, the research acknowledged the various migration routes and strategies which African players mobilised to drive their migration aspirations abroad. Among these were relocating to family members or social visits, furthering of education, through schools and colleges system, personal adventure by road, local clubs and leagues exposure, national teams and international competitions, football academies (structured and non-affiliated), Colts' teams and juvenile leagues. These developments helped construct a typology of players' migration itineraries that is linked to the shift in perspective of African football and the growth of the European football market. This led to the identification of interconnections of players' strategies, football structures, network profiles and other resources that were available to them. A thorough analysis of these resources invested in players' migration project helped to develop the three main itineraries, that is: (a) individual resource-based itinerary, (b) collective resource-based itinerary and (c) formal networks resource-based itinerary.

Before elaborating on the itineraries, a schema is provided in Figure 5.1 to illustrate further the migration process of African players to Europe.

A model of African footballers' migratory itineraries

This model explains the approaches African players adopted to achieve their professional football dreams in Europe. From their local communities, they combined the various essential parts including street football activities, the shift in African football and the growth of the European football market. Street football events were seen as a social activity in the locales which supported their social integration and inclusion in their social groups. A grey ground for identifying football talents and prospects for development. Young boys' initial contact with football did not just impart social norms and cultural values but also improved their physique. In their communities, football played a social role as they converged to have fun and leisure within their social groups. Boys have access to free space in their communities and competed among themselves in inter-street competitions which also strengthened their social relationships. The pathways toward young boys' migration process abroad are outlined in Figure 5.1.

1. At stage one, young boys meet in their social groups to have fun with the ball as a social activity in the communities where some even walk several kilometres to play with boys from other towns or villages within their districts and beyond. Young boys learn to play football in the informal and hard way due to their passion for the sport.
2. The second stage involves the placement of identified talents and prospects from the street football to be introduced to formal and informal bits of training by football academies including the Afro-European partnership model, private and philanthropies model, federations' academies (Darby, Akindes, and Kirwin 2007), Colts' teams and juvenile leagues. The focus here is basically on refinement and development. Structured football academies provide formal training for their football recruits. The informal training is acquired from those juvenile teams that are non-affiliated and without proper structures but feel obliged to support the nurturing and developing of football talents in their communities. Mostly, they are football enthusiasts or fans or retired footballers and their passion signifies a social contribution to help foster integration and inclusion among young boys in the locales. Through this platform, some boys are able to get the opportunity and play for clubs in the local leagues.
3. At the third stage, the best talents are able to attract the attention of clubs and leagues that seek after their services locally and internationally. Others also join community-based football clubs, corporate-owned clubs, private ownership or national juvenile leagues organised by federations to improve on their quality. Some local leagues expose and provide the chance for football recruits to attract the attention of national team authorities and other leagues across African countries. These exposures improve their confidence level towards the European football markets where they can entice big offers in exchange for their quality (Acheampong 2018). Activities of intermediaries

including informal and formal networks intensify to secure football contracts for players across the various clubs and leagues in Africa. After the leagues' experiences and exposure, the next destination of play for them is the search for a professional opportunity abroad. This is because most leagues in Africa are not professionally organised.

From the three stages, football recruits have a greater chance of moving to Europe depending on the kind of resources they can mobilise. This includes human, material, and social relations or network resources acting as a 'cling' to their professional ladder abroad (Acheampong 2018). That extends to intermediaries, in this case, parents, families, extended family, agents and sports agencies, scouts, club officials and social relations and networks. Intermediaries' (agents, scouts, sporting directors) activities are crucial because of their important role in expediting professional contracts for players in Europe. So are the roles of significant others like parents, families, extended family and social relations who contribute to their migration project in the needful ways (via relocation abroad, normal or social visits, reunion and schooling abroad, and enrolling them at football academies).

Football agents or sports agencies collaborate with their scouts and networks to facilitate direct transfers and negotiations with clubs for the release of players to leagues abroad while families, relatives, and the community determine who should move or not (Carter 2007). After the achievement of a professional status abroad, players still maintain transnational relations with their localities via sending remittances, going for holidays and supporting the migration of others both in their communities of origin and abroad (Acheampong 2018; Carling 2007). Contributions from the players to families, relatives, and the communities reflect their unique social assistance to the larger society in return for the support they have received from them.

Typology of migration strategies

Here, we discuss in detail the typology of players' migration strategies as introduced in the latter part of the section on 'Migratory process: Itineraries and strategies typology' above. The focus is on how players were able to organise resources in pursuit of their professional dreams abroad. They include the following; individual resource-based itinerary, collective resource-based itinerary and formal networks resource-based itinerary.

(a) Individual resource-based itinerary: This involves those players who take their own initiatives and efforts to move abroad by bringing together their own funds, personal and social relations and networks. Players' decisions are to fulfil personal aspirations and desires so as to feel self-esteem in their professional career. It is an adventurous and risky itinerary. It can be linked to the 1980s strategy of players as they explore their surroundings to become footballers.

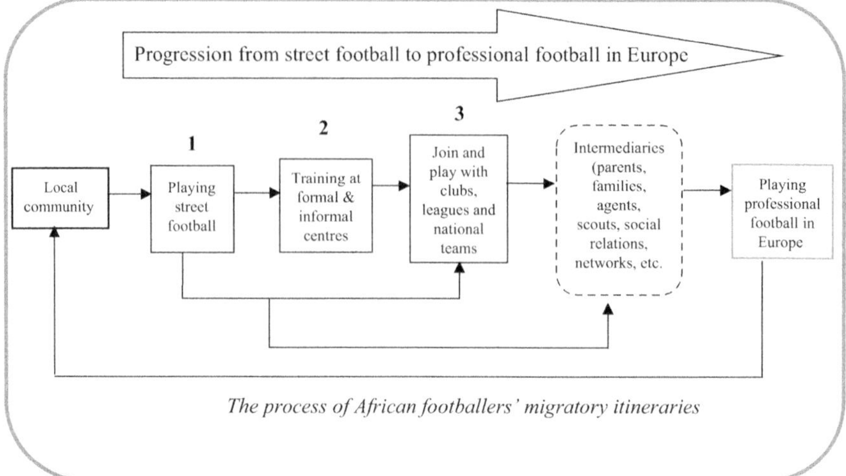

Figure 5.1 Schema of African footballers' process of migration to the European Leagues

(b) Collective resource-based itinerary: In this category, players arrange resources from families, extended family, and many distant relatives that can support them to achieve their professional aspirations abroad. Contributions and support from their family members are in various forms including but not limited to studying abroad, relocation overseas, reunion with family members or reconnecting with their exiled and expelled parents or families. Through that, some have the opportunity to join football academies or lower division leagues where their talents are refined and advanced due to better conditions or environment that support their overall development. This can be related to the 1990s strategy of players as they assumed the entrepreneurship approach by looking for professional opportunities abroad.

(c) Formal networks-based itinerary: This embraces players who are connected by intermediaries like scouts, agents, sports agencies that arrange for the needed supportive services and documentation to facilitate their movement abroad. It also includes club officials, local managers, coaches and teammates acting as recruitment referrals for their foreign managers (Engh and Agergaard 2015). In this itinerary, both collective and individual resources bases are used since agents or sports agencies act as a 'broker' for players and their host clubs. This trend is prominent in the 2000s, as players strategise to increase their financial resources and social recognition by opting for better contracts that commensurate with their talent and qualities.

Table 5.2 Typology of migratory itineraries of African players

Typology	*Human*	*Material*	*Social networks*	*Periods*	*Strategy*
Individual-based itinerary	personal, friends	funds, skills, knowledge	friends, community, teammates, local club officials.	The 1980s: football vs. school	exploring their social environment
Collective-based itinerary	parents, families, extended family members,	funds, school, accommodation, sports gears, education abroad, etc.	distant relatives, friends, social relations, etc.	The 1990s: football structures, international competitions and socioeconomic opportunities	business resources: socioeconomic opportunity
Formal networks-based itinerary	Agents, friends, parents, families, relatives, club officials, local managers, scouts	funds, skills, knowledge, sports gears, travelling documents, contracts, videos, CVs, etc.	friends, sports agencies, community, teammates, local club officials, distant relatives, social relations, networks, etc.	The 2000s: huge financial potentials, social recognition and family support improved	managerial instincts: ways of increasing their financial benefits

Overall, the various resources invested in players' migration itineraries have a greater chance of influencing their contributions and assistance (give back phenomenon) to families, relatives, friends, and their community members. The typology of players' migratory itineraries is summarised in Table 5.2.

Conclusion

The purpose of this chapter was to illustrate and analyse the process of African players getting to the big stadiums in Europe from their communities of origin by providing a theoretical context for its application. As this aspect has eluded many scholars, we highlighted the approaches adopted by the young boys with the passion and love for playing football in the streets among their social groups. Some young boys or locale boys even travelled several kilometres to play and have fun with other social groups in the villages, towns and districts. We saw how the street football events provided avenues for best talents to be scouted and integrated into juvenile clubs. This approach was based on informal training and practising of football which gave them exposure to be scouted by the community-based clubs, private owned clubs, non-affiliated and unstructured clubs, football academies, etc. The process of professionalisation began in the streets of Africa and ended in professional leagues abroad. The crafty strategies adopted, including other resources, players mobilised to the European professional clubs, resulted in one specific evolution of their migration dubbed as 'periodisation' of the professional football evolution.

This was classified into three different periods: the 1980s, 1990s and 2000s. These periods represent the fluctuating outlooks of the professional opportunities available in Europe and the evolution of African football and social structures, explaining how football evolved regarding each period: from a social activity to creating socioeconomic opportunities and professional activity. In the 1980s, football was contentious as parents, families, and the communities were not aware of their young boys given sporting talents but only knew of schooling as the best way of achieving adapted social success in society. Some boys were resilient and adopted a crafty approach of becoming football players within their social environments to pursue further on their football dreams. Until the 1990s, when youth and senior national teams from Africa performed very well at the FIFA World Cup competitions, which gradually changed the seeming perception of parents, families, and the communities to accept that, football could offer socioeconomic opportunities for their young boys with sporting talents. Ultimately, young players adopted emerging and deliberate strategies (Mintzberg and Waters 1985) to becoming professionals abroad with the support of intermediaries. African players assumed entrepreneurial status as they relied on the professional opportunity that could increase their economic value in the European football market. This set the tone for parents, families, and communities to support the development of their young boys with football talent. Entering into the 2000s, football growth intensified with huge financial prospects. Professional players gained more authority in the international transfers market and began to accept mobility opportunities that could increase their financial resources, positioning them as managers with the view of increasing their resources to maximise profit on their quality and talent along with their circulation and mobility in leagues abroad. Are we to expect a new evolution in global football?

Knowledge of players' migration and mobility project contributed to understanding their various itineraries to become professionals abroad. Based on this logic, we concluded on a typology of players' migratory itineraries namely: individual-based itinerary, collective-based itinerary and formal-based itinerary. Each has peculiar characteristics that helped classify them based on the kind of human, material, social relations and networks they mobilised to facilitate their football migration abroad. In all these processes, players started from their communities after passing through the various stages to acquire either informal or formal training or both leading to them achieve their football ambitions. Finally, embracing the contributions and support of parents, families and communities in their migratory itinerary process may have a great influence on their Give Back Behaviour to society. This migratory itinerary process tends to improve our understanding of the concept of the give back phenomenon of African professional players to their communities of origin.

Notes

1. Interview with C. K. Akunnor, on 1 September 2015.
2. Interview by Bah Abdoulaye with Eto'o, on 24 February 2013.
3. His interview was recorded and transcribed from Kwesé TV Sports Show, on 23 August 2017.
4. Interview by Owusu Willian with John Utaka, on 22 June 2011.
5. Interview with Anthony Annan, on 13 April 2016.
6. A Colts team is the nursery ground for juvenile players in Ghana from U-10–U-17.
7. See note 5.
8. Interview with Prince Ikpe, on 9 December 2015.
9. See note 1.
10. Lazy people who do not want to go to school and are aimless but only interested in playing football.
11. Interview with Kwadwo Wilberforce Mfum, on 15 September 2017.
12. Interview with Jean-Claude Mbvoumin, on 7 October 2015.
13. See note 8.
14. Interview with Sam Ayorinde., on 18 December 2015.
15. Interview by J. Masters and B Anderson with Mo Salah on CNN, on 24 April 2018.
16. Interview with Edema Fuludu, on 2 February 2018.
17. See note 12.
18. This was an important decision on the free movement of labour among the EU Member States and had a deep impact on the transfers of footballers within the EU territories.
19. Interview with Nii Odartey Lamptey, on 8 August 2015.
20. Interview with Abedi Pele, on 9 March 2016.

21. Interview with Rueben Ayarna, on 20 January 2016.
22. Interview with Zakaria Isa Suraka, on 22 December 2015.
23. Interview by Reddy Melissa with Sadio, on 8 November 2016.
24. See note 14.
25. Ibid.
26. Interview with Stephen Appiah, on 10 July 2013.
27. See note 21.
28. Interview with Bouna Coundoul, on 14 July 2013.
29. See Orr 2007.
30. Interview with Yaw Yeboah, on 26 March 2016.

Bibliography

Acheampong, E. Y. 2017. 'Socioeconomic analysis of the Give Back Phenomenon: Professional footballers in Europe and their assistance to the communities of origin in Africa.' PhD diss., Université Grenoble Alpes, France.

Acheampong, E.Y. 2018. 'Giving back to society: evidence from African sports migrants', *Sport in Society*, doi:10.1080/17430437.2018.1551367.

Büdel, M. 2013. 'An ethnographic view on African football migrants in Istanbul', Ankara Üniversitesi SBF Dergisi, *Cilt* 68 (1): 1–20.

Carling, J. 2007. 'Transnationalism in the context of restrictive immigration policy.' PhD Thesis, University of Oslo, Oslo.

Carter, T. F. 2007. 'Family networks, state interventions and the experience of Cuban transnational sport migration', *International Review for the Sociology of Sport* 42 (4): 371–389.

Darby, P. 2002. *Africa, Football and FIFA: Politics, Colonialism and Resistance*. London: Frank Cass.

Darby, P. 2007. 'Out of Africa: The exodus of African football talent to Europe', *Working USA: The Journal of Labour and Society* 10 (4): 443–456.

Darby, P. 2010. '"Go Outside": The history, economics and geography of Ghanaian football labour migration', *African Historical Review* 42 (1): 19–41. doi:10.1080/17532523.2010.483793.

Darby, P. 2014. 'International football migration and Africa: Feet drain or feet exchange', *More than a Game, Sports, Society and Politics: Panorama Insights into Asian and European Affairs*, January 2014.

Darby, P., Akindes, G. and Kirwin, M. 2007. 'Football academies and the migration of African football labour to Europe', *Journal of Sport and Social Issues* 31 (2): 143–161.

Engh, H. M., and Agergaard, S. 2015. 'Producing mobility through locality and visibility: Developing a transnational perspective on sports labour migration', *International Review for the Sociology of Sport* 50: 974–992.

Gleeson, M. 1996. 'The African invasion. Kick-off: African Cup of Nations 1996', *Fans Guide*. January, 106.

Lanfranchi, P. and Taylor. M. 2001. *Moving with the Ball. The Migration of Professional Footballers*. New York: Berg.

Mintzberg, H., and Waters, A. J. 1985. 'Of strategies, deliberate and emergent', *Strategic Management Journal* 6 (3): 257–272. doi:10.1002/smj.4250060306.

Orr, T. 2007. *No Hands Allowed: Jay Jay Okocha*. Mitchell Lane Publishers.

Poli, R. 2006a. 'Migrations and trade of African football players: Historic, geographical and cultural aspects', *Afrika-Spectrum* 41 (3): 393–414.

Poli, R. 2006b. 'Africans' status in the European football players' labour market', *Soccer and Society* 7 (2–3): 278–291.

Poli, R. 2010. 'African migrants in Asian and European football: Hopes and realities', *Sport in Society* 13 (6): 1001–1011.

Reddy, M. 2016. 'Sadio Mane's story: How I went from torn boots and shorts on Senegal's streets to a Liverpool sensation.' http://www.goal.com/en/news/2466/goal-50/2016/11/08/29293582/sadio-manes-story-how-i-went-from-torn-boots-and-shorts-on. [Accessed on 12 May 2018].

Skogvang, B. O. 2008. 'African footballers in Europe. Social and cultural diversity in a sporting world', *Research in the Sociology of Sport* 5: 33–50.

Van der Meij, N. and Darby, P. 2014. 'No one would burden the sea and then never get any benefit: Family involvement in players' migration to football academies in Ghana.' In Richard Elliott and John Harris (eds), *Football and Migration, Perspectives, Places, Players*. New York: Routledge.

6

Professional players, relationships, and typologies of Give Back Behaviours

Introduction

Footballers' established relationships with the local community are observed from their social and cultural embeddedness in society. Apparently, players' modest beginnings in the communities reproduce the behaviour embedded in social norms and cultural values, which tends to frame their lives and connect to their origins irrespective of wherever they may be. Maintaining such ties with parents, families, relatives, and the communities is an integral part of their culture. Others who are unable to maintain this vital connection with the community members may be regarded as 'ungrateful' or ridiculed (Acheampong 2018; Van der Meji and Darby 2017), as insensitive to cultural norms and values of the people. The aim of this chapter is to demonstrate how an understanding of African players' deep connection with the communities can influence their GBB to society. This enables us to carefully consider players' relationship with the communities of origin as critical in responding to societal causes via their Give Back Behaviours. To acknowledge this, first, we explain in detail what underpins African players' relationships through the various economic and non-economic projects which they referred to as giving back to the communities of origin. Their GBB is classified according to the purposes they serve in the communities. Next we move on to discuss 'Giving back' as a socioeconomic phenomenon; 'Give Back Behaviour'—an emerging African culture; 'Give Back Behaviour' and social and cultural embeddedness; 'Give Back Behaviour' and institutionalised networks; and 'Give Back Behaviour' and economic rationality. All these together optimise players' deep connections with their parents, families, relatives, friends, grassroots teams and the community at large, which in turn supports the construction of a typology of African players' GBB. The final section provides revelations and reflections on how some community members can manipulate cultural norms and values to exploit some players' investments.

Professional footballers' relationship with their communities of origin

The humble beginning of African players reflect their community embeddedness showing how social norms and cultural values can shape or reshape their lives in the environment they may find themselves in.

As soon as footballers consider keeping their relationship with their community, they must respect the latter's social rules and cultural norms. Thus, the socio-cultural values may play a role impacting on the behaviours of players concerning whatever they do in relation with their communities because of the respect for their culture. This is also ingrained in the family systems as they deliver support to individual members via social welfare coordination. It extends to their transnational relations shown over the regular contact with families, parents, friends, and the community people, a way to strengthen their social bonding. This could be one of the main reasons why African players make frantic efforts to maintain such relationships before, during, and after their post-playing careers.

Essentially, their ability to sustain economic community relationships supports players' easy reintegration after a change in situational status abroad. Yet, there are other forms of conduct that determine players' interconnectedness with their localities of origin after becoming successful professionally abroad. According to Carling (2007), this can be observed via remittances, sending family members or friends for holidays and supporting the migration of others in the community. Through this support, community ties and social relations in the larger society are reinforced. This was the overwhelming response from all interviewees who admitted that they send regular remittances in addition to other things. Ayarna, with over 12 years of professional experience abroad explained that their behaviour is a community norm which cannot be underestimated.

> Unlike the Europeans, everything is yours though some will help their family out when they are in a better position but most often a European footballer signs a contract the dad says good luck, African player you sign a contract this is not good luck now, you have a responsibility to yourself, family, friends, extended family, former teammates, and others in the community and I don't think any footballer complains about that.[1]

Alongside, others sponsor some family members, friends, relatives and people in the community as cosmopolitan migrants or settlers or returnee migrants. A typical case is narrated by Akunnor:

> We were six and one has passed on and I managed to send them overseas where they live now. They were also happy for my career and encouraged me with their support. However, as the 4th child, I wasn't happy because I became like the 'breadwinner' for the family and I didn't like that way.[2]

Being in a better position in African settings tends to bring along with it associated responsibilities for players. To them, achieving a giver-position enables a player to support the well- being of others in his social environment (Ungruhe and Esson 2017) as explained by Akunnor, though he did not like being the fourth born among his siblings, which shows the transfer of the eldest responsibilities after he turned professional footballer abroad. This puts a responsibility on those successful financially to support the entire family tree as they might have contributed in various ways to facilitate their migration abroad. In the future, researchers can also explore what can best explain the 'Give Back Behaviour' of female professional players from Africa to their communities of origin.

Giving back as a socioeconomic phenomenon

Most African professional players invest their football earnings in different socio-economic projects in their countries of origin and abroad. Some of their economic investments include dealing in properties, telecommunication networks, sporting facilities, training centres, food production, bank savings and shares, real estate, football academies, hospitals, sports promotion, oil and gas, transport and garage businesses, microfinance, large-scale farming, oil and logistic businesses, schools, education and coaching, and sport administration, gaming business (Casino), lending capital to banks, bank auctions, leasing of plots of land, apartment rentals in home country and abroad, hotels and hostels and other private/personal businesses which some decline to mention. George Seyi, who won two gold medals with the Nigerian senior national team declined to mention some of his personal business but spoke about the ones he has done publicly with friends. He said:

> The only investment I want to talk about is what I did publicly not my personal one. We have a football academy right now with two colleagues from my former university. We came together and started a football academy which we're still running until now. I have a foundation in my mother's name because my mum died just before I started my university degree. Absolutely, I also invested in my human capital including furthering my education to the master level.[3]

Clearly, apart from his economic investments with his university friends, he has established a charitable foundation in the name of his late mother who was a philanthropist. To him, it is a way to appreciate his mother's social commitment to the needy in society. So, he is picking up many youngsters off the streets and placing them into his football academy rather than allowing them to do bad things as this is the only way he can also give back to support the community.

Other non-economic projects besides sport include health centres, clinics and provision of hospital equipment, sporting kit or gear and equipment, investment in human capital— scholarships, building and renovation of schools, donations to orphanage homes, installation of well water/pump water, intellectual capital, cultural capital, gifts, free health insurance schemes, community library and financial support to the needy. These are some of the social supports professional players from Africa tend to offer their communities of origin.

Didier Drogba, a social role model for many African youths has recently established another school in the village of Onahio Pokou-Kouamekro to advance the level of children's education aside from the five clinics built in Ivory Coast. He recalled:

> The belief of my foundation has always been if we give children access to health and education, we will build future generations of doctors, scientists, businessmen and women and that is how we build a better Africa.[4]

This demonstrates the important meaning Drogba attaches to such social projects in the area of health and education, because a sound mind resides in a healthy body. Therefore, a solid foundation in the fields of health and education can give hope of a better future to the village people. That is, they are essential components in the developmental process of communities. Hence, developing the human capital of individuals can be a step towards building a better society in Africa. Drogba's behaviour is based on an affection action which is coherent with his values and objectives to achieve a socioeconomic goal (Bouhaouala 1999, 2007).

The economic and non-economic projects of African players to their communities are informed by their embeddedness which replicates their values, conceptions, objectives, and economic interest. This is essential because it shows how the rationalities of players are redirected into the various socioeconomic investment initiatives which tend to deepen their connections with their communities.

In sum, players' socioeconomic investments in their local communities determine how they can support the different activities of society especially their families, parents, and the extended family. That also replicates the influence of their social norms and cultural values or the economic returns to families, communities, and societies, by using their talents, skills, finances, knowledge, and experiences acquired from their football profession to make sure they help others who were like them before their situational change abroad. This is expressed by how players' rationality differs in perspectives regarding the importance they assign to their economic and non-economic behaviours to their countries of origin. Yet, the establishment of those socioeconomic projects can reveal a form of appreciation and/or the distribution of the resources invested in their migration projects by families, relatives, communities, and the grassroots' teams.

Give Back Behaviour in the African culture

Analysis of the interviews revealed an important phenomenon that all the players confirmed as an integral part of African culture. This justifies the regular contributions (remittance) and support of families, relatives, friends, and the communities as an existing norm in African societies, because their localities are built on social and cultural embeddedness which tends to frame and define their social activities and family identities. Players supported their argument with the fact that those in better positions are either obliged to assist people or must be ready to do so, especially when they migrate abroad. This is reiterated by Ayarna who explained how African players have come to accept this as part of the broader culture. That is, 'we have the African culture, if you have it, everybody joins you'.[5] This clearly confirms the assertion of Ungruhe and Esson (2017) that those in a giver-position have some social responsibilities which are bestowed on them after achieving a professional footballer status abroad.

Again, players stressed that their successful migration projects abroad are based on the 'collective efforts' and contributions of significant others from their localities. That alone can oblige them to reciprocate this gesture by sending regular remittance to support their social welfare or livelihoods in the communities. To

De Vasconcellos Ribeiro and Dimeo (2009), the returns are considered as lasting provisions for families who anticipate the financial rewards from their migrant footballers. Giving such support is regarded as 'a collective project on social mobility, mainly by families or relatives who select among the talents viewed as appropriate for the exploit of football migration' (Rial 2014).

Beyond that, players' social status and achievements enhance a family's image and reputation, social recognition and sometimes, a person is decorated with a prestigious local title always conferred on him by the chief or opinion leaders in the community for his contributions and support to the good cause of society. Some African players have been awarded various honours back home in their countries or elsewhere in Africa. Eto'o, one of the most accomplished African footballers was installed as paramount chief in Kaffu Bullom, a chiefdom in Sierra Leone in November 2015.[6] This cultural honour was for his social contribution towards the fight against 'Ebola' programme in the country and on Africa soil.

However, those who refused to support some of these social programmes and activities can be ridiculed or tagged as 'ungrateful being' (Acheampong 2018; Van der Meij and Darby 2017) and above all, bring shame to parents, families, relatives, and friends. In some cases, the community may deprive them of certain local benefits and can also become bad stain on their family.

Give Back Behaviour and social embeddedness

Street football is a common social activity often associated with early childhood play in many African communities. All the players admitted to this fact when they described their football career paths starting from the communities through to achieving a professional status abroad. Thus, players explored their social environment to become footballers using their social connections and social groups to their benefit. Graduates of street football must participate in inter-street competitions including walking long distances to towns or villages to play with other social groups. This deepens their social integration and inclusion among their peers and in the communities that organise those events for them.

With the social support of the community, football talents and potentials can find ways to nursery grounds for their refinement and development. The regular organisation of football activities in the communities provided the players with an opportunity to practise football often, which eventually exposes their raw talents to football fans. This inspired their social groups' integration in the locales where they spent their leisure time. Through those social activities, young boys became members of the social group that defined and reinforced their social identity (Tajfel 1978). In this context, football events played a social role for young people to have fun and improve their talents. On the whole, the social support of the community in different ways—via encouragement, accompanying them to matches, providing footballs, sport kits among others—helped some young boys to achieve their professional dreams abroad, with others becoming financially successful professionally. In other words, the various kinds of support they had enjoyed in their communities made a big difference to players' economic behaviours. George Seyi recalled how the community people organised street football events for them which they always look forward:

> The consistency in the organisation of tournaments because we looked forward to it. Not like they put money down to help us buy boots, anklets or others, none of that, but the fact that they still loved the game that much as they made sure they organised this tournament.[7]

Some of these tournaments indirectly built their confidence and prepared them for other tryouts into clubs and national teams locally. Sam Ayorinde also narrated the support he had from his friends in the community that linked him to several football trials which got him into a club finally.

> So, I went for trials there to play for the feeder team (Julius Berger FC) and I think we were many, but I was able to *make it* because they selected only 10 of us and then I 'damaged' this team. Then from there, after school, I went running for trials around and ended up signing for NEPA Lagos FC the only professional team I played for in Nigeria and left for Europe.[8]

His social relations paved the way for his series of trials and finally landed him a club before he was able to move abroad and continue his professional career. The social integration characteristics provide young boys with the opportunity to interact and make new friends as they play football together. This makes them feel embedded in a set of relationships with others whose choice can influence their own interest as well (Granovetter 1985).

Players' affiliation with the community before turning professional abroad make them aware of some challenges young boys must handle in their environment in order to get through to their football dreams. This familiarity is a common feature to which all the interviewees testified. As Victor Wanyama[9] explained, 'you need to remember where you came from and do as much as you can to help them especially the kids who are in need so, is a great initiative'. All the players interviewed revealed how ecstatic it is to support the kids who have the talent but without any hope of making it in football. For the players, contributing to this good cause is a great feeling and demonstrates their social inclusiveness and deep connection to the community. This reflects their economic behaviours in terms of social influences through their Give Back Behaviours to the community.

The players admitted that their social bonding with the community people always supports their easy reintegration in societies. This tends to create opportunities for players to speak on the various media platforms such as radio stations where they always acknowledge the community people for their social supports offered them. Rising from the village to becoming the only professional footballer, Lumor Agbenyenu, a member of the Ghana senior national team narrated how he intends to give back to his village people by setting up a football team in return for their support. Thus, 'everybody wants to play football especially, the kids in the area and with this, it will help them, and they will be happy and make them remember me all the time'.[10] This proposed project will make him be involved as well as able to manage it properly because of his football background. In the same vein, the project can serve as a legacy for him in the community and motivation for aspirant young boys who want to take football to the highest level. Similarly, Rabiu, a gold medallist for Ghana in the U-20 tournament held in Egypt 2009 mentioned the need to support this community people. He said; 'I followed these young boys to this football exercise to give them my support and motivation'.[11] Even though Rabiu was nursing an injury, he accompanied his community boys to the trial to give them support and inspiration to play and get selected by the organisers. Rabiu's behaviour demonstrates his social connection with the community and replicates the same way that he was supported by Sulley Muntari, a former member of the Ghanaian senior national team. Beyond that, players' networks promote their social interaction which has the tendency to influence the economic behaviour embedded in social relations in their communities (Granovetter1985).

Surprisingly, professional footballers' social connection with the community people also influences their wives, who tend to contribute to the decision-making process about their Give Back Behaviours. Some advised their husbands to restrain from giving out money and rather invest in social enterprises that can offer the community people sustainable jobs, making them become self-reliant. In a way, it was to ensure the sustenance of their investments so that the people can continue to have regular earnings rather than being idle or dependent on others.

Other footballers are made ambassadors for their social embeddedness and cultural values that connect them to the larger society. Jay-Jay Okocha is an ambassador for SOS Children's villages where he often talks to the kids and gives them some assistance and support (Orr 2007). He admits that supporting a social cause is a great and beautiful initiative. Thus, the vital role of people in the social environment is critical and the desire to support charity activities is fantastic insofar as it impacts on the needy in society. Okocha did not hide his feelings about how '[Football] is religion in his country. It unites the whole country as one.'[12]

The deep social connection of African footballers with their communities affect some decisions of players in terms of their league choices abroad. This is essential because they recognise their views as an important part of the support they continue to enjoy from them. For instance, Dede Ayew moving from Olympique Marseille (Ligue 1, France) to Swansea City (Premiership, England) reiterated how excited Ghanaian fans would be to see him in that prestigious league with a global viewership. He recalled:

> When I returned to Ghana, I felt the warm welcome from all my people. They are people who really trust me, push me and want me to get to the highest level. I have been in the national team since I was 17 years old, so all

> the Ghanaian people have seen me grow up as a person and as a player. They wanted me to go to the Premier League and although I took this decision also for myself, I took it for a lot of people in my country because they wanted me to be here.[13]

Dede's social connection with the Ghanaian people played a role in his decision to join the Premiership in England. Showing the social dimensions to his behaviour determined which European league to join and that increased his fan base in Ghana and for the new club too. The social embeddedness of African players is demonstrated via their social contributions and support to the communities.

A collection of high-profile African footballers including Michael Essien (Ghana), Aaron Mokoena (South Africa), John Utaka (Nigeria), Mohamed Aboutrika (Egypt), Nwankwo Kanu (Nigeria), Didier Drogba (Côte d'Ivoire), Samuel Eto'o (Cameroon), etc. have undertaken various social projects in sport and/or out of sport to support their community people. Some of these projects include but are not limited to building libraries, public toilets, providing clean drinking water, involvement in the 1Goal initiative, Heart Foundation, charity foundations, schools and health care centres, hospitals, Ambassadors against Hunger and UNDP Goodwill Ambassadors among others; these are some of social contributions towards bettering the lives of their community people in various forms.[14] This exhibits their social embeddedness as they reciprocate their contributions and support through their giving back behaviours. The players' gestures determined the significant meaning they assign to their social behaviour in relation to their values, objectives, conceptions, and interest to society. These social projects may be independent of any social forces due to their deep connection with the local communities. They are a reproduction of their economic behaviours influenced by social connections with societies in which they are embedded (Granovetter 1985).

Indeed, others identify the need to use football as an effective tool for solving social issues in the communities. This is one of the main concepts behind Mbvoumin's CFS project spreading across Africa in educating young boys being lured abroad through football human trafficking (Esson 2015). He cautioned professional players not to be focusing too much on the financial rewards of the game at the risk of the communities breeding social vices in the youths which could be disastrous for their future in Africa. The majority appreciate football as an instrument that can promote social development, education, and many things in their communities. Some actions of the players are observed in their various social projects which seek to engender and protect the youth from being trapped into illegal migration abroad through football. Thus, getting closer to the grassroots through their social integration and deep connection with them can minimise some of these social issues in Africa. However, exploring how unsuccessful African migrant players abroad can reintegrate into their local communities may contribute to providing useful information for the youth on their career choices in football.

Give Back Behaviours and cultural embeddedness

Apart from social embeddedness influencing footballers' Give Back Behaviours, cultural dimensions play a critical role in their economic behaviour as well. This was observed with some players visiting individuals in their local communities to show them their appreciation in return for whatever they have contributed to their football careers, which is an accepted cultural norm. Noah, a member of the Zambian winning squad in AFCON 2012 recalled paying regular visits to the local people when he was on holidays.

> The main important one is just to help not in terms of material thing but sometimes to pay visits to them by making somebody smile. You know with some people just being around them you talk with them they will feel privileged and important as well, so I do that more often, and I never get angry at somebody… I just want to be somebody who makes a difference in someone's life.[15]

Away from the provision of economic projects for families, friends, relatives and teammates, players' behaviour could be related to cultural norms and beliefs which may oblige them to offer support because they are in a better position to do so. Thus, players' earnings tend to escalate in their destinations of play abroad. Others are inspired by religious principles of giving to people including the needy in society and that also affects players' choices in their giving back behaviours. Analysis from their choices of some projects can demonstrate aspects of cultural values that help to shape and reshape society for the better. Paintsil recalled how cultural values informed some of his decisions and he ended up establishing charity foundation to teach and educate kids from 8–12 years, to teach them the values of tolerance, peace, love, respect and discipline in their communities.

> So, the kids play football together and after we teach them how to comport themselves, listening to their teachers, and wait for the opportunity to come and give themselves to God especially those who believe in God. But we have Christians and Muslims and they should also know that we are the same people. That is what I'm trying to teach the kids because those words I have mentioned have helped me in my career and brought me far to this level and I think this is better and good to also share it among the kids.[16]

He believes that when such values are inculcated into kids, they will pick them up and grow up with them. To some, there are more blessings in giving than always receiving. The cultural embeddedness of many African players is shown through their religion as well. Thus, the Protestants and Moslems have a strong religious belief that 'the more you give to the needy or disadvantaged people, the more you receive from your creator'. Their social activities and integration with the people provide players with the opportunity to interact and identify some issues of their communities for possible redress. With this, others provide support as a means of commitment to their religious belief, which according to some, means that they have a religious obligation to help the poor and the needy in society. Still, a board member of the Professional Footballers Association of Ghana (PFAG) and a licensed football coach, Ahinful explained how he gave out freely a parcel of land for the construction a church in his community.

> I didn't build the church, but I gave them the land and all of us, church members contributed to putting up the structure. After giving my land, I still contributed financially so were other members of the church. Where they were worshipping before they were being sacked from the place and I had a plot of land somewhere that I wasn't ready to use so I gave it out to the church.[17]

Ahinful's providing the land to the church could be related to the belief that the more you commit resources to the work of God, the more you continue to enjoy benefits from Him (according to the Protestants' belief). Most of the players admitted that their communities' norms and cultural values have gone a long way to influence their situations for the better because it has created a conducive and supportive environment for them to achieve their professional football dreams. Cultural embeddedness also drives some players to support and nurture young football talents from villages, towns and distant areas to be exposed to formal training and development. Cultural norms and values within the communities have moulded and reformed players' economic actions in terms of supporting the good causes of societies through their give back behaviours. Evidence was seen from some players who invested in different social projects including the establishment of community libraries, health centres, scholarship schemes, charity foundations among others to support and contribute to the education of the communities in different ways. Born a natural leader, Appiah united the Black Stars team on a magical run that steered her country to its historic World Cup in 2006. He explained:

> I remember after the FIFA World cup Germany 2006, I was just walking around the locale and then something came to my mind that the locale where I grew up (Chorkor in the capital of Accra close to the sea) and said to myself the people have supported me a lot or done a lot for me with their prayers and all that, so I have to give something back to them. [...] I registered 200 people for free National Health Insurance Scheme (NHIS) and went on to create this "StepApp Foundation". I have built a Healthcare Center for mothers in Chorkor, to receive free medical attention. In the same locality, I had also built a community library.[18]

Appiah's projects were in response to some of the challenges affecting his former locality where his football career started from. All these were to improve the standard of the people in the locality as he was a victim dropping out of school. Chorkor, a suburb of Accra, is noted for its fishing activities and a locale that has also produced famous and world boxers for Ghana including the legend Azumah Nelson, Ike Quartey among others.

Other players were able to reconnect with their social groups back in villages or towns, which depicts positive cultural embeddedness. Some also supported their grassroots teams, setting up social projects in sports to replicate a culture in their former schools. The captain of the Ghana senior national team Asamoah Gyan expressed satisfaction after following the steps of some members of his former School Alumni Association culture of giving back in various ways to improve teaching and learning at the school. He recalled before constructing the AstroTurf pitch for his alma mater (Accra Academy Senior High School, Ghana) which was officially opened in June 2017.

> About 5 months ago, I told everybody about this Astroturf, it just comes to my mind when I came for a visit at the school and I just said it to the students that I'm here to do the Astroturf for the school that is to give back to the school and I think giving back is a good thing, and am not the only person who has given back to the school. But this project will be an example for my fellow students who are coming up and I'm sure they won't let the school down.[19]

These initiatives serve as an example to students and young players that when they become gainfully employed and successful professionally, they should also support their schools and grassroots teams. This has become a cultural norm among professional players due to the cultural morals associated with such kinds of assistance to the community.

African players affirmed that no amount of money can compensate for the values of respect, love, commitment, togetherness, tolerance, friendliness, and selflessness gained from the local communities. It continues to strengthen their social relationships back home in their countries of origin. Some players described how their childhood or youthful football experiences have culturally shaped their values and behaviours in societies. In his autobiography Didier Drogba explained how he learned the value of sharing and caring for one another (Penot 2008). Indeed, some of these values could also mirror the kind of social projects he undertakes for society.

African players' socio-cultural connections are also observed in the transfer of their cultural experiences abroad to the community. These are reproduced in their give back behaviours to the game including the acquisition of new languages, culture and social remittances that tend to enhance their technical abilities (Williams 2014) on coaching and training aspects of football in their communities. Some players acknowledged that cultural meanings do not restrict themselves to the mind but also influence their conduct and reveal themselves through the organisation and regulation of social practices (Hall 1997).

Support for the people is also a kind of solidarity because of socio-cultural differences that can explain the significance of their give back behaviours in the communities. Players believe that apart from becoming professionals, they count themselves blessed to have a favour from their creator, and these manifest in their economic and non-economic behaviours to society. Beyond that, it inspires their religious belief which affects their conceptions, objectives, values, and interests to the people and societies. Lastly, players in their bid to sustain family reproduction and the future include the local people in creating employment opportunities, which are influenced by cultural norms since they do not want to be scorned. Players' socio-cultural ties are embedded in the institutionalised networks as they play significant roles in their migration projects and tend to affect investment behaviours to society.

Lastly, in African communities, religion is very important in education and society, and this generally influences professional footballers' vision and GBB as well. This showed in the players' rationale as most of the behaviours were more focused on local culture and economic strategy for satisfying the larger society.

Give Back Behaviours and institutionalised networks

The football labour market provides a medium for clubs and agents to negotiate on the release and engagement of international footballers. This makes the activities of intermediaries crucial to the functioning of the football market, they rely a great deal on their personal relationships, scouting networks, club officials, social relations and other networks. These agents act as a 'hub' because they hold the football market together by managing confidential information on potential openings and negotiation processes, and leveraging their social networks with other agents and club officials (Poli and Rossi 2012). This is essential because agents do not work in isolation in the modern management of football but through intermediaries such as social networks (scouts, other agents, club officials) and personal relationships with clubs, families, friends, former footballers, and local managers.

With the support of intermediaries, football has seen a growing pattern in the mobility of international players to the various leagues abroad. The steady involvement of intermediaries has generated a pivot of institutionalised networks that support and facilitate the migration of football talents in Africa to leagues abroad. Alongside this, the significant role of families, relatives, friends, clubs' owners, extended family and more distant relations in this process of migration cannot be disregarded. Thus, most of the players revealed that their transfer abroad was brokered by their respective networks comprising agents and with a few from club officials and self-initiative. Nii Odartey Lamptey explained how his strong desires for a professional career facilitated his search for a local manager in Nigeria.

> I think through that competition [FIFA U-17 World Cup], Anderlecht SC [Belgium] spotted me and they wanted me, but they did not know how to contact me. At that time, the late Stephen Keshi was with RSC Anderlecht, so they contacted him to try and get me because Nigeria is the closest Anglophone country to Ghana, making it easier to contact him… So, he informed his local manager in Nigeria to come and look for me in Ghana. This local manager came to Ghana and delivered the news to me.[20]

Anderlecht club used their player, Stephen Keshi as a link to reach Nii Lamptey after he had a successful tournament during the FIFA U-16 World Cup in Scotland in 1989. His initial visit to the local manager in Nigeria deepened his relationship with Keshi who later became more than a family member to him. That charted his professional football journey to Belgium after migrating from Ghana to Nigeria in search of the local manager. Around the late 1980s, FIFA regulations on minors were a bit relaxed and that made some football agents exploit some young African players who were desperate to move and play abroad. This early development identified the role of intermediaries as situated in the institutionalised networks, showing the importance of networks and social relations as an integral part of footballers' migratory itineraries to leagues abroad. Indeed, this re-emphasised how African footballers' migratory routes are embedded in institutionalised networks.

Others recalled how helpful their colleagues have been by passing on useful information and opportunities (Bale 1991) that enabled them to secure new contracts with clubs after they were made redundant. Ahinful, a former Ghanaian international with over 15 years of professional experience and a holder of CAF licensed 'A' coach narrated how he got back to active football after the cancellation of his contract from an Italian club.

> I had then cancelled my contract with the club. Then I spoke to a friend in Turkey with a football club. He also informed his coach that I was a free agent and upon that I was invited to a trial with their team and later, they signed me, and the rest became history.[21]

Alongside those official football agents, social relations and networks of players can act as recruitment referrals (Engh and Agergaard 2015) by using their informal networks and mobility within the leagues to transmit relevant information of possible opportunities for colleagues in clubs abroad. In effect, Ahinful used this exchange to his advantage as he was able to secure a place in the club. Afterwards, the necessary procedures governing international players' transfers were evoked to facilitate his licence and permit to continue his career in Turkey.

Others shared the way they got to Europe to pursue their professional aspirations. Sam Ayorinde started his professional football adventure by road through the various borders of Africa and with the support of social networks' directive, and he played for over 14 years abroad. He recalled:

> Before Austria I went to Greece, it was also through somebody (some Nigerian who had been there for a long time) for some months to try and see if they can fix me a club so, he can make some money. Finally, they arranged for me a trial with Thessaloniki FC, it went well anyway.[22]

Sam used his social relations in a win-win situation and that facilitated his migration to a league in Greece. Indeed, the migration of African players abroad is often supported through the mobilisation of resources from families, extended family, social relations and networks of agents, scouts, club officials, and local managers. Prince Ikpe described the influential role of his local manager who negotiated everything that enabled him to move to the Italian league in 1995.

> So, when they came and organised a game for us to play and Techie (my local manager) now invited me again …I went, played, and scored the only goal that we used in defeating the other team. Because we were selected players and I was the youngest and smallest among them. I was the only one that Techie was managing… I performed so well, and the match video was taken to Italy. That was when they asked for me. It was between my local manager and the Italian club's scout.[23]

The local manager acted as a link between the player and the foreign scout and later, he was offered a four-year contract. After signing his first professional contract in Italy, he recalled:

> It was the most important moment of my life, and I knew that it was the beginning of my career. Because not hearing that I wasn't going back to Nigeria, but I have made it and they had offered a contract what else will be greater than that for a boy that has gone through hardships, hot times, and was hoping and dreaming every day and finally, a contract has been given to me. I didn't care how much was the money even though it was so small but for the moment, I have the platform to exhibit my abilities, skills and potentials that were fit for me.[24]

Through the efforts of his local manager's network, the player had an opportunity to showcase his talent abroad. He ordered the local manager to take his first contract money and ensure that he sorted out his family, by instructing him to give his share of the money to his family and relocate them from the 'den neighbourhood' to decent accommodation and find them a productive business to operate. The use of the 'den neighbourhood' refers to the way some people in the locale perceived him as a 'bad and lazy boy' because of football. They were against his football career though he did not like it either. Later, he realised that those locale people did things out of ignorance, yet he visited them and gave them food and money and they were shocked and amazed by his social support and gifts to them. The player's Give Back Behaviour reflected his deep connection and a way of getting reintegrated after turning professional footballer from that community. Incidentally, the behaviour of the community people towards his football desires might have challenged him to put in more efforts to reach his professional football dream abroad.

There are instances where young and upcoming players recognise those professional players ahead of them as 'senior colleagues', some of whom eventually become their role models and advisors depending on how they are able to get along with each other. This tends to foster their social relationships especially when they find themselves in the same club abroad. Senior players may provide various kinds of support and assistance to the young ones due to their vast mobility experiences in leagues. Alozie shared his experience and that has strengthened his relationship with the senior player ever since. Through that positive social relationship with the senior player (Laumann and Pappi 1976), he learned a lot of things both in the game and business perspectives. He recalled the tremendous improvement in his investment activities back home with the fruitful advice from his senior player:

> I have a lot of housing projects, into oil business thanks to Julius Aghahowa, he advised me on that. I learnt a lot from him for like I knew him for over 10 years and within that one year, I had to learn so many things from him that I never knew. I thought I knew something about the game but no, he taught me a lot of things I never knew and was already like 28 years when I met him. And it was like I am a baby in the game and he opened my eyes to see the real football and understand how it is to live with the people of Nigeria.[25]

Beyond playing in the same team, Alozie established a positive relationship that has provided him with a lot of benefits including improving his game quality and identifying new investment opportunities in Nigeria. The social relation has enlarged his perspectives on how to support the community people and manage his various investments without recourse to cultural values and social norms. Alongside his new business ideas, he has also learned to manage his social relations and networks in the communities. All interviewees acknowledged that the various social and network resources have played a significant role in facilitating their migration and mobility abroad. Anaba clarified how he felt at home in Spain after meeting a Ghanaian player in the same team.

> Fortunately for me, there was one Ghanaian player (Boakye Yiadom) who was by then playing for Elche CF, even though I had my own apartment, but I was always doing everything with Boakye. So, it was more like Boakye who received me in Elche, I was feeling at home. Everything was okay.[26]

Anaba had been to Europe before for international competitions but living alone was quite different. Meeting another player from Ghana supported his easy integration and he ended up developing a positive relationship with him. He again benefited from various advice which reinforced his social inclusion in the team and enhanced his stay in Spain. The institutionalised networks situated in social relations tend to manifest in the migration and mobility of African players in the leagues abroad. Sam Owusu, a young player with less than three years' experience described how the institutionalised network created an opportunity for him to begin his professional career in Europe.

> There was a guy called Darko in Europe who was a friend of my local manager. After I returned from France with the Red Bull Academy, I became

> famous. My local manager spoke with me about Darko, who wanted to help me travel to Europe, but he didn't mention the specific country, until the last few days to my travel.[27]

Through the social networks of his local manager, he finally moved to Europe and pursued his football professional aspirations. Aside from the local manager using his networks to facilitate his migration process, he also benefited financially from both the agent and the young player's transfer transactions.

Others have maintained their social relationships with friends and social groups from their locales even after situational changes in status. George Seyi recalled the contributions of his school and locale friends to his professional career and projects back in Nigeria.

> You don't need 20 people around you. You might need two or three, they will be the ones to facilitate and push others on your behalf. So, I was very lucky in that regard like I said, there are few of them that I grew up with, play football together, and supported ourselves together. They facilitated all those things I did in Nigeria. I used the right professionals with the support of my school friends.[28]

The former Nigerian international with a master's degree in Sport Directorship from Manchester Metropolitan University, UK, used the various social relations and networks established from his childhood and schools to provide him with information on investment opportunities in Nigeria. In the end, he has partnered some of them to invest in productive projects including a sports agency, scouting and player management. As George Seyi puts it, 'we have a football academy right now with two colleagues from my undergraduate university. We came together and started a football academy project which we are still running until now.'[29] Seyi's action is quite different from some African players who could neither maintain their childhood or school friends nor locales' social groups or schoolmates. It is not surprising as he wants to study for another master's degree in Sports Management after his active football career to equip him with enough knowledge in the area of football management.

Some players' situational changes in social status can become negative for them since they may see themselves as a different social class and therefore tend to avoid their former social groups or friends (Acheampong 2018). Apparently, this was exposed by Cofie who thinks that they should be humbled despite the fame and wealth achieved:

> One thing about some of us is that when we start becoming important that is, famous, winning cups, playing important games, we become too arrogant and forget our old friends saying, now I'm at this level, and now you are no more my friend, and I have to go along with those at that level.[30]

This kind of attitude can let them lose some opportunities from their grassroots social group and friends as well as school colleagues. Apart from that, it limits their social relations and networks back home and can have negative effects on their social reintegration and social inclusion.In other words, their new social class level will have an influence on their social and economic behaviours because of changes in social preference.

In Africa, a few structured football academies continue to facilitate the migration of recruited trainees to leagues abroad. They do this through the established social networks and contacts (scouts, agents, and clubs) to assist them in the transfer of their graduates to the European football market. These processes support their breakthrough abroad and some may reciprocate this opportunity by offering various financial and sporting resources to the former football academy.

African players' migration and mobility is demonstrated through broader institutionalised networks integrated into complex nodes ranging through parents, families, extended family, more distant relations, grassroots teams, football academies, non-affiliated teams, local managers, scouts, agents, clubs' officials, sports agencies, federations, coaches, and friends, all aimed at enabling development and stimulating the migration of football talents to leagues abroad.

Give Back Behaviours and economic rationality

African players gained migration and mobility opportunities abroad through the various resources they were able to mobilise including social relations and institutionalised networks. In return, professional players benefit from financial rewards that considerably increase their economic value in exchange for their football talent. Some of these economic returns (football-related revenues) are remitted to families, households, relatives, and the communities while others invest in Africa and Europe. Professional players make rational investments in diverse ways in order to sustain the future of their families, relatives, and friends among others in society. Abedi A. Pele, a former Ghanaian international who won his first AFCON trophy in 1982 at age 17 and went on to win the UEFA Champions League trophy with Marseille in 1993 recalled planning far ahead during his professional career by investing in his country and this has sustained him after his retirement from active football.

> I was always saying to my other players and colleagues that I am going to Ghana immediately I stopped my professional career. So, I was investing here in houses, real estates and everything that I bought was in Ghana and I never did anything abroad. So, it was not difficult for me to stop football today because I had prepared the ground for my future. It was not very difficult for me also to integrate into society because everything was okay. I had done my homework when I was playing abroad. My wife was very instrumental because she was coming down to take control and supervise all the projects when I was playing.[31]

Alongside his role as an ambassador for Polio on the continent, Abedi carefully planned his investment activities together with his wife when he was actively playing abroad. His early investment approaches supported him to reintegrate easily after discovering business opportunities within the communities. This enabled him to strategically position his investments to support his post-transition playing career. He made rational choices for the future with the backing of his wife who was instrumental by serving as a point of contact and information transfer to identifying business opportunities in the communities.

Others have invested in their countries of origin because they intend to spend the rest of their life there after active playing careers are over. They think that their communities provided them with an opportunity and reinvesting all their acquired resources back can help improve livelihoods via the provision of jobs, employment, etc. Thus, their GBB is reproduced by the series of support and contributions they had from the community people which added value to their human capital development. Alozie, having spent over 12 years playing professionally in Ukraine, stated that 'mostly, all my projects are in Nigeria because that is where I am from, because one day, everybody will go back home'.[32] All his projects in Nigeria are under the care of his family with some hidden from people as advised by his senior footballer (Julius Aghahowa). This is because he wants them to respect him more after his active career when he starts to expose these hidden economic businesses. His rational strategy is in preparation for his post-transition career abroad. It is also the reason why he visits home (Nigeria) every year when club football is on a break.

One high-profile African footballer chose to spread training centres (projects) across the African continent to help improve livelihoods and develop football talents as a part of his GBB which to him occurs naturally. That is, he is not selective about which specific country to invest in but hopes to cover many countries on the continent with his training centres (projects). Eto'o explained his actions to that effect:

> My latest project is in Kenya, specifically in Nairobi where we opened a training centre. As I said earlier, I am a child of Africa. I do not choose and have no preference. Whether Guinea, Gabon, Cameroon, I am a child of Africa, I feel good all over. Today is Guinea, tomorrow will be another country …This is done naturally. I hope God will give me a long life to bring this project in most African countries.[33]

Eto'o hopes that investing in those training centres in different countries across Africa can provide the right conditions for adding value to the talent of youth in the future. In the long term, this can produce the next football stars on the continent. Eto'o disclosed that his motive for investing in Guinea, consequently, is a self-conviction that one day, an African country can win the senior FIFA World Cup tournament.

> I am convinced that Africa has the potential to win the World Cup tomorrow but that we must have some basis. We have a lot of luck because our mums made us have some talent while Europeans learn football at football academies. However, we go to the streets to find ourselves in big stadiums.[34]

His sport projects are interesting and community-centred but they may have economic intentions as well. Can this help stop the illegal migration of young talents abroad and contribute to strengthening the unity among African countries? The various sustainable sport projects of players can support infrastructure improvements in Africa and concurrently, equip and develop sporting talents as well as serve as a source of leisure and recreation centre for the communities, thus developing the human capital of young African talents to make them productive and beneficial to the larger society (Becker 1993).

Some professional players' investment in their countries represents a symbolic meaning to their children, family, extended family, and the community. Marcel Desailly explained the reason for his economic investment in his country of origin.

> All the considerations I got towards my kids was to show them who I was and the money that I was having. There were no physical structures to give consideration and that is how I was going to transmit something to my children because I could not transmit (show) my victories in the UEFA Champions League or my FIFA world cup to them. This magnificent sporting facility is also for my kids as a big example to show them that their father was an entrepreneur. I have worked hard and set something for their future if they want to come back and work in Ghana.[35]

Desailly's investments represent a legacy for his children as they never watched him achieving those laurels from his playing career. Apart from his children, he recognises the economic investment in a physical structure to show some of his achievements to society and the generations thereafter. This demonstrates the transmission of cultural values through his GBB to his family, extended family, and that also supports his social integration into the communities. Other economic investment activities can be likened to managers and entrepreneurs of businesses. With over eight years of professional experience in Europe, Cofie recalled the inspiration behind his economic investment in the communities.

> In my country, I'm investing in houses (properties) for rentals. I do invest in buildings because, the risk is minimal and day in, day out, people are giving birth so you can always get somebody to occupy your apartments. You can always get your rent and those are the driving forces.[36]

Cofie reiterated there is *no place like home*. He has his family, relatives and everybody there and that informed his main decision to invest in the communities for the future because no one knows tomorrow. His investments are geared towards economic gains as he identifies opportunity in properties business as a deficit in Ghana and something that always appreciates all the time. A Zambian international footballer and a gold medalist in AFCON 2012 explained the reason for his investments in properties away from his country of origin. Noah Chivuta recapped how he relocated his business to South Africa.

> My family stays in South Africa where I have most of my properties in Johannesburg. The reason for these investments, you know our career is a bit short and you need to do something after football. It is a good way of investing your money because the properties don't depreciate easily, it can maintain you. For example, I buy a car today and drove off, the dealership has started to depreciate but the house, it will never be that. I would like to be comfortable, but I have a limit because I wouldn't go for the sake of, I just want to drive Lamborghini cars, and I will be sitting alone with one person on the side. So, I'll never do such kind of investment.[37]

Noah's investments are in preparation for his post-playing career and that of his family. He admits that giving your children a better education is the right direction for their future. To him, investing in South Africa is a good choice because it is more developed than Zambia, yet his wife commutes there for business purposes. However, he gave reasons never to invest in luxurious cars at the expense of his family's future. Others took advantage of the business opportunities within their social environment as a rational choice to increase their financial capital. Noted for his role against racism in football, in Germany, Tony Yeboah narrated how he quickly converted one of his properties to a hostel to meet the demands of a private university shortfall in accommodation within the locality of his economic project.

> This building we are sitting in, it used to be a hotel (Accra) but now I changed it to the hostel because there are a lot of students around this community. I have a big hotel in Kumasi too. Apart from these, I have a lot of properties in East Legon, cantonments in Accra, and some apartments in England. All these are from football money. The money I had from football I used it to do investments.[38]

Tony exhibited entrepreneurial behaviour by cashing in on the university challenge after converting his hotel building to a students' hostel. He has invested in some apartments in Europe at a location that is very attractive to holidaymakers and for leisure time. To him, these economic projects are for the future of his family and the extended family and provide jobs opportunities for the community people especially those in Ghana. The former captain of the Ghana senior national team (Black Stars) and now a football licensed coach, C. K. Akunnor[39] is among the few African players that have investments in Europe.

> I have most of my investments in Germany and I get returns on it here while in Ghana. But in Ghana, I did something small and am still doing a lot of different things. I'm into the transport business, auctions — thus you work with the banks, and the banks manage your money, buying shares, lend capital to microfinance companies, but it is not easy. Sometimes, I had been in a situation where I lost a lot of money because of what happened at the World Trade Centre in the USA. If I tell you how much I lost...

His decision to invest abroad was based on political stability because, initially, he was not convinced about his country's political stability or reacting according to investment opportunities available during his playing career. There is a possibility that because of the huge capital lost through the America World Trade Centre incident (11 September 2001), he has become cautious of investing outside his country of origin. Investing in financial businesses is due to his belief that you *never know tomorrow, and it is for tomorrow's sake.* Akunnor's rationality behind his investments was for the future of his kids and what will provide a good foundation for them, as well as serve as an example for them to follow suit.

Bearing in mind investment dynamics, African players must rethink and reposition their economic investments towards equipping individuals becoming independent so that they can sustain their welfare. Beyond that, players should be taught how to manage their talent and make a living from it because it can provide them with regular earnings for life after football. Yet, it will be interesting to determine how African players' football-related incomes and sporting resources are impacting on the community people in their countries of origin.

Typologies of African professional footballers' Give Back Behaviours.

In developing the typology for African professional footballers, we considered five main categories of factors which assisted in identifying the GBB typology. These are:

1. Involvement of social structures (family, community, etc.) and football institutions (academy, clubs, etc.),
2. Social norms and values and cultural beliefs
3. Economic interests and ROI
4. Nature of resources mobilised
5. Targets of the give back phenomenon.

In general, many African players make economic investments despite their social support to their families, relatives, friends, and others in the communities. Their action produces different GBB depending on a series of variables including social obligations to support their families and the community members or ROI for those who have contributed economically and socially to players' migration project. Indeed, the regular sending of remittances in support of families, households, friends, and others in the communities depicts an emerging norm, thus, an African culture rooted in the socio-cultural construct. This according to De Haas (2010, 246) plays a role in the migration decision that is embedded in the concept of the extended family system (Adegoke 2001, 27) including what the players tag as 'good people'. The typology of African players also measured their values, objectives, conceptions, and interests, aside from the role of significant others as crucial to their 'Give Back Behaviours'. It ruminates on the role of community members and the value they put on their activities which are important determinants of 'Give Back Behaviours'.

There are other factors that affect the fortitude of the GBB. Among them can be social constraints identified through media, social networks, social groups, etc. These have an emotional impact on the decision of many African players and the kind of projects to establish in their communities. In the same way, players make sure they satisfy the latter, in order to safeguard and protect their interest in building a positive image in the eyes of Europe and African societies. That is, a player's inability to offer support after achieving socioeconomic status internationally may cast doubt on his socio-cultural connection with the local communities. This development is still not obligatory, but it is relevant and must be properly managed otherwise it can cause serious damage to one's reputation and family members in the community. That may involve players being ridiculed and tagged as ungrateful (Acheampong 2018; Van der Meij and Darby 2017). It is different in the 'Western world' but it is important in African communities, which are based on socio-cultural identity. Indeed, footballers achieving social recognition, social status, and fame should not only serve their economic and social interests but also support the communities, fans, employers, and sponsors which may drive local and regional development. Otherwise, they stand to be accused of ungratefulness and may lose their social status for not contributing in return to their communities' needs, which can have a negative impact on their image and family's reputation.

Invariably, footballers' social and economic interests are not only linked to the Give Back Behaviours but also based on several rationalities that combine different levels of economic interests, values, and social objectives. The identification of good reasons for their action (Boudon 1995) in relation to every 'give back' approach allows a description and explanation of this complex phenomenon. This supports the construction of a typology of the Give Back Behaviours targeting four types of groups with specific actions: (a) hybrid family, (b) cross-closed family, (c) shared family and (d) shadow family. Detailed elaboration on the typology is provided below.

Hybrid family

African players in this category make decisions based on an all-inclusive approach of the extended family structure comprising the close family, wife's family, and others in the community. They consider the effects that their giving back may produce on the family, clan, and the society in a longer term. Their rationalities reflect all types of investments from different businesses to social projects with the tendency of supporting the family's future and the extended family structure, which makes it obligatory. In addition, professional players often invest in social project either in or out of sport while some engage in both. Players have had between 8 and 18 years of professional experience abroad and migrated from the cities or regional capitals to Europe. Their giving back is rationally based even though some values play a role. It replicates the objective of social and economic changes.

A few of them have high-profile status and migrated from the towns or villages to the cities or regional capitals in search of professional activity. The age category ranges between 26 and 55 and with a close family size of between four and eleven, and either married with a child or having fewer than six children. Former players dominate this category due to their vast mobility experiences abroad. Professional players' actions demonstrate their embeddedness in the communities as a collective culture rather than their individuality. The majority of them are Protestants and there are a few Moslems. They believe in giving to the needy or underprivileged people as directed by their doctrines. The majority of the players' give back action includes economic/financial (Entrepreneurship and Patrimonial investments (E), Social projects and Charity (Sc), remittance for the family/community (R), Social project in sport (Sp), Social and business in sport (Sb) and Social project (S)).

Those into sport projects, particularly football academies, feel more comfortable in that area due to their familiarity and easy way of transferring their expertise to the young ones in the communities. This demonstrates their cultural transfer by 'giving something back' to the game with the acquired knowledge to enhance technical ability (Williams 2014) in their football academies. It contributes to impacting young talents and potentials by empowering and making them productive individuals for themselves and society. Others who return home upon completion of their European professional career were given ambassadorial roles to champion social issues in the local communities and Africa. Certainly, the role of their wives and family members is indispensable regarding the various contributions of close family to the different socioeconomic investment initiatives. That is why those married footballers continue to appreciate the support and efforts of wives in their businesses.

Beyond the acquisition of personal investments and the use of his financial capital for philanthropic purposes, Eto'o offered a cheque for $200,000 for the construction of a hospital for the local people in his mother's village Ngambe in Cameroon, and gave an additional $1million for other projects, donations to orphanages, etc. He was crowned paramount chief in Kaffu Bullom, a chiefdom in Sierra Leone in November 2015.[40] This was part of his commitment towards fighting against Ebola in that African country. There is a plethora of examples of African footballers' contributions to the cause of the larger society. This category involves more active footballers than former players investing in such projects for the benefit of the close family, extended family, and others in the community.

Away from their direct support and assistance, most of them are high-profile players with an educational background ranging from a master's degree to high school level, with a few dropping out of school. They played/play in elite European leagues, with mouth-watering earnings (wages /salaries) in exchange for their talents. At this level, almost all former players get involved in football management such as agents, coaches, administrators, club owners, and welfare officers. This is a familiar field for them, and they mostly invest in football activities.

Cross-closed family

This applied to those professional players whose actions are toward the close family of parents' siblings and some community people. In this category, players' give back is rationally based and towards the family, clan, and society but for short and medium terms. They engage in projects from business investments including social projects of all kinds to support children education, donations to orphan homes, solidarity, etc. Age ranges from 22 to 32 with over two to 14 years of professional experience abroad. The majority of them lived in the cities or regional capitals, with a few migrating from the villages and towns.

Most of them are unmarried and those with spouses have fewer than four children. The close family size is around six members with a strong family bonding and a desire for social commitments. Their give back is based on the objective of social commitment to the family, clan, and society at large. It is based more on norms and cultural values, as an integral part of the local community. Players' give back is also rational and more directed towards the benefits of the larger society. Here, their socioeconomic and educational level is lower than the first group. Their give back actions vary from remittances for the family/community (R) and Social project in sport (Sp), Social projects and Charity (Sc) and Social and business in sport (Sb).

This group is dominated by Protestants with an educational background ranging from first degree to high school level. There are some who could not go to school but stuck to only football. Players are often found in leagues 2 and 3 with a few in the top leagues. Their wages are far higher than what they used to earn in their domestic leagues. The majority are active with a limited number of former players who are working as scouts, coaches, technical support staff and directors of their own football academies.

Shared family

As well as undertaking business investments, players are also keen on social projects whether in or out of sport. They include those with rationality for supporting the extended family of wives and their family members and a few others in the community. In this group, the ages are from 30 onwards with a close family size of four to ten, some unmarried and those married with fewer than five children. They have over 11 years of professional experience abroad and include a limited number of high-profile players. They often began their football careers in the towns or villages before migrating to cities or regional capitals. Here, their socioeconomic and educational level is lower than the first and second groups. Their economic investments are rationally based and focused towards themselves and their families with a little attention to social activities. The give back actions are for a longer term.

Little as their contributions could be, it might, somehow, support the community because they have played a role to help them reach that level of their professional careers. Level of education varies from secondary school (Senior High School) to elementary school. Their give back actions range from remittances to family/community (R), Social project in sport (Sp) to Social projects and Charity (Sc). Most of them are married and Protestants, with a few being Moslems. Alongside support for families and community people, some invest in real estate or properties, transport business, and oil and logistics businesses for their post-playing career. This group is dominated by active players with a few former players. They often played/are playing in the top leagues as well as league one with substantial wages for their talent. Former players in this category are into football organisation and administration, and some are employed as scouts, coaches, welfare officers, etc.

Shadow family

This relates to those players with the rationality of impacting the social lives of friends, coaches, more distant relatives, adopted family and others, who might have directly or indirectly contributed to their professional careers. They offer them basic economic benefits and support with social projects out of sport. Most players are unmarried, some have children but are not married and those with spouses have a family size fewer than three children. A close family size of between four and 14.

The majority of them migrated from the towns or villages to seek their fortune in the city or regional capitals with the ball. Players are mostly found in leagues 2 and 3 with substantial wages in excess of what leagues in Africa could offer them. They invest in real estate (apartments), bank shares, regular sending of remittances to family, friends and others, which they recognise as a social obligation to people's lives because someone supported them to reach where they are now. Their socioeconomic and educational level is higher than the third group. The GBB is based on social and moral obligations that are linked to human capital theory. In this group, social commitment is high towards their grassroots clubs, coaches and others in the localities. But it is always for short-term purposes. On top of their remittances to the family/community (R), their give back action focused more on the Social project in sport (Sp) and Social projects and Charity (Sc).

Considering the level of their leagues and age, they can still play for a long time provided they are able to take strategic economic decisions while actively engaged. Players' educational backgrounds vary from polytechnic to high school. This is dominated by young players between the ages of 19 and 26 with less than four years of professional experience. A few are in the elite European leagues. Protestants are dominant with some Moslems. Some players could not play for long in Europe and returned home to continue in leagues in Africa.

Synthesis

The various migration patterns and approaches of African professional footballers abroad supported the development of the typology which also revealed two additional sorts of typologies of sport migration to the earlier studies: thus, duality and education switch, as explained in Chapter 2. We vividly identified how African professional players make economic and social investments to support their families, relatives, friends, and others in their communities. The book revealed how players' Give Back Behaviours differ according to their profiles and that also determined their remittance value and support to families, extended family, friends, coaches, and others, which is an integral part of social norms and cultural values in African communities. In a way, it obliges them to contribute and support those parties mentioned above. The typology of African players was consistent with their values, objectives, conceptions, and interests regarding the community embeddedness as critical to their Give Back Behaviours. Their behaviours were translated into several types of socioeconomic activities undertaken in the communities. However, elements of social forces (media, friends, social groups and people in the locales) influenced the rationality of some players in terms of their Give Back Behaviours to the communities. For players to enjoy continued support and avoid being tagged, shamed and ridiculed among their other professionals, some make sure they protect their reputation and social interest by undertaking economic and social investments in the communities.

Players with a Protestant background exhibit an approach typical of the sixteenth and seventeenth centuries' concept, with a special tendency of developing economic rationalism (Weber 1930; Schroeder 1992). But the present-day Protestants tend to support the needy or disadvantaged in their communities. This belief shapes their religious faith and improves the moral behaviour of members and that is like the beliefs of Moslems, which also obliged the wealthier people in society to support the needy.

Outside their migration abroad, players acquired knowledge and skills, influential relations, social and cultural remittance returning to their countries of origin (Al-Ali *et al.* 2002). All these sporting, capital and intellectual resources play an important role in their diverse activities where some can transfer their knowledge and ideas to their established football academies and clubs in the communities. Generally, African players provide football equipment, training kits and some financial support to their grassroots teams and that strengthens their deep connections with them. The study discovered how some professional players' economic and non-economic actions are strategically undertaken to avoid societal pressures and a bad image for their families. That is, the community tends to differentiate those without any economic or non-economic projects as not responsible and this may negatively affect their social status in society. Such behaviours make families see their initial investments in them as a waste of resources which could have been channelled to support and develop other family members' human capital. So, for those concerned to avoid being labelled as such, they are forced to contribute something to minimise pressures from social groups in the communities.

Reflections

The community sometimes forgets to appreciate how some professional players have spent so many resources and efforts in supporting others in the localities. However, when they do not have any more, community members tend to accuse them of not planning their lives properly. In Africa, the belief of locales is that migrants abroad must succeed and anything short of this is not pleasant for their ears. That outlook tends to oblige African players abroad to give back and their inability to fulfil that can affect their social identities and embeddedness. Helping families and communities may not be a bad idea *per se*, however, it must be done in a way that makes them independent or self–reliant, having a sustainable livelihood. The current perception concerning footballers and migration that is shared and predominates in African communities has a long life before moving on to a post-modern model.

Perhaps African professional footballers may be able to build real socioeconomic partnerships involving the local forces with skills and competencies that can support local development. This can promote their self-sustainability and enable them to better support society for a longer term. Migration has been and still is an important driver for changing the social dynamics that can transform people's lifetime and cultures. Concurrently, it should not be an opportunity for African players to reject cultural values, customs, beliefs and norms. Yet some professional players are conscious of the risks that certain cultural values, norms and customs that may stifle social and economic local developments.

It is interesting to note that classical migrants from Africa often form an association to support their communities with developmental projects and socioeconomic partnerships with local communities. This is unusual for professional footballers who seem more individualist and concerned about their social recognition and may have low interest in joining such associations. Based on this, we conclude that African professional footballers' Give Back Behaviour is a way to promote their popularity as well as maintain their social relationship with their communities. With the major global and climatic changes in African countries, African professional footballers in Europe must be more conscious and dynamic in their socioeconomic approach. That is, they can focus on those investment initiatives that may drive regional and national development through an effective 'give back' approach to the benefit of the larger society. The question is, how would the future generations of African professional footballers be expected to behave regarding this fundamental issue? Especially when we observed that female football is the next driver for European football economic growth.

Table 6.1 Give Back Behaviours typology

	Players	*Education*	*Family size*	*Objectives*	*Target group*	*GB span*	*Give Back rationality*
Type 1 Hybrid family	Age: 26–55 years with 8–18 years' professional experience.	Second degree to High School/ School dropout	Close family (4–11), married with a child or fewer than 6 children	Economic and social changes	Close family, extended family and community	For long term	Based on the players' interests and values
Type 2 Cross-closed family	Age: 22–32 years with 4–14 years' professional experience.	Lower than type 1. Some only stuck to football	Close family (4–6), unmarried / married with fewer than 4 children	Supporting financially and socially their close family	Close family (parents and siblings), extended family and community	For short and medium term	Based on social and cultural norms
Type 3 Shared family	Age: 30 years onwards with 11 years' professional experience.	Secondary to Elementary school	Close family (4–10), unmarried / married with fewer than 4 children	Supporting financially and socially their wives' families	Extended family to wife's family members	For long term	Based on social and cultural norms
Type 4 Shadow family	Age: 19–26 years with 2–12 years' professional experience.	Polytechnic to High School	Close family (4–14), unmarried / married with fewer than 3 children	Remittance and recompense	Friends, teammates, coaches, adopted family	For short term	Based on ROI or reciprocity

Conclusion

Some studies on African footballers' migration to leagues abroad exposed how economic potentials obtained from their professional career have supported their households and improved their social welfare as a way of giving back to society (Acheampong 2018; Darby 2014; Lanfranchi and Taylor 2001). Professional football status is recognised as a means that can assist African players to achieve their aspirations and ambitions to climb the social ladder in society. In this chapter, it was revealed that players' relationship with the community can influence their GBB to society. We appreciate the diverse contributions of society towards their professional career abroad, which consistently played a role to affect players' sending of regular remittance to parents, families, relatives, and the communities through the giving back phenomenon. This new development was observed from the various socioeconomic investment initiatives of players in the communities, which they assigned significant meaning to their economic behaviour. Furthermore, players giving back were classified according to the economic rationality of that specific action based on their economic and non-economic support to society. Thus, giving back as socioeconomic phenomenon; give back behaviour—an emerging African cultural norm; give back behaviour reflecting their social and cultural embeddedness; give back behaviour based on institutionalised networks; and give back behaviour determined by economic rationality and interest.

Knowledge of the typology of African players was consistent with their values, objectives, conceptions and interests regarding the community embeddedness as critical to their Give Back Behaviours. Recognising their investment initiatives, it is important for African players to build real socioeconomic partnerships involving the local forces with skills and competencies that can support local development. This can promote their self-sustainability and enable them to better support society for the longer term.

Notes

1. Interview with Rueben Ayarna, on 20 January 2016.
2. Interview with C. K. Akunnor, on 1 September 2015.
3. Interview with George Seyi, on 10 December 2015.
4. A report extracted from Africanews.com, on 17 January 2018.
5. See note 1.
6. This was part of activities promoting the FIFA '11 for Health and 11 against Ebola' programme in Sierra Leone, in February 2016.
7. See note 3.
8. Interview with Sam Ayorinde, on 8 December 2015.
9. His interview was recorded and transcribed from Kwesé TV Sports Show, on 23 August 2017.
10. Interview with Lumor Agbenyenu, on 10 January 2016.
11. Interview with Mohamed Rabiu, on 2 February 2019.
12. Interview with FIFA.com, 2015 after his participation in 12th Match Against Poverty organised by Zinedine Zidane and Ronaldo. (http://www.fifa.com/world-match-centre/news/newsid/259/429/9/). [Accessed on 30 April 2015].

13. Interview granted Swansea reporters when he signed for their club. (http://www.swanseacity.net/news/article/swansea-city-andre-ayew-ghana2545061.aspx). [Accessed on 15 July 2015].
14. These players have undertaken several social projects in their communities as reported by K.N.S Mensah (June 2010) from goal.com. (http://www.goal.com/en/news/1717/editorial/2010/07/21/2035384/ten-african-footballers-with-a-social-conscience) [Accessed on 15 May 2015].
15. Interview with Noah Chivuta, on 23 April 2016.
16. Interview with John Paintsil, on 23 July 2013.
17. Interview with Augustine Ahinful, on 11 August 2015.
18. Interview with Stephen Appiah, on 10 July 2013.
19. Interview with Gyan Asamoah, on 26 November 2015.
20. Interview with Nii Odartey Lamptey, on 8 August 2015.
21. See note 17.
22. Interview with Sam Ayorinde, on 18 December 2015.
23. Interview with Prince Ikpe, on 9 December 2015.
24. Ibid.
25. Interview with Alozie, on 10 December 2015.
26. Interview with Anaba, on 7 December 2015.
27. Interview with Sam Owusu, on 22 December 2015.
28. See note 3.
29. Ibid.
30. Interview with Cofie, on 22 January 2016.
31. Interview with Abedi Pele, on 9 March 2016.
32. See note 25.
33. Interview by Bah Abdoulaye with Eto'o, on 24 February 2013.
34. Ibid.
35. Interview with Marcel Desailly, on 14 June 2013.
36. See note 30.
37. See note 15.
38. Interview with Tony Yeboah, on 10 August 2015.
39. See note 2.
40. See note 33.

Bibliography

Acheampong, E. Y. 2018. 'How does professional football status challenge African players' behaviour?', *Soccer & Society*, doi:10.1080/14660970.2018.1541797.

Adegoke, A. A. 2001. 'Pubertal development and traditional support systems in Africa: An overview', *The African Journal of Reproductive Health* 5 (1): 20–30.

Al-Ali, N., Black, R. and Koser, K. 2002. 'Refugees and transnationalism: The experience of Bosnians and Eritreans in Europe', *Journal of Ethnic and Migration Studies*, 27 (4): 615–634.

Bale, J. 1991. *The Brawn Drain: Foreign Student-Athletes in American Universities*. Urbana, IL: University of Illinois Press.

Becker, S. G. 1993. *Human Capital: A Theoretical and Empirical Analysis with Special Reference to Education*. 3rd edition. Chicago: The University of Chicago Press.

Boudon, R. 1995. *Le juste et le vrai: études sur l'objectivité des valeurs et de la connaissance*. Paris: Fayard. [2001. *The origin of values*. New Brunswick/London: Transaction.]

Bouhaouala, M. 1999. 'Micro-mentalités et logiques d'actions des dirigeants des petites entreprises du tourisme sportif: contribution à une sociologie économique du sport.' Thèse de Doctorat de l'Université Joseph Fourier Grenoble 1.

Bouhaouala, M. 2007. 'Micro-mentalités et logiques d'action des entrepreneurs dirigeants de petites entreprises', *Revue Internationale PME*, 20: 2.

Carling, J. 2007. 'Transnationalism in the context of restrictive immigration policy.' PhD Thesis, University of Oslo.

Darby, P. 2014. 'International football migration and Africa: Feet drain or feet exchange', *More than a Game, Sports, Society and Politics: Panorama Insights into Asian and European Affairs*, January 2014.

De Haas, H. 2010. 'Migration and development: A theoretical perspective', *International Migration Review* 44 (1): 227–264. doi:10.1111/j.1747-7379.2009.00804.x.

De Vasconcellos Ribeiro, C. H., and Dimeo, P. 2009. 'The Experience of migration for Brazilian football players', *Sport in Society* 12 (6): 725–736. doi:10.1080/17430430902944159.

Engh, H. M. and Agergaard, S. 2015. 'Producing mobility through locality and visibility: Developing a transnational perspective on sports labour migration', *International Review for the Sociology of Sport* 50: 974–992.

Esson, J. 2015. 'Escape to victory: Development, youth entrepreneurship and the migration of Ghanaian footballers', *Geoforum: Journal of Physical, Human, and Regional Geosciences* 64: 47–55. doi:10.1016/j.geoforum.2015.06.005.

Granovetter, M. 1985. 'Economic action and social structure: The problem of embeddedness', *American Journal of Sociology* 91 (3): 481–510.

Hall, S. 1997. *Representation: Cultural Representations and Signifying Practices*. SAGE.

Lanfranchi, P., and Taylor, M. 2001. *Moving with the Ball. The Migration of Professional Footballers*. New York: Berg.

Laumann, E. O. and Pappi, F. U. 1976. *Networks of Collective Action: A Perspective on Community Influence System*. New York: Academic Press.

Orr, T. 2007. *No Hands Allowed: Jay Jay Okocha*. Mitchell Lane Publishers.

Penot, H. 2008. *Didier Drogba: The Autobiography*. Aurum Press Ltd.

Poli, R. and Rossi, G. 2012. *Football Agents in the Biggest Five European Markets. An Empirical Research Report*. Neuchâtel: Centre International d'Etude du Sport (CIES).

Rial, C. 2014. 'Circulation, bubbles, returns: The mobility of Brazilians in the football system.' In: R. Elliott and J. Harris (eds), *Football and Migration: Perspectives, Places, Players* (61–75). Abingdon: Routledge.

Schroeder, R. 1992. *Max Weber and the Sociology of Culture*. London: Sage.

Tajfel, H. 1978. 'Interindividual and intergroup behaviour.' In H. Tajfel (ed.), *Differentiation between Groups: Studies in the Social Psychology of Intergroup Relations* (27–60). London: Academic Press.

Ungruhe, C. and Esson, J. 2017. 'A social negotiation of hope. Male West African youth, "Waithood", the pursuit of social becoming through football', *Boyhood Studies* 10 (1): 22–43. doi:10.3167/bhs.2017.100103.

Van der Meij, N. and P. Darby, P. 2017. 'Getting in the game and getting on the move: family, the intergenerational contract and internal migration into football academies in Ghana', *Sport in Society*, doi:10.1080/17430437.2017.1284807.

Weber, M. 2001 [1930]. *The Protestant Ethic and the Spirit of Capitalism*. New York, NY: Routledge.

Williams, J. 2014. *Women, Soccer and Transnational Migration*. London: Routledge.

Conclusion

Concluding thoughts

In this book, we have introduced readers to the concept of economic sociology that underpins the Give Back Behaviours of African players abroad. We moved on to highlight the 'Give Back Behaviour' of African professional footballers who migrated to European leagues, viewed as the most attractive socioeconomically. The identification of their migration process and professional itinerary, the role of the communities' support and the football networks in their itinerary were important points in this book. These points reflected how 'Give Back Behaviour' is connected to the context of European football evolution and African football development. Analysing the development of the European football labour market significantly supported the rise of African players' movement to the European leagues as observed in the 1990s (Acheampong and Bouhaouala 2019; Poli 2010; Poli, Ravenel and Besson 2015). This also transformed African footballers' migration process and their strategies of becoming a professional footballer in leagues abroad. The new development substantially increased African footballers' level of incomes and positively modified their social status and social recognition in their countries and on the international front as well.

The transformation of leagues abroad has improved greatly football players' socioeconomic importance and made them become one of the major actors of African football, social cohesion and local policies. At the same time, these professional players had to maintain a strong link with their communities of origin and family members back home due to the cultural, social norms and values, or economic interests or personal goals. This socio-cultural responsibility and shared values to their communities assigned them an important role that prompts high socioeconomic demands from their communities of origin. For instance, migrants who moved for economic considerations, with a mission to gain money for assisting their families, used to remit regularly to these latter. This demonstrates the strength of African footballers' connection with the classical migration and communities' social rules of origin in terms of 'Give Back Behaviours'. The book explained how professional footballers supported their communities through the various socioeconomic investment initiatives offered to society. Indeed, their behaviour demonstrates the significant meaning they assign to their socioeconomic actions that are reflected through their economic rationality. This justifies players' economic behaviour which determines the values, objectives, conceptions, and interest they attach to their contributions and support to the community.

A thorough analysis revealed how classical migrants from Africa to Europe basically realigned their economic considerations to their families and communities, because of their social norms, cultural values and the commitment towards their families and the social status they want to achieve. In some cases, most of them are obliged to give back having enjoyed diverse support and financial contributions pertaining to their migration process, which indirectly make family members and the community expect ROI because they objectively supported them in their process. The understanding and explanation of African footballers' Give Back Behaviours inspired us to examine the key hypothesis including past and current studies on migrants' relations with their communities of origin, particularly with reference to the context of professional football. The book relied on the contributions of theoretical models to understand the influence of social, economic, and cultural determinants which enlightened us on the African professional footballers' remittance and support actions they offer their communities.

Regarding the specificities of footballers' process of migration, social status, and level of incomes, their GBB varied and was subject to differentiation regarding their level of leagues abroad and embeddedness. Based on the above observations, we described different socioeconomic causes that tended to affect their GBB. This book adds new knowledge and information to clarify how cultural, social, and economic factors underpinned the GBB of African footballers in Europe. Beyond that, it provides insight into understanding the evolution of African football, and identifying the strategies and resources that football players mobilised in facilitating their migratory process and professional itineraries. In comparison, after migrants and professional footballers achieved a high social and economic status, they managed their Give Back Behaviour in relation to their communities of origin. The GBB of African footballers resulted from their economic rational choice because of the complex socioeconomic phenomena which informed the interaction of economic and non-economic factors as an individual or a collective logic.

We established here that the GBB is consubstantial to migration from the South to the North and migrants' communities. This was observed via the role of their economic and non-economic factors (social and cultural) that oriented African footballers' Give Back Behaviours toward their families and communities. Their Give Back Behaviours were determined considering the return on investments (Becker 1993), or values and norms (Weber 1922) or embeddedness in social relations (Granovetter 1985, 2017) or the institutionalised networks (North 1990; Volery 2007) which are related to footballers' migration. In sum, African players' GBB are based on the combination of social, cultural, and economic factors in their socioeconomic approaches (Swedberg 2003). Indeed, we should not consider only one way to explain their GBB; in some cases, contributions were made in reference to the human capital model (Becker 1993). The ROI approach was not the only way footballers chose to give back and to justify their behaviour, because non-economic causes also played a part. Besides, giving back could be a condition for footballers to maintain their social status and relationship with their communities of origin. The GBB of players, for instance, might be considered as a social and economic contribution to confirm their success as a migrant by responding to their communities' expectations. The study's socioeconomic approach together with the contribution of Weberian methodology (Bouhaouala 1999, 2007) supported our meso-analysis in combining individualist and holistic causes in the determination of footballers GBB.

The book detailed the utilitarian rationality and socio-cultural determinants, the interests and values intermixed in the decisions and choices of African players. Max Weber's (1978) theory contributed to understanding why the individual player is not totally independent of society or totally submitted to it. The Weberian ideal-types of behaviours showed how economic and non-economic causes played a role in orienting human actions in relation to their economic and non-economic behaviour. The results showed that African footballers' behaviour regarding their giving back depended largely on the complex socioeconomic logic of actions determined by their economic interest, social norms, and cultural beliefs. The book summarised the three main outcomes;

1. *Social and economic evolution of African football:* The communities and families' perception of football, specifically, as a professional career has evolved positively. Concurrently, football structures and sporting facilities including football academies (Darby, Akindes, and Kirwin 2007), modern training gyms, juvenile leagues, etc. in Africa have been developed by local and international agents parallel to the growth of the European football labour market. This allowed us to identify one evolution with three major periods from the 1980s to the 2000s showing the evolution of social perception, football structures and migration strategies: Thus,
   (a) Controversial vision: football vs. school (the 1980s).
   (b) Shared vision: football's gradual shift from social to professional activity (the 1990s).
   (c) Professional football as an opportunity (the 2000s).
2. *Typology of players' migration itineraries:* These are linked to the evolution of African football and the growth of the European football labour market. It created a platform to identify the interconnection between players' strategies, football structures, network profiles and other resources provided from the communities. In this book, we identified three itineraries of players' migrations:
   (a) Collective resource-based.
   (b) Formal networks resource-based.
   (c) Individual resource-based.

3. *Four types of Give Back Behaviours:* These were identified based on five main categories of factors that structure the GBB typology. These are:
   (a) Involvement of social structures (family, community, etc.) and football institutions (academy, clubs, etc.).
   (b) Social norms and values and cultural beliefs.
   (c) Economic interests and ROI.
   (d) Nature of resources mobilised.
   (e) Targets of the give back phenomenon.

In general, many African professional footballers make economic investments and contribute social support to their families, relatives, friends, and others in their communities. The give back differs depending on many variables such as a social obligation to support their families and the community members or ROI for those who contributed economically to players' migration project. For instance, the regular remittance to support families, households, friends, and others in the local communities can be described as an African culture rooted in the socio-cultural construct. The typology of African players was derived from their values, objectives, conceptions, and interests, yet they consider the role of significant others as a crucial to their Give Back Behaviours. African players often consider the role of community members and the kind of value they placed on their activities is a crucial determinant of the Give Back Behaviours.

Similarly, there are other factors that affect the determination of the GBP. We observed social constraints identified through media, social networks, social groups, etc. These go a long way to influence many African professional players' behaviour and the kind of projects to establish in their communities. In the same way, as African professional players tried to satisfy the latter, they often seek to safeguard and protect their interest in building a positive image in the eyes of Europe and African societies. Thus, players' failure to support based on their achieved socioeconomic status internationally and across African countries may cast doubt on their socio-cultural connection to their local communities. This development though not obligatory was also relevant and must be properly managed otherwise it can cause serious damage to one's reputation and family members in the locality. This is different from the 'Western world' but it is important in African communities built on socio-cultural identity and community belonging. Certainly, footballers achieving social recognition, social status, and fame should not only serve their economic and social interests but also support the communities, fans, employers, and sponsors who may promote and drive local and regional development. Otherwise, they stand accused and may be labelled as ungrateful persons, who do not contribute in return to their communities' needs and that can have a negative impact on their social image and economic value (Acheampong 2018).

Invariably, footballers' social and economic interests are linked to their Give Back Behaviours which are based on several rationalities that combine different levels of economic interests, values, and social objectives. The identification of good reasons for the action (Boudon 1995) in relation to every 'give back' approach permitted us to describe and explain the complex phenomenon. This supported developing a typology of the Give Back Behaviours targeting four types of groups with specific actions: (a) hybrid family, (b) cross-closed family, (c) shared family, and (d) shadow family.

Beyond the identified typology, the research revealed one constant: African players' remittance decision was mostly coerced by social and cultural norms or religious belief that may impact on their behaviours to society. This is because, in African communities, the social and cultural norms of the community take priority over individuality and therefore, tend to impact the rationality of locale people, which was observed through the behaviours of professional footballers. Thus the Give Back Behaviour represents a form of obligation for African migrant players to give back to their local communities of origin considering their contributions toward their professional careers abroad.

Again, analysis of the typology of African players' behaviour can improve our understanding of the 'give back' concept, showing that it is a way of providing either tangible or intangible support in the interest of responsibility via (economic or non-economic activity) to affect social lives of people in society. The tangible or intangible support includes but is not limited to intellectual and cultural capitals, skills and knowledge, finances, efforts, time, social networks, sporting capital, and other things that can make people's situations in the local communities better. Some of these findings were achieved after the application of economic sociology approaches that provided a conduit to solve the complex social phenomenon of players' Give Back Behaviour which may be based on the same individual but with different determinants such as economic, social, cultural, etc. (Lahire 2011).

The book contributes to the knowledge of African footballers' behaviour regarding their migration strategies and how they invest their football-related revenues after achieving professional status abroad. It again provides a new prospect for development on the concept of Give Back Behaviours that may interest researchers as they move away from the pull and push factors of sport labour migrations. Interestingly, African players used crafty tactics and other strategies to become professional footballers and how this stratagem plays out in their post-playing career transition either as sports entrepreneurs or football managers would be a welcome subject to be studied.

Weberian methodology produced a good contribution to resolving the combination of different theories coming from the social sciences and other multidisciplinary areas. With all these, the research could not cover the entire 55 UEFA countries and those African footballers in the lower leagues. The research was limited in terms of getting African professional footballers from all the CAF zones for the interviews, especially those from the North and East of Africa, yet some contributions were extracted from their previous interviews in the sports papers, clubs' websites and on television which were directly related to the subject. Further studies on this work should move beyond the application of social sciences but with other fields that can add a new dimension on the subject. Based on the research outcomes, it could be interesting to describe the relation of African and European football, the evolution of the football labour market, and the evolution of the GBB depending on the evolution of African football.

Studies of African migrant players abroad have concluded on various findings such as underdevelopment and lack of professionalism and other administrative lapses among the main challenges of African football development. This research identified hardships some African migrant players grappled with regarding their new clubs and leagues abroad. This includes lack of orientation by their new clubs and football agents not giving them a pre-departure briefing on their new environment. Thus, most of them encountered a lot of problems in adapting to the language, food, weather conditions, administrative and social issues to get them well integrated into the new environment. This is predictable because many African communities are characterised by a sort of togetherness and deep connection premised on collectivity rather than individuality. That reflects the sense of belongingness and cultural embeddedness which often affect football players relocating from their home country. Socio-cultural affiliation among members of the locales transcending the community borders can create a hindrance for many players in their new environment with a different culture and orientation. African players' established relationships with the close family, extended families, friends and others tend to play a significant role in their social lives as proven through their values, objectives, interest and conceptions to society.

The rise in migration reaffirms Poli *et al.*'s (2015) studies showing African talents as the second largest donor of foreign players to the European leagues after UEFA. Moving forward, families, communities and society should understand that every footballer has his own destiny and as such, it is not every African migrant player who can succeed in their chosen profession, thus, *many footballers are called but fewer would become professional and financially successful*. Yet, the community sometimes forgets how some professional football migrants have spent so much money in supporting others, and if they do not have any more, must cooperate with them rather than turning against them. It does not mean they did not plan well or did not do things well; such is life, and players should hold whatever they have tight and give support intelligently in the best way they can to the benefit of friends and the communities. Because providing for others may not be a bad idea but helping them become more independent is the best form of support players can offer their locale people to improve their social welfare.

Migration has been part of the changing social dynamics and transformation of people's lifetime. It is part of their adventures of rising but it should not mean that a prolonged stay in Europe can affect African players' cultural values, customs, beliefs and norms. However, some professional players warned against families and community people hiding behind cultural values, norms and customs, as a pretence to promote their selfish interest at the expense of the society. Thus, society must change its mindset of self-seeking for their own pockets rather than focusing on the deep cultural ties that characterised their social behaviours in the past. Without a change in people's attitude within the communities, it becomes difficult to improve their livelihood in the various African communities, no matter the efforts and support professional footballers may offer to society. For the African professional players, it is time everybody stops thinking about themselves (self-interest at the expense of people) because they were not brought up like that in the communities. Such an attitude can breed cultural proliferation by shifting their cultural collectiveness towards the individualistic approach. The research revealed that the best legacy an African professional footballer can leave their local communities may show through their giving back behaviour provided it will have a meaningful impact on people's welfare.

Critical approach of African footballers' migration

Historically, the migration of African footballers was linked to colonial exploitation from the 1920s through to the 1960s (Lanfranchi and Taylor 2001; Murray 1995). Some of those players exported to the various leagues in France and Belgium became nationals of their former colonisers (Broere and Van der Drift 1997; Darby 2010; Murray 1995). In the 1970s, Darby (2010) reported that some players attracted foreign clubs because of their exploits and popularity on the African continent. Regarding the earlier migration processes, football was not more prominent until the 1980s when European football evolved, shifting the approach of African football and its players' migration abroad.

In the latter part of the 1980s, young boys' passion for football increased as they explored the social environment of becoming footballers. Various barriers to football in the communities were handled and became like a step for boys to achieve their anticipated professional dream abroad. Through the crafty approach, some boys got scouted from their street football experiences (informal training) and events. The evolution of European football gave a new vision to football in many African communities. Exposure of young African boys' raw talent at the FIFA youth and senior competitions in the early 1990s changed the football wave in Africa. Foreign scouts flooded the continent in search of talents for the European football market as well.

The families and football structures played an important role in the decision making towards the migration of young boys to leagues abroad. Socioeconomic benefits of football became evident for parents, family members, and the community as they took a keen interest in supporting young boys with sports gear and training kits and going further to enrol them in football academies. All towards a better professional football career due to their sporting talents together with education. Alongside this, some players were able to mobilise football structures, getting into national teams including human and network resources to achieve their professional ambitions. Players adopted both emerging and deliberate strategies (Mintzberg and Waters 1985) in their quest to become visible to the new market of football in Europe.

The exploits of some African players in leagues abroad provided an incentive for scattered football academies in Africa (Darby 2002). This is why member associations of CAF need to intensify their efforts by developing a strategic policy that will regulate and monitor the rampant growth of football academies across the continent. Here, they must consider local content in the academies' curriculum in developing their talented recruits. For instance, RTD academy has a structured educational policy that seeks to produce both professional footballers and academic graduates. This vital aspect of recruit trainees' development, if not properly checked, can affect their future especially those in the mushroom and unlicensed football academies without appropriate educational structures to support their growth in the communities.

Strong economic opportunities and high social position of football have fuelled society's interest in the sport. Parents and communities employed strategies toward securing a professional career for their young boys as they provided them with social and material support. This influenced families' vision leading them to adopt rational strategies as they could anticipate the prospects of the sport. The investment in the human capital of young talent through structured football academies got a huge boost from families and the community, because formal football structures can provide an opportunity for developing young people and integrating them into society through a job opportunity. The professional activity of football gained more recognition in the 2000s as African players rationally exhibited a managerial approach by using resources of families and football structures to reach their professional aspirations abroad. All in all, African players mobilised the necessary human, material, and social resources as a viable impetus towards their professional career in football overseas.

Bibliography

Acheampong, E.Y. 2018. 'How does professional football status challenge African players' behaviour?', *Soccer & Society Journal*, doi:10.1080/14660970.2018.1541797.

Acheampong, E. Y. and Bouhaouala, M. 2019. 'African footballers' life cycles according to the analysis of transfer value along their career path: a case study of Ghanaian players', *Sport in Society*, doi:10.1080/17430437.2018.1551366.

Becker, G. 1993. *Human Capital: A Theoretical and Empirical Analysis with Special Reference to Education*. 3rd edition. Chicago: University of Chicago Press.

Boudon, R. 1995. *Le juste et le vrai: études sur l'objectivité des valeurs et de la connaissance*. Paris: Fayard. [2001. *The origin of values*. New Brunswick/London: Transaction.]

Bouhaouala, M. 1999. 'Micro-mentalités et logiques d'actions des dirigeants des petites entreprises du tourisme sportif: contribution à une sociologie économique du sport.' Thèse de Doctorat de l'Université Joseph Fourier Grenoble 1.

Bouhaouala, M. 2007. 'Micro-mentalités et logiques d'action des entrepreneurs dirigeants de petites entreprises', *Revue Internationale PME*, 20: 2.

Broere, M., and Van der Drift, R. 1997. *Football Africa!* Oxford: Worldview Publishing.

Darby, P. 2002. *Africa, Football and FIFA: Politics, Colonialism and Resistance*. London: Frank Cass.

Darby, P. 2010. '"Go outside": The history, economics and geography of Ghanaian football labour migration', *African Historical Review* 42 (1): 19–41.

Darby, P., Akindes, G. and Kirwin, M. 2007. 'Football academies and the migration of African football labour to Europe', *Journal of Sport and Social Issues* 31 (2): 143–161. doi:10.1177/0193723507300481.

Granovetter, M. 1985. 'Economic action and social structure: The problem of embeddedness', *American Journal of Sociology* 91 (3): 481–510.

Granovetter, M. 2017. *Society and Economy, Framework and Principals*. Harvard, MA: The Belknap Press of Harvard University Press.

Lahire, B. 2011. *The Plural Actor*, translated by David Fernach. UK: Polity Press.

Lanfranchi, P. and Taylor, M. 2001. *Moving with the Ball. The Migration of Professional Footballers*. New York: Berg Publishers.

Mintzberg, H., and Waters, A. J. 1985. 'Of strategies, deliberate and emergent', *Strategic Management Journal* 6 (3): 257–272.

Murray, B. 1995. *Football: History of the World Game*. Aldershot: Scolar Press.

North, C. Douglass. 1990. *Institutions, Institutional Change and Economic Performance*. Cambridge University Press.

Poli, R. 2010. 'African migrants in Asian and European football: Hopes and realities', *Sport in Society: Cultures, Commerce, Media, Politics* 13 (6): 1001–1011. doi:10.1080/17430437.2010.491269.

Poli, R., Ravenel, L. and Besson, R. 2015. 'Exporting countries in world football', *CIES Football Observatory Monthly Report*, 1–10.

Swedberg, R. 2003. *Principles of Economic Sociology*. Princeton and Cambridge: Princeton University Press.

Volery, T. 2007. 'Ethnic entrepreneurship: A theoretical framework.' In *Handbook of Research on Ethnic Minority Entrepreneurship: A Co-Evolutionary View on Resource Management* (30–41). Cheltenham: Edward Elgar (30–41). ISBN 978-1-84542-733-7.

Weber, M. 1978 [1922]. *Economy and Society: An Outline of Interpretive Sociology*, translated by Ephraim Fischoff *et al.*, 2vols. Berkeley: University of California Press.

Index

Printed in Dunstable, United Kingdom